The Essential Royster

THE ESSENTIAL ROYSTER

A Vermont Royster Reader

Edited by

EDMUND FULLER

ALGONQUIN BOOKS
OF CHAPEL HILL
1985

ALGONQUIN BOOKS OF CHAPEL HILL
Post Office Box 2225
Chapel Hill, North Carolina 27515-2225

Unless otherwise noted, the essays reproduced in this book first appeared in *The Wall Street Journal*.

© 1954, 1955, 1956, 1963, 1964, 1966, 1975, 1976, 1977, 1978, 1979, 1980, 1981, 1982, 1983, 1984 by Dow Jones & Company, Inc., publishers of *The Wall Street Journal*.

© 1974 by The American Enterprise Institute for Public Policy Research: "The American Press and the Revolutionary Tradition." Presented as a lecture in 1974 at Stanford University; published in *America's Continuing Revolution* (Anchor Books/ Doubleday, 1976) under the auspices of The American Enterprise Institute.

© 1974 and 1983 by the United Chapters of Phi Beta Kappa: "The Public Morality: Afterthoughts on Watergate" and "Watching the Pendulum in Education." Both essays first appeared in *The American Scholar*. Reprinted by permission of the publisher.

© 1979 by The Heritage Foundation, publisher of *Policy Review*: "On the Freedom and Responsibility of the Press." Reprinted by permission of the publisher.

© 1979 by The New York Times Company: "Europe Revisited: A Nostalgic Tour with Grandchildren." Reprinted by permission of the publisher.

LIBRARY OF CONGRESS CATALOGING IN PUBLICATION DATA

Royster, Vermont, 1914–
  The essential Royster.

  1. United States—Politics and government—1945–   —Addresses, essays, lectures. 2. United States—Civilization—1970–   —Addresses, essays, lectures. 3. World politics—1945–   —Addresses, essays, lectures. I. Fuller, Edmund, 1914– . II. Title.
E839.5.R68 1985   973.9   85-1302
ISBN 0-912697-19-9

10 9 8 7 6 5 4 3 2 1

Printed in the United States of America

CONTENTS

VIII. Trials on Trial

IX. School Days

X. Persons in Their Places

XI. The Sexes

XII. Of Earth and Energy

XIII. Nights at the Opera

XIV. Purely Personal

FOREWORD

In April 1984, Vermont Royster received his second Pulitzer Prize. His first, in 1953, for editorial writing, was presented during his long tenure as editor of *The Wall Street Journal*. The second was for commentary, awarded for his columns under the heading, "Thinking Things Over," a weekly feature of the *Journal* for many years, from which a great part of the present collection is drawn. In happy circumstance, prize number two very nearly coincided with his seventieth birthday, upon which canonical milestone he ruminates in an essay included here, "Three Score and Ten."

In a loose sense this book is a continuation of, and is a natural companion to, an earlier collection, *A Pride of Prejudices*, first published in 1967 and reissued in 1984. Mr. Royster himself chose the contents of that volume but did not wish to undertake again the somewhat subjective task. The material available for the present book was of such abundant quantity and quality as to test sorely even the relative objectivity of the colleague and friend to whom he entrusted the choice this time. The peeling off of late-stage eliminations, a process not unlike eating an artichoke, often was painful.

As designated selector, I owe readers a brief account of the factors which guided my choices. I've sought the broadest representation of Vermont Royster's thinking and writing. Thus, excellent columns appropriate to any of the headings in the book had to be sacrificed not only because of limits of space but in order to permit a reasonable balance among subjects. Those chosen represent the most lasting, the least time-and-topic bound. Although, *sub specie aeternitatis*, all things are temporal, topical, and transitory, the largest frame of reference, the themes that seem most persistent amid the flux of events, were sought.

Even the matter of headings presented difficulties requiring some arbitrary decisions. One cannot easily separate the essays in "Windows on the World," which concern international events, from those in "Of

Peace and War," or both groups from the essays gathered under the heading "Of Politics." Though these columns from *The Wall Street Journal* and other essays reflect an acute sense of history and a philosophical bent, Mr. Royster disclaims the formal title of historian or philosopher. Yet as compiler, I felt compelled to stress, in two sections, the qualities here called "The Historian's Eye" and "The Philosopher's Eye," in which such elements, present throughout the book, are particularly evident.

Naturally a major segment deals with the press. Mr. Royster has always cast a maverick's eye upon the brotherhood and sisterhood of his craft. On this subject, in addition to four *Wall Street Journal* columns, he examines his profession at greater length in two longer pieces. One traces the history of newspapers in this country from Colonial times to our own. The other is a meditation on "The Freedom and Responsibility of the Press."

He has much to say on education, justice and our courts, economics, energy, women and men, together with some purely personal views. "Persons in Their Places" offers appraisals of some major world figures, including the U.S. presidents he has known. As a distinctly different facet of his interests, the group called "Nights at the Opera" shows us that had not politics and world affairs been at the heart of his professional concerns we would have had an excellent critic of grand opera. The earliest articles included here, these reflect Rudolf Bing-time at the Metropolitan Opera House.

In his essay "Journalism as History," Mr. Royster remarks: "I am simply a journalist writing about the ephemera of our time. But a curious thing happens with ephemera. A newspaper article is dated and forgotten within a week, sometimes the next day. But let a decade pass, or certainly a generation, that same article takes on a new life. The interest in it, and perhaps even its value, increases, just as that old Tiffany lamp fell into scornful disfavor only to find itself in time sought out to decorate the newest of homes."

"Ephemera" written by one possessing the historian's and philosopher's eye, as perceived in this collection, are indispensable treasures to the later historian. They record events and attempt to assess them before the writer can yet know the outcome. With one exception, none of the essays in this collection has appeared in a book before. "Of Men and Angels," which appeared in *The Wall Street Journal* on December 23, 1965, was included in Mr. Royster's first collection, *A Pride of*

Prejudices. He used it again in the *Journal*, for its seasonal appropriateness, on December 24, 1975. It seemed so suitable a beginning to the opening section of the present book, "The Philosopher's Eye," that the exception was made for it. All the pieces gathered here retain relevance and value in their subjects and themes, for readers today and for those in an indefinite future who will be seeking clues to what it was like to live in Vermont Royster's time and to view it with his capabilities and sensibilities. Together with the contents of *A Pride of Prejudices*, these essays are properly part of his record of what his recent autobiography calls "My Own, My Country's Time." They are "the essential Royster" as being the essence of the man.

Chapel Hill, N.C.   EDMUND FULLER
September 1, 1984

I

The Philosopher's Eye

OF MEN AND ANGELS

The late Thomas F. Woodlock, whose thoughts on things used to fill this space many years ago, was wont to return often to a search which was once thought worthy of the perplexity of philosophers. The search was to answer the simple question, What is man?

The question was implicit whenever he wrote, as he did voluminously, on very practical matters that seemed remote from metaphysics—on monetary policy, for example, or speculation in the stock market or on foreign policy problems of war and peace.

"We chatter fatuously of dictators and democracies," he remarked on the eve of World War II, "as if it were merely a matter of governmental forms or, even, economic theories that is in question. It is not rival forms but rival substances that face each other—the most fundamental of all ideas, man's idea of his own nature, man's concept of himself and his destiny."

So he urged his readers to see the brewing war as a conflict over the nature of man. So he saw many political issues, as a reflection of the conflict over whether the state should be the master or the servant of men.

Sometimes at Christmastide he would state the question explicitly: Man is either nothing more than a collection of atoms shaped in the form of an animal, or he is the man of the Psalmist, "a little lower than the angels . . . crowned with glory and honor."

Today the very form of the question would strike most people as quaint. To our generation angels are no more prevalent than witches.

As for the substance of the question, enlightened intellect is supposed to have settled that. In the graphic words of a scientist eminent in Woodlock's day: "All natural traits and impulses of human beings must therefore be fundamentally good. . . . Cruelty, selfishness, lust, cowardice and deceit are normal ingredients of human nature. . . . Intrinsically they are all virtues."

This is no mere recognition of the natural frailties of men. Cruelty and deceit are not imperfections which we may all be brought to simply because we are not gods; the plea is not even that these are failings to be understood and forgiven. Sadism and dishonesty are virtues to be acquired as they are useful. For animals—is it not so?—love and lust are one, and being one are indistinguishable.

Such is the modern lesson taught under the aegis both of scientists renowned for their knowledge and of philosophers reputed for their wisdom. It is not only a rejection of angels to aspire to; discarded also along with man's divinity is the conception of man's uniqueness or that his destiny is any greater than that of beasts.

Thus Socrates, the rationalist, is as outmoded as St. Paul the mystic. Spinoza, to whom man's special status was the human mind, is as out of the common course as Buddha, who saw in man a special spirit. The concept of sin, which for Thomas Aquinas was the fruit of man's first disobedience, is as insubstantial as the superego, which to Freud was the inner measure by which man tells good from evil action and which, in lieu of God, punishes the way of the transgressor.

If such is the lesson, why should anyone lament the animal behavior of men?

Yet lamentations are being heard in the land, and the sound of them comes from strange places. Clerics who debate whether God is dead give sermons decrying the mores of their flocks. It is no longer unusual to find articles in the intellectual magazines, both popular and esoteric, bemoaning the alienation of man from society and the crumbling of society's ethics.

The American Scholar, one of the more reflective quarterlies, mirrors such reflections. In a single issue here is Joseph Wood Krutch sadly puzzling over the modern cult of the Marquis de Sade. Storm Jameson, in a little essay on the writer in contemporary society, confessing that the attack on conventions "which can be gay and salutary" begins to shock "when it becomes an attack on self-respect and decent self-love." John Morris expressing pleasant surprise at a writer who can use words like "gentlemen" and "honorable" without "somewhere a trace of irony."

Finally, there is Hiram Haydn offering a jeremiad against our society "in which violence and cruelty and vindictiveness flare openly every day" and where sexual exhibitionism concentrates on "sadism and fifty-seven kinds of perversion."

Mind you, these are not the voices of the bourgeoisie. All these writers have impeccable credentials as intellectuals—rational, progressive and non-mystic. The heralds of the Enlightenment have joined the Puritans at the wailing wall.

While that in itself is interesting, the strange thing about it is that these new criers of "O Tempora, O Mores" seem to see no connection between the ideas about man and the behavior of men.

Yet if man, in the words of the anthropologist, is "a predator whose natural instinct is to kill with a weapon," can we decry the instinct which, being natural, is thereby virtuous? We may fear the predator for ourselves, as the lamb does the lion, but what moral reason can there be for condemnation?

An old man is sliced up on a park bench by a pack in human form for the joy of seeing him bleed, and our sympathy is not for the dead but for the unfortunate young with nothing else to occupy their time. A tortured woman stands on a window sill and the gathering crowd below yells "jump" for a lunch-hour thrill. Why not?

Lust, cruelty, selfishness are indeed instincts we share with the beasts. If this be all, as the new philosophy dreams, then what point is there in kindness, courtesy, charity, chastity, respect or honor?

Still, if wise men today lament the consequences they may one day look to the causes. And if they do not recover the vision of the Apostles, they may at least share with an ancient pagan the view that "humanity is poised midway between the gods and beasts." That, after all, is not too far from where once the angels dwelled.

December 24, 1975

THE MEN ON MARS

Those of us of a certain age who were reared on the Martian tales of Edgar Rice Burroughs are bound to have some mixed feelings about the results of the exploration of Mars by that Viking robot.

Burroughs had never been to Mars any more than he had been to Africa but that didn't stop his imagination from peopling that distant planet with strange creatures—bold warriors and exotic maidens— any more than from creating in Africa talking apes and a boy as at home in the jungle as we in our own backyards.

We can still believe, somehow, that Tarzan learned to read by plucking at "bugs" in a picture book, and that he mastered Numa the lion and Tantor the elephant. Burroughs had a touch of the poet and he was offering us a joyful song to the ingenuity of the human species.

The scientists, though, have killed what imagination made of Mars. They long ago took away the mystery of those Martian canals. Now, with their ingenuity, they have robbed us of the myth of Martian men. The photographs of Viking show nothing on that planet but a desolate wasteland, its groping finger picks up nothing but lifeless dust.

Thus while we marvel at what science has done, we are stripped of our youthful fantasies. If we are richer in knowledge, we are poorer in dreams. So we are left with mixed feelings about the wonders of the exploration of space.

But what science has taken away from imagination it has given back to philosophy. It seems that, after all, this planet of ours is alone with life in the solar system, that at least within the reach of our marvelous probes, we the human species are unique.

In that sense, anyway, the exploration of space has challenged the Copernican revolution which took away from man his special place in the scheme of things.

Since the beginning of time men have wondered about our place in the cosmos. Were we a unique accident of evolution or, in different terms, were we created the chosen of God to have dominion over earth and heaven? Or was this planet but one among many with life, were we the human species not matchless of our kind?

Long before there were Christian theologians, Lucretius the Roman was saying there must be elsewhere beyond the earth "other combinations of matter like to this which ether holds in its greedy grasp. . . . There are other earths and various races of men and kinds of wild beasts."

Lucretius made his argument on mathematical probability. "In no wise can it be deemed probable . . . that this single earth and heaven have been brought into being." Chance produced this world and the life upon it; so it must have produced others.

Jewish prophets and Christian apostles would have none of this. This earth, created by God out of chaos, was the center of things, around which revolved the sun and the moon and the stars. Man, created in the image of God, was at the center of this center.

It was Copernicus who destroyed this egocentric view, not by challenging its theology but its cosmology. He did no more than prove that the earth moved, that it was not the center of the universe.

But in so doing, he shook the foundation of man's egocentric view of himself. How could man be the culmination of God's actions if the earth was only one planet among many to rotate around the sun, if the sun itself was only an insignificant star among innumerable galaxies?

So began that questioning that has not ended to this day. If our little home was only a bit of dust in an infinite macrocosm, if there was the mathematical probability that somewhere out there was another planet, another bit of dust, where the same concatenation of circumstance must have produced a like life, a like species, could man still claim his holy privilege as the only begotten in the image of God?

The end of mysticism and the birth of rationalism had begun. Can anything be so ridiculous, said Montaigne, than that "this miserable and wretched creature . . . should call himself master and emperor of the world." How absurd, he thought, that man could imagine himself "above the circle of the moon and bringing heaven under his feet."

To Freud, that prophet of our time, the cosmology of Copernicus displaces man from his vain place and shrinks him to a banal biological entity. Man cannot hold to his naive self-love, he said, once man knows that earth is "not the center of the universe but only a tiny speck in a world-system of a magnitude hardly conceivable."

Yet now there is a certain irony, and perhaps even a little comfort, in man's exploration of the cosmology of Copernicus. We have made only a small beginning, but already we have climbed above the circle of the moon and brought at least a part of heaven under our feet. And in exploring that Copernican cosmology we have, if anything, increased the wonder.

Not on the moon, not on Mars, have our probes found a hint of life, not a lichen, not a microbe. For aging romantics, no Martian men. Thus pass those fantasies of my youth.

Still, there are—are there not?—men on Mars. The real marvel is that they are us. Man, that miserable and wretched creature, is proving himself a master and emperor in a way philosophers of old never dreamt of.

Of course there remains mathematical probability. No one can prove a negative, that somewhere out there in the infinity of space there are not creatures like us, probing their heavens. But a probability, for all its pretense at mathematical precision, is only a possibility, leaving the unknown and the mystery.

That mystery must wait until we reach the stars. Until then, within this solar system which is ours, we, the human species, are restored to our special place, alone upon this little planet.

September 1, 1976

CIVILITY AND MADNESS

If there were one word that could encompass such a man it would be civility. If there were one word that could describe the manner of his murder it would be madness.

Charles Frankel was best known to the general public through his television series that traced mankind's journey over the centuries in pursuit of liberty. It was, as Dr. Frankel showed us, a long journey of many twists and turns and also, as he reminded us, a journey not yet ended.

If we have come close to finding it in our own country, and have it at least as a grail devoutly to be sought, we need only look around us to see how far beyond hope the dream of liberty lies for so many of the peoples of our earth. That is brought home to us every day in the news of the world.

But it was not only the pursuit of liberty that Charles Frankel preached, though he did that superbly. He was a philosopher as well as a historian, a teacher of both in classrooms, in books and wherever he could gather a few who would listen; then he would tire the sun with talking and send it down to bed.

Indeed I suspect that, to him, liberty was as much a means to an end as a thing desirable in itself. He knew that liberty by itself can be abused, turning into an anarchy as oppressive as tyranny. What he sought from liberty was the freeing of the human spirit because he believed, above all else, in the dream of civilized man.

Civility and madness. They met one night in the quiet village of Bedford Hills, N.Y. There some person or persons—made, as Charles would put it, in the image of God—went on a wanton spree of violence. They broke into two houses and killed all the occupants of each. Among the dead were Charles and Helen Frankel.

You will search in vain for a motive. The intruders were not professional burglars. They killed first, slipping quietly into bedrooms to put bullets in the heads of their sleeping victims. When they afterwards ransacked the houses it was in aimless fashion, leaving fingerprints everywhere. Much of what they took they left in their stolen car, casually abandoned later in Brooklyn.

Nor were they of the familiar breed of terrorists bent on vengeance or, in the fashion of our times, on spreading fear to make some political point. There was no connection between the two houses, other than proximity; they were simply chosen at random. All the available evidence suggests the murderers did not even know whom they had killed until, perchance, they read about it in the morning paper or heard it on the TV news.

Madness, then, seems the only word for it. The police say the killers were either psychopaths or junked up on dope, killing in a frenzy, shooting some of their unknown victims many times.

What is one to say about such madness? There is a temptation to think this kind of madness endemic to our times, something spawned by these times alone, a sign of a breakdown in our culture, one more manifestation of our moral degeneration. After all there have been other such senseless killings, a man in a college tower or in a shopping center shooting randomly at strangers.

Charles Frankel the historian would not, I think, have succumbed to that temptation. He knew madness and killing have never been strangers to our species, any more than oppression, tyranny, avowed terrorism or the vengeance of revolutionists. Iran's is not the first revolution to devour itself in bloody slaughter. Man's inhumanity and madness are a recurrent cancer on our species.

There is also, I must confess, a temptation to weep the more at the tragic irony that in this case the random victim should be one who believed so much in the ability of man to overcome his barbarism and madness. He had a deep and abiding faith in the rationality of man, in the power of civility in discourse and disagreement.

Yet Charles Frankel the philosopher would have known that there was as much tragedy in the death of his neighbors as in his own, for all that he was famous and they were not. And he would not, or so I think, even in death lose his faith in the worth of man's struggle to, someday, civilize himself.

To believe in the ultimate goodness of man, he once wrote, "is not to say that men's good deeds outnumber their evil deeds, or that benevolence is a stronger disposition in man than malice." His faith, rather, was to keep looking for cures to the human ailments that lead to evil "and of refusing to take No for an answer."

He himself would never accept such an answer. In what were to be his last days he was the moving spirit in founding The National Humanities Center, a place where scholars can gather seeking new light on the human condition. In his vision their search will be not alone for knowledge about the physical universe in which we live but for something equally and perhaps more important, an understanding of what we are as a human species and of our relation to each other and to that universe.

It is there that Charles Frankel built his own monument. For he built well and what he began will endure. Those whom he brought together with his vision will see to it that the vision is not lost.

So much, then, for the public place of Charles Frankel, historian and philosopher. But there is one more thing to be said. Most of us who knew him had not his gift for civility in all things. To have lost in such a manner a good and gentle friend makes us think how thin is that veneer called civilization, and we can only cry out in helpless anger at the madness in man that will not be exorcised.

May 30, 1979

THE PREVALENCE OF EVIL (I)

For those of us who spend our time contemplating what goes on in the world there come events that defy any rational comment.

What is one to say about an earthquake that kills people by the hundred thousand—or about devastating floods, hurricanes, tornadoes or volcanic explosions—except to say they are terrible and to mourn the dead?

We are no less paralyzed when, sometimes, the catastrophe is not from the violence of nature but the violence of men.

What is there to do except express horror at the Nazis who stuffed other human beings into gas ovens in wholesale slaughter? It begs the question to say that Hitler was a madman. That kind of madness itself defies rational explanation. And the horror is compounded because that was not the work of one man alone; it was done only because thousands of other human beings shared in the brutality against their kind.

So it is with what came to pass in Guyana. That horror too came not from a single madman bent on murder; with murderous madmen we are familiar enough on our city streets.

As the bodies were unpiled—some poisoned, some with slashed throats, some with blown-out brains—we were numbed as from a holocaust. What manner of people were these who could butcher each other or walk senselessly to death, some holding their own dead children in their arms?

Our minds are paralyzed because we live in a time when they are gripped by a belief in the rationality of man, in the relativism of right and wrong, and we feel betrayed. We no longer believe in the prevalence of evil. Indeed, we doubt any longer that there is such a thing as evil.

Nietzsche, the German philosopher who became the herald of the Nazis, long since proclaimed God dead. Thus there can be no measure of right and wrong to which all men must repair in fear of being judged no more than beasts. Each of us is entitled to make his own measure.

"To talk of intrinsic right and wrong," said Nietzsche, "is absolutely nonsensical. Intrinsically an injury, an oppression, an exploitation, an annihilation can be nothing wrong inasmuch as life is essentially . . . something which functions by injuring, oppressing, exploiting and annihilating."

From this comes the modern catechism that, since we are merely animals, cruelty and brutality come naturally to us. And these being the normal ingredients of human nature, there can be no evil in them. In the words of an anthropologist, S. J. Holmes, "they are all virtues."

Or perhaps Hamlet put the new philosophy as well as any modern philosopher when he said, "There is nothing either good or bad but thinking makes it so."

This is no mere recognition of the frailties of men, that being weak creatures here below we could not always obey a higher moral law even if we professed it. In the "scientific" view vice is not an imperfection to which we may succumb because we are not gods. It does not exist because today the commandments on Mount Sinai have been repealed.

There are, then, no longer any sins, not even murder. Murder is at most misbehavior against man-made law. An old man is sliced up on a park bench by a pack in human form for the joy of seeing him bleed and we are asked not to judge them evil but simply unfortunate in having nothing else to occupy their time.

To the rationalist no man does evil; he is at worst misguided in his actions. But I have no doubt that Jim Jones in Guyana thought he was doing "good" when he led his flock to slaughter; in death he thought to save them. I have no doubt that those who followed him thought they were following the path of righteousness.

I have no doubt either that Hitler thought he was doing good trying to annihilate the whole of the Jewish people—or that those terrorists loose in the world today think to make a better world by indiscriminate killings.

Yet simply to call all that paranoia, which it is, is to affix a label that explains nothing. We are left with horror inexplicable.

There was a time when men would have thought Guyana explicable if no less horrible. From the fruit of that forbidden tree, so they believed, came man's knowledge of good and evil and the free will to

choose the one or the other. His woe, in that ringing voice from Ecclesiastes, is that "the heart of the sons of man is full of evil."

That is to say they found evil a palpable presence in the world because they recognized its seed in themselves. But that presupposes a
belief in a moral law higher than man-made law and that man is something more than an animal. "If I am not an animal," so went the ancient cry, "what am I? If I am only an animal, what am I?" Even pa-
gans once thought "humanity is poised midway between the gods and
beasts."

If it is otherwise, why should anyone lament the behavior of men, as
in Guyana? A thousand dead, more or less, is nothing in a crowded
world; no more than die with each day's sun.

It is not fashionable any longer, I know, to believe in sin, that there
are things wrong simply because they are wrong. But I submit—not by
way of argument, for it cannot be settled by argument, I can only make
an assertion—that in Guyana we saw the face of evil plain.

The crime was murder. The evil lay in its cause, the perversion of
love by one man usurping the role of God and others bowing before
him as if he were. That transgression is the only thing that can explain
such a horror.

December 6, 1978

THE PREVALENCE OF EVIL (II)

The list is long of man's inhumanity to man. It by no means began in our own time with the holocaust of Hitler, nor has it been confined to any one place or people. Massacres of innocents were already old when Herod the Great ordered the slaughter of the male children of Bethlehem. Cruelty and casual killing have marked the history of those who preached mercy and the goodness of God—the followers of Abraham, Jesus, Mohammed.

Massacres are certainly nothing new to the avowed godless in the communist countries of either China or the Soviet Union. In China, more than twenty million "counter-revolutionaries" were massacred between 1949 and 1965. In Russia, nineteen million died in the early Stalin slave-labor camps, eight million in the great purge of 1936–38. In the Ukraine, seven million were deliberately starved in the government-induced famine of 1931–32. How many have been liquidated in the years since World War II, nobody knows.

By such measures, the murder of 269 persons on an airliner becomes a footnote in history; what makes it especially shocking is that it's a figure the mind can grasp.

What is new in our time is not the constant reappearance of mankind's inhumanity but the disappearance of the concept of evil—that quality that breeds this cruelty, brutality and disregard of human life.

In past times, philosophers argued about the nature of evil, but they had no doubt it existed. What man, asked Socrates, would choose evil over good? And he urged his disciples to seek above all "to learn and discern between good and evil" so that they could choose.

To the writer of Ecclesiastes, the "heart of the sons of men is full of evil," which may be why in prayer we ask the Lord "to deliver us from evil." To later Christian philosophers, evil was a palpable thing that posed a theological problem. In a world created by a good and omnipotent God, how could it exist? The best they could answer was that it was born with man's first disobedience that lost him forever the innocence of Eden. God let evil exist as punishment for the descendants of Adam.

In our more enlightened time, the "problem of evil" has vanished because evil itself doesn't exist in a world of moral relativism. Everything now is a matter of subjective value judgments. Spinoza abolished the ideal of "good" as well as evil, as many after him have also abolished God. Anything, Spinoza taught us, can at the same time be good or evil—or both. Hamlet put the same idea succinctly when he remarked that nothing is either good or bad "but thinking makes it so."

The result of this moral relativism, which today you can hear preached even in churches, is that everyman is now free, in the popular phrase, "to do his own thing," effectively repealing the laws of Moses or any other prescriptive behavior.

Among other things, this has altered our idea of crime and punishment. The mugger or the murderer has at most violated a civil law that can be, and is, frequently changed. His deed may be "bad" because it frightens us by disturbing our sense of safety, but since it may be prompted by an unhappy childhood or economic misfortune, it cannot be morally condemned. With no canon of morality, how can it be?

I've no doubt Hitler didn't consider himself evil. He put Jews in gas chambers to serve what he thought a noble purpose, "purifying the race." So with Stalin, who thought the slaughter of millions was justified in building a new society. If there is no concept of good and evil to which we human beings may repair, how do we condemn either?

Indeed, if evil does not exist, how do we understand the world around us? What else moves Black Septembrists to shoot up a peaceful Olympic village? Or the Irish Republican Army to blow up their neighbors? Or terrorists anywhere to assassinate indiscriminately? In their own minds, all of these people think they act to serve a higher purpose. By their own value judgments, the lives of innocents are of lesser importance.

For that matter, how are we to judge that shooting down by the Soviet Union of a Korean civilian airliner packed with innocent people? The fighter pilot who fired the missile was only carrying out orders; had he not done so his own life would have been in peril. Those who gave the orders thought they were acting in the "national interest." Although we know they were mistaken because it was not in fact a spy plane, they may well have been misled by an inadequate response from the commercial pilot to the military challenges. Any defense attorney would have, at the least, the argument of mitigating circumstances.

I'm sure none of those people think themselves evil men either, and in fact they may not be in all other ways. What we have, all the same, are haunting questions about the nature of evil that can lead men to the murder of innocents as a casual decision. Their deed was morally wrong simply because it was wrong, and that is not altered by the explanation that the Soviet Union is paranoid with suspicion and the perpetrators acted within their value judgments, though that explanation may be true enough.

The ancients for whom evil was a palpable reality knew that evil could exist independent of the men in whom it lodged; it can even, and sometimes does, lead men of good will to inhumanity to men when they think they act in a worthy cause, such as the burning of heretics.

What those philosophers never solved is what evil is or why it is. Nor can I. All I know, looking at the world we live in, is that it is as prevalent today as it was in the beginning, when Cain killed Abel.

September 29, 1983

THREE SCORE AND TEN

It begins, so I'm told, when your eyes turn routinely to the obituary columns in the day's newspaper. If that's the case, then I have had for a long time some intimations of mortality.

Sometimes it's about a friend, or even more poignantly a schoolmate of long ago, leaving us at sixty-seven. Sometimes yet another near contemporary with whom I have shared many hours who made it to eighty-seven. Or perhaps a famous person with a long obituary at ninety-one, catching me by surprise that he had lived so long quietly out of the public eye.

Sometimes, of course, it's a different story in another part of the paper about a neighbor, or perhaps a once celebrity, celebrating a ninety-fifth birthday with grandchildren and great-grandchildren gathered to help mark the occasion.

Whichever way it is, or whomever the news item is about, such stories often hold my attention more than the latest news of Lebanon, Latin America or the progress toward the Democratic nomination. The latter I read because that's my business. The others I read because, of late, longevity holds a more personal interest.

We are all, I think, more conscious of those birthdays that mark the passing decades. A young person feels more grown up at twenty than at nineteen. At forty, or even more so at fifty, you are conscious of beginning a new stage in life. And so you are, or at least so am I, on reaching the biblical three score and ten.

This is not, be assured, a gloomy thought. There was a time, it's true, when a man of seventy was ready for the discard. Not any more. In my time I've seen the life span of our species stretch beyond the imagination of our forebears. Those cut off untimely are the exception rather than the rule.

And not just longevity only. Thanks to the amazing medical progress of our time, even old age need not incapacitate. Along my way I've lost my appendix, my gall bladder, one kidney. I've suffered a "small" stroke and had some of my ancient arteries reamed out. Yet here I am, as is my long habit, still putting one word after another, hale if not hearty.

How long I can keep this up, I naturally don't know. But I have many cheering examples before me. Thomas F. Woodlock, the man who started this column, kept it up well into his seventies. So did his successor, William H. Grimes. Woodlock, in fact, wrote his last column from his hospital bed, having lost neither his interest nor his touch, and it was published posthumously.

Then there are more famous writing folk. Will Durant completed his monumental history of civilization with the age of Napoleon, his own age being ninety. Mark Sullivan, whose six-volume compendium of the early years of this century was a favorite of my youth, was still writing journalistic commentary when he was pushing eighty.

But more pertinent to my present musings are those nearer contemporaries who have shared my time and remain active scribblers for the public press.

Several come to mind. James Reston, two-time Pulitzer winner, is still interviewing presidents and traipsing around the world for *The New York Times* at seventy-five. By comparison Mark Childs, veteran observer of Washington, is a mere youth of seventy-one.

Then there are two former colleagues who set before me durable examples. John Chamberlain, one-time writer on just about anything for *The Wall Street Journal*, has been just as wide-ranging in his current syndicated column at eighty. So also Ray Cromley, seventy-four, the *Journal*'s Tokyo correspondent before World War II.

The doyen of all, however, must be Richard Strout, who for many years wrote for the *New Republic*. He first went to Washington for the *Christian Science Monitor* during the administration of Calvin Coolidge and was still there to greet the administration of Ronald Reagan. I wouldn't be at all surprised if he turned up at this summer's political conventions, notebook in hand, at the age of eighty-six.

As we elder journalists like to say, the legs give out long before the sap stops running.

And speaking of elders, I mustn't forget that at three score and ten I have a president even older than I, and one with a vigor I can only envy.

I'm not sure I'd go so far as to say with Browning's Rabbi Ben Ezra that "the best is yet to be." In my case, it would be hard to think of anything better than a life of rich memories. Of growing up in a small Southern town in a way forever gone. Of the delight to a young man in first exploring Baghdad on the Subway, and surviving its challenges. Of surviving, too, a great depression and the greatest war yet in history. Of the excitement at age twenty-two of attending a Roosevelt press conference. Of nearly a half-century writing for *The Wall Street Journal* with a license to write as I please.

And most of all, of a long and happy marriage fruitful of children and grandchildren.

Of all such things are my memories compounded. I can only tell anyone who will listen that it has been a full and interesting life and that I doubt the future can match it.

If I have any melancholy in facing that future on a seventieth anniversary, it has nothing to do with the past or even with those intimations of mortality. It comes only with the unease that someday I may lose the enthusiasm for watching the world around me and the eagerness to inflict on readers my thoughts about it all.

I'd gladly settle right now for Dick Strout's durability. But I suspect I'll weary long before eighty-six. And when that time comes, whenever it is, I hope I'll have the wit to recognize it before others do.

May 5, 1984

II

The Historian's Eye

JOURNALISM AS HISTORY

I am not an accredited historian. The most I can claim is that I have been a journalist writing about national, and sometimes world, affairs for nearly half a century. I have thus lived through much history and have had a chance to observe history in the making. This gives me some credentials, I hope, for discussing the role of journalism, in all its forms, in both the making of history and the recording of some parts of it for the benefit of future historians, or for any who wish to know how it was in some past time.

As a journalist with, happily, a ringside seat to observe this half-century, I have come to agree with Carlyle that history is the sum of innumerable biographies. Sometimes, as Emerson thought, this means the biographies of a few men—a Napoleon, let us say, or a Franklin Roosevelt or Winston Churchill. Theirs are the deeds that fill many history books. But to understand history the biographies of the great and the famous are not enough. It is revealed also, and sometimes more clearly, in the lives of the innumerable people who lived through it including journalists who tried to record it.

For those too young to remember, who wish to know about the Great Depression, it is not enough to read economic histories or even the many Roosevelt biographies. The young should ask their parents or grandparents how it was. Or read Studs Terkel, who gathered together the memories of just "ordinary people"—nameless so far as learned histories go—of that time long ago.

So also if you would learn about World War II it is not enough to read Eisenhower or Churchill. A journalistic account, such as *The Longest Day*, will tell you much about that global conflagration because it tells what happened to the men who actually fought it, landing one morning in the face of the enemy on a Normandy beach. Or read the memories of those who were at Pearl Harbor that fatal Sunday, whether Japanese in the sky or Americans on the exploding ships below.

I am not alone in thinking thus. In the archives of our great libraries there are, of course, the letters and papers of the famous, of presidents, governors and others who led us in troubled and stirring times. They make interesting reading for those who would know our past. But these are not the only letters or papers in such collections. Those in charge who wish to preserve our past have also collected letters of innumerable people who fit no such categories. These are the letters, diaries and other papers of people without renown—farmers, merchants, laborers, wives, mothers, who tell of their daily living. These can be equally fascinating, and often more instructive. For they tell how it actually was to live through the American Revolution, through the early days of state and nation, through the turmoil of the War Between the States, through the pains of the Reconstruction period. They tell us how they earned their livelihood, how they fared when their livelihood was meager, how they met sickness and death in the family, what they thought of the men and events that swirled around them.

These papers are sometimes poorly written, almost always unpolished in style because their writers did not know they were writing the stuff of history. They are simply sons telling a mother how it was to be at Gettysburg. Or mothers speaking their grief at the loss of a child. Or a farmer telling a distant friend how the crops were that year and what the prices were on the local market. But such papers are invaluable. Without them the historians would be deprived of much they need to know to restore life to the past.

There are other writers too who provide the stuff of history. For lack of a better word I will simply call them "the observers." That is, those who observed their times and set down their observations without benefit of hindsight, which is what journalists do. One of the most famous of these in antiquity was Thucydides. Today he is admitted into the pantheon of historians, but in fact he wrote a strictly contemporary account of events that he lived through, the most notable being his account of the Peloponnesian War, in which he fought as one of the Athenian commanders.

In more recent times we learn much about our nation in its early days through the writings of Alexis de Tocqueville and, for that matter, of Charles Dickens, both of whom traveled throughout our country and set down their account of what they saw and thought about at that time. If you read de Tocqueville, especially his *Democracy in America*, you will learn very little about his own life. You will learn a great deal about our early penal system, about the institution of slavery, about the way we governed ourselves in the middle of the nineteenth century.

So with Dickens, who traveled to America at about the same time, and whose impressions of us were less than favorable. He found more vulgarity and sharp practice here than he expected or than we would like to admit. But Dickens had a keen eye. If you would know how life was in England in that nineteenth century, or how we impressed foreigners of that time, he too provides raw material for more formal historians.

Both de Tocqueville and Dickens were essentially writing journalism, Dickens consciously and professionally, de Tocqueville unconsciously—although the latter might have scorned the designation. It is journalism because the essence of that craft is the setting down of observations on the current state of things. It is not written out of delving into musty tomes in a library, which is and must be the task of any who would write a history of some distant past.

Of course journalism can influence events as well as record them. Tom Paine with his pamphlets had an enormous influence on his time. So did de Tocqueville, inserting his opinions into his observations. But this is true also of those other observers we don't always think of as journalists—the letter writers. They influence those they are writing to and help shape "public opinion." Examples of this abound in the Committees of Correspondence in our pre-Revolutionary period.

Later times may alter any contemporary observer's perceptions. Diligent research may show that at times he got his facts wrong; even Thucydides hasn't escaped unscathed. All of us can only write what comes within our purview and none of us can avoid the personal views which may color our accounts; that is, our prejudices, if you prefer that word. But without such journalistic writing (called by whatever name) the historian would flounder.

The faded files of newsprint, or the even more faded ancient letters or diaries of those who lived in the time under scrutiny, are part of the raw material of the historian's research. To discuss intelligently the origins of the First World War, a Barbara Tuchman must not only read the official files in Britain or in Germany, the reports of statesmen and generals, but also the diaries of lesser officials, the newspaper records of the time, and even the letters of those "ordinary" people who wrote to each other about how it was with them.

If anything, this is more true of recent times than those of antiquity, for the simple reason that there is more such material available. We know little about the Trojan War except what Homer tells us—and most of that was doubted until Heinrich Schliemann excavated Troy and finally convinced scholars that Homer knew what he was writing about.

As we come down to our own times, if you would understand "the South that was" you must read Gerald Johnson and W. J. Cash. Southerners may not find either palatable to their tastes—or their prejudices. But no historian of the South can ignore them. If you would know how it was in your town "just yesterday" you cannot ignore the perceptions of those who wrote long ago in your newspapers.

Here, of course, I must confess my own prejudices. I am not in any sense a scholarly historian. I am simply a journalist writing about the ephemera of our time. But a curious thing happens with ephemera. A newspaper article is dated and forgotten within a week, sometimes the next day. But let a decade pass, or certainly a generation, that same article takes on a new life. The interest in it, and perhaps even its value, increases, just as that old Tiffany lamp fell into scornful disfavor only to find itself in time sought out to decorate the newest of homes.

There's a simple explanation for this journalistic phenomenon. As we live our daily lives we know how it is—in fact, we are inundated with the news of events and of opinions on it. So Vermont Royster or James Reston or Ed Yoder or James J. Kilpatrick sees events this way and has this opinion of them. So what? Everyone has his own point of view. But years later those still living may enjoy looking back to recall how the events were first recorded and viewed. Those too young to remember can find it interesting to learn how it was "in the olden days." This is especially true of historians who wish to recreate the past. Thus it is that we journalists also serve—albeit modestly—in the making of history as the future will see it.

Marcus Aurelius in his *Meditations* put it well. If we are discoursing about men and events, he said, "we should look at them in their assemblies, armies, agricultural labors, marriages, births, deaths, noise of the courts of justice . . . feasts, lamentations, markets, a mixture of all things." And whosoever records these things, whether he be called a journalist or no, is a servant of history.

Plutarch, that great historian of antiquity, understood this when he wrote that he would endeavor to bring together "such things as are not commonly known and lie scattered here and there in other men's writings . . . found among the archives."

I assume that for older readers I need not dwell on the value to present times of recalling past times. I am not so sure that the young feel the same way. When we are young we tend to think the world began when we first paid attention to it, and to think the past has nothing relevant to say to us about these present times.

So I hope I will be forgiven one more quotation, this one from the great Roman orator, Cicero. "What is a human life worth unless it is set in an historical context? To remain ignorant of things that happened before you were born is to remain a child."

I make no apologies, then, for the role of the journalist in recording, as best he may, the events of the day which, upon some other day, will be that raw material for history.

Talk presented to the North Carolina Historical Society,
October 4, 1983

OLD, AFFECTIONATE FRIEND

For a good many years it was the custom of a good many news-papers, including *The Wall Street Journal*, to reprint George Washington's Farewell Address on the occasion of his birthday—the real birthday, not that one contrived to give us a long holiday weekend.

The custom fell into disuse in the late 1930s. In part, no doubt, this was because Washington's formal and solemn prose falls quaintly upon the modern ear. He wasn't a very charismatic figure even in life. He seems less so to posterity, staring at us from those frozen-faced portraits and laden in school-children's memory with the fable of the little boy who wouldn't tell a lie to escape a whipping.

But another reason, I suspect, was that Washington said things that sounded very quaint by the 1930s and more so today. One of the things he urged upon his country, for example, was that it avoid permanent alliances with foreign nations. He was also constantly adjuring Congress to have some care with the public purse.

In time, of course, we did erect a monument to him, the choice though being not some brooding statue but a cold and faceless obelisk. Today, amid all the festivities of the Bicentennial, he remains the forgotten man. The talk is all of the fiery Jefferson, the fatherly Franklin, the romantic John and Abigail. For inspiration a sitting president burrows into the words of the tempestuous Tom Paine, not into those of his own somber first predecessor.

No wonder, I suppose. In his first inaugural Washington declined the "emoluments" of office as "being inapplicable to myself." He recognized that financial vision must be "indispensably included" for presidents lest the office fall only to the rich and well-born but he thought it ill-advised that public offices should be sought for their pecuniary rewards.

That's hardly a thought to commend itself in a time when congressmen richly reward themselves and our presidency costs us more than the sovereign of that kingdom against which we rebelled.

Nor was that all. Washington also said, and the senators of that day agreed with him, that the foundation of the new Republic must be the "principles of private morality," that if "individuals be not influenced by moral principles it is vain to look for public virtue." He might not be surprised, looking around him today, to find the people complaining of a want of public virtue.

But he had more to offer than such quaint homilies. It's surprising, in fact, how much he had to say on matters of his own time that are not irrelevant to current controversies.

Faced with the problem of what to do with a large body of citizens who had rebelled against the laws of Congress, he decided there are times when amnesty is better public policy than Draconian judgment and so he granted "a full, free and entire pardon to all persons" who had participated in what is known to history as the Whiskey Rebellion.

Faced with a demand from the House of Representatives that he provide all the correspondence and documents relating to negotiations with Great Britain, he declined with the observation: "The nature of foreign negotiations requires caution, and their success must often depend on secrecy, and even when brought to their conclusion a full disclosure of all the measures, demands, or eventual concessions which have been proposed or contemplated would be extremely impolitic." To do so, he said, would have a "pernicious influence" on future negotiations, "producing mischief in relation to other powers."

Faced with the problem of educating a citizenry for this novel experiment of a self-governing people, he proposed the "establishing of a national university" to be supported out of the public treasury and open to all of demonstrated ability "who are to be the future guardians of the liberties of the country."

Faced with the problem of peace in a perilous world, he concluded that to be prepared for war is the most effectual means of avoiding it. "If we desire to secure peace . . . it must be known that we are at all times ready for war."

So it was that in 1796 as he came to the end of his service he sought to offer to his countrymen "as an old, affectionate friend" both precepts and example from those years of experience reaching back long before 1776.

The example—that eight years was long enough to entrust any man with the powers of the presidency—we finally came to embody in a constitutional amendment against those who might not follow it. The precepts have been hardly heeded by anybody.

"The great rule of conduct for us in regard to foreign nations is, in extending our commercial relations to have as little political connection as possible . . . to steer clear of permanent alliances with any portion of the foreign world. . . . There can be no greater error than to expect or calculate upon real favors from nation to nation. It is an illusion which experience must cure.

"Cherish public credit . . . avoiding the accumulation of debt, not only by shunning occasions of expense but by vigorous exertions in time of peace to discharge debts . . . not ungenerously throwing upon posterity the burden which we ourselves ought to bear."

These were not precepts then, any more than now, to gain universal acclaim. At the time, his farewell to public service moved one Philadelphia newspaper to comment: "The man who is the source of all the misfortunes of our country . . . is no longer possessed of power to multiply evils upon the United States. If ever there was a period of rejoicing, this is the moment."

Today, to be sure, children troop up his monument and his face adorns our dollar bills, 600 billion of which measure the public debt. But it's no wonder indeed he's little quoted in those Bicentennial orations. What you do wonder, is how he would have fared on those hustings in New Hampshire.

February 25, 1976

AND OUR POSTERITY . . .

This being our Bicentennial year the countryside is dotted with speakers recalling our Founding Fathers and their handiwork in the Declaration of Independence and the Constitution. As a young lady in my family remarked, we are going to get Bicentennialed to death.

A purist might contend that what we are celebrating is our Bicentenary, the word Bicentennial having been an adjective until the advertising and promotion people converted it to a noun. No matter. A birthday by whatever name is a time for taking stock, for recalling the past, looking at the present and wondering about the future.

So we are going to hear a lot about all men being created free and equal, about the rights of free speech, freedom of religion, habeas corpus, trial by jury and all those other things incorporated in the Bill of Rights, those first ten amendments to the Constitution.

There will be much discussion about the American Experiment, what it is and whether it can endure. There will be quotations from Jefferson, Hamilton, Franklin and the others who had a hand in designing our system of government. The meaning of this phrase or that in the Constitution will be examined, praised, criticized and generally tormented. And out of it all will come, we hope, a new sense of pride and faith in this experiment which is not yet ended.

Of course there will be a certain selectivity in what is cited, depending on the current view of old ideas. As with other sacred writings the selections vary with the gospel to be preached.

For example, with all the attention heaped on those first ten amendments which are proclaimed as the foundation of our liberties, little will be said of the tenth. This is the one which says that "the powers not delegated to the United States, nor prohibited by it to the states, are reserved to the states respectively, or to the people."

That view has long been confined to oblivion. Today the idea is ex-

actly reversed. We think it self-evident that powers not specifically prohibited to the national government are delegated to it.

Much will also be said of that phrase in the Preamble to the Constitution which speaks of the intent to "promote the general welfare."
Hardly anyone will carry the quotation further where it also proclaims
the intent "to secure the blessings of liberty to ourselves *and our
posterity.*"

For one thing, we now wonder whether the blessings of security are
not more the purpose of our government than those of liberty. But
what really seems quaint today is that the men of those times should
have been concerned in what they did not only for themselves but for
those who should come after.

That is not the attitude of our times. We look to the problems of
today and care not what we may create of problems for tomorrow. Let
the next generation, or the one after, worry about them.

The difference in attitude is reflected in many ways but nowhere
more noticeably than in the conduct of public finances. The Founding
Fathers and their immediate successors took great care not to shift the
burdens of the public treasury to future generations. Though theirs
was a poor country they were frugal with debt. Operating budgets were
balanced; until the Civil War there was no public debt to speak of.

Even as late as 1910, just before World War I, the public debt was
barely $12 per capita. Two World Wars and a depression raised it to
$1,700. By 1975, after many years of prosperity, every baby was born
with a debt of $2,500—never to be paid off, to be sure, but the interest
on it to be paid out of his taxes forever.

We think nothing of adding to it. Deficits of $50 billion or $70 billion a year hardly make us blink. With such deficits we still propose to
cut our own taxes, depreciate our money. Let our children deal with
the consequences.

The chief cause is not, as you might suppose, from the burdens of
defense or general government costs. The cost of our general government (the legislature, the executive and administrative departments) is
almost exactly the same percentage of our national income today as in
1968; defense costs are a little more than half as much. The great increase has come in interest on that public debt and, most especially,
in all the things called social programs, the things we do for our generation to be paid by the next.

The most dramatic example is Social Security. Experts differ whether the actuarial deficit for the Social Security fund is one trillion dollars or two trillion. In either case, it is *trillions*. For the future there must be astronomical tax increases or less Social Security. Either way a future generation must pay for our generosity to ourselves.

We cannot blame all this on our politicians. We the people demanded it. Anyway, such figures are but symptoms of a change in spirit.

Men once fought at Lexington and Gettysburg not because it profited them but to secure for others the blessings of liberty or a more perfect union. Today we look no further than for peace in our time. Women once bore the hardships of the mountains and the prairie dreaming of a future for their children and grandchildren. Now many dream of no children at all.

Once, in our families and our nation, we spoke of building generation after generation. Now we hear voices proclaiming, to each its own.

Yet we ourselves are the posterity of those who began the American Experiment, and if there are blessings from their handiwork for us to enjoy it's because they thought not just of the day but of the morrow.

Surely that's a thought worth remembering with gratitude amid all the celebrations of our Bicentennial. And it might be worth reflecting, now and then, that if this experiment they began is to endure we should give some thought to what we do to those who will come hereafter.

March 3, 1976

THE SWINGING PENDULUM

So now we enter the third century of American independence, or at least the declaration of it, while approaching the third millennium of the Christian era and something like the tenth millennium since civilization first began in the Mesopotamian valley.

It's hardly surprising, then, that the American Historical Association in convention should have paused to reflect on the American experience, what it means and what it portends for the future. Or, as Arthur Schlesinger, Jr. has noted, that these reflections should lead to meditation on the perishability of republics, the subversion of virtue, the transience of glory and the mutability of human affairs.

For the questions are not only what the third century holds for the American experiment, still on probation, but also what the future holds for civilization itself in an atomic age.

These are natural questions on our national anniversary, and the reflective mood is no doubt deepened by the coincidence that we begin a new national century with a new president to mark symbolically the end of one time and the beginning of another.

The two questions are inextricably entwined. Obviously the American experiment cannot survive if civilization collapses. And one does not have to be a chauvinist to feel that if this experiment in liberty fails then the future of civilization will be altered.

One thing that makes them anxious questions is the ever-present possibility that mankind will blow itself up. But that is not all. As historians know, all civilization is precarious, poised ever on the edge of barbarism by which it can be overrun as tilled fields untended revert to jungle.

About all that, there are certainly ominous signs. Only the word barbarism can describe what's been happening in Lebanon, the very cradle of civilization; in Ireland, where Christians kill each other in the name of the Cross; in Africa, where blacks senselessly slaughter their brothers; indeed everywhere that terrorism against the innocent is thought no more than a mode of expression.

Nor have we escaped. The violence in our streets, bombs in airports, madmen shooting at passersby, the prevalence of assassinations, all these things are remarked and deplored. But they no longer surprise. And it is this want of surprise that tells us what has changed. Violence our country has always known. What is new is that it is now casual, indiscriminate and indifferent, and so becomes an ordinary hazard of living.

About all that, there is little we can do, you and I. We can only hope that somehow terrorism will be conquered and pray that our leaders can spare us atomic war. But there are other things, too, to give pause. Our times have also seen changes in morals and manners, in our perceptions of ourselves as human beings and in our value judgments about what is right or wrong in human behavior—and these also can threaten society.

"Everybody must develop their own standards of sexual morality." The quotation is from a medical psychologist. It could be from almost anyone and it reflects a prevailing attitude not merely about sex but about all human behavior.

Note that this does not merely criticize old standards of morality, be they of Puritan ethic or middle-class values, those standards much scorned as outmoded. Rather it says there are no standards at all to which all may repair. Each makes up his own.

We see this mirrored in many ways. The family declines because people no longer feel bound by a sense of responsibility, one to another. There is no inner voice to trouble the young who cheat in classrooms, the businessman who bribes, the politician who accepts. And so on. If everybody is free to develop his own standards, why should it be otherwise?

There have been Cassandras crying peril at this for a long time. Lothrop Stoddard called it a revolt against civilization. To Ortega it was the revolt of the masses. Spengler saw in it the decline of the West. That they may be proved right is undeniable. That they will be is by no means certain.

For civilization has in fact stood on that razor's edge between preservation and destruction since, some seven or eight thousand years B.C., the species first gathered in numbers larger than a family group or tribe. Once it had done that it had to try to create the means of social order to separate civilization from barbarism. Since then the barriers between have always been fragile.

In those millennia nations have risen and fallen, societies have been born and died, some destroyed by wars, some by pestilence, some by internal decay of the social order. None has proved immutable. At least once, during what we call the Dark Ages, civilization itself almost vanished when its decadence made it prey to barbarians.

Yet in due time it was born again, and out of that rebirth came what we know as Western civilization. It is an accumulation not only of ideas about political organization and of technical knowledge but also of time-tested social values. Its crowning glory is political liberty. Its underpinning is a moral idea, that man of all the animals is touched with some kind of divinity and so answerable for his life to something outside himself, be it to God or to his fellow human beings.

If we lose that moral imperative, as the Cassandras warn, neither our country nor its civilization can stand unaltered. Losing faith in what made us, we sink or are overrun. But it is, let us hope, a far more durable moral view than is dreamt of by the doomsayers.

Anyway, there are everywhere signs of another change. More and more people—including, ironically, the rebellious young now rebelling against being cast adrift without standards—are seeking more fixed stars to steer by. Perhaps it is not even foolish to think some part of Jimmy Carter's appeal was a hunger for our society, too, to be born again.

If so, historians will not be surprised. The swinging pendulum is a constant of history. The hope for America in this third century, and of its civilization, is that while one generation may forget old lessons, in time another relearns them.

January 12, 1977

AN AMERICAN CENTURY?

"At the beginning of the 14th Century France was the most powerful, the most populous, the most active, the most rich of the realms of Christendom; her interventions were to be feared, her arbitrations respected, her protection sought after. One might have thought there was opening up for Europe a French century. . . .

"Forty years later that same France was crushed on the field of battle by a nation five times less populous. Her leaders were split into factions, her middle class in revolt . . . her roads ravaged by crime, all authority flouted, her commerce paralyzed, misery and insecurity everywhere. Why such a collapse?"

The words are those of Maurice Druon, French historian and novelist. But with some changes in words and dates they could apply equally well to other nations which in the past had their day of preeminence—or at least the promise of it—only to find their power, their influence, their riches transitory.

For a time it was the turn of Spain. Made rich by her conquests in the New World (she once controlled nearly all of South America and much of what is now the United States), she seemed to be a permanent fixture among great powers. Britain may be said to have had two "centuries," that of the first Elizabeth and the period between the Napoleonic wars and World War I before she finally sank to second-rate status. History is replete with other examples of the rise and decline of nations.

Just when the United States emerged as a major world influence, economic and military, can be debated. Some would begin with World War I, largely because the then great European powers—France, Germany, Britain—exhausted themselves in that struggle.

But no one will dispute the fact that by 1945 the U.S. was the world's preeminent and unchallenged power. It was not only that we emerged victorious from World War II with a military might unmatched among victors or vanquished. We were also the richest, in and out of Christendom, with our interventions to be feared, our arbitrations to be respected and our protection sought after. One might have thought, and many did, that there was opening up an American century.

Today, less than forty years later, it can no longer be said that we are universally respected, wooed or feared.

Economically we are challenged by nations we defeated, West Germany and Japan. Politically we are challenged and often bested by a nation we helped save, the Soviet Union. Just of late we have been defied, militarily and politically, by one of the world's smallest nations.

So whatever else may be said about our position in the world, we no longer stand astride it like a colossus.

Some of this change was inevitable. We could not expect the rest of the world to stagnate. Indeed, we did not desire that and we gave much of our treasure to rebuild both former enemies and allies and to stimulate growth in underdeveloped countries. We never had any ambition to be the Rome of the world, ruling the whole of it as once did the Caesars.

Nonetheless, our decline from the pinnacle lies not entirely in such stars. We have, as other nations before us, contributed to it with our own follies.

The decline of nations is a phenomenon that fascinates historians, and none has been more probed than that of Rome. Some (Gibbon) emphasize the destruction of old mores under the impact of Christianity. Some (Max Weber) the decline of cities. Some (Westermann) the collapse of its economic system. All agree that, in one way or another, internal causes led to its fall.

Maurice Druon, writing of that French century that never came, blames the mediocrity of her rulers. Surrounded by such seeming riches they imagined them boundless. They spent so much that soon there was no recourse but to cheapen the coin, to pile taxes upon taxes. Among the results was a demoralization of the army, an unravelling of the social order. The French people collapsed under the "excess of taxes . . . the money degraded."

Thus it was, in Druon's view, that France was broken within before, in 1356, it was defeated by a small English army on the field at Poitiers.

Historical analogies should not be pushed too far. The American republic, for all its troubles, remains a rich nation economically, a strong nation militarily, an influential nation politically. Yet it ought to give us pause that our decline from the pinnacle has been paralleled by a decline in old mores (not from a new religion but from a secular view that the old mores are outmoded), by a decline in our cities with our streets ravaged by crime, by corruption in high places, by heavy taxation and, not least, by the degradation of our money.

Moreover, in a year in which we are to choose new leaders we can't help wondering, I suspect, whether we are not in fact choosing among mediocrities. Anyway, none of those presently before us seems to have impressed the people as a leader of exceptional ability or of great vision. And, as Druon observed about France, there can be no greatness in the political order, or at least none that will endure, without leaders whose character and will can inspire and direct the energies of a people.

Under the best of fortune, of course, there is nothing that predestines America to remain forever the America it was in its place among nations. With nations, as with other organisms, there seems to be an immutable law of growth and decay. There is no reason we should be an exception.

That we must accept. But there is no predestination—only our own follies—if the promise of an American era lasts not even half a century.

January 9, 1980

THE LEGACY OF LUTHER

This week the world is taking note of the 500th anniversary of the birth of Martin Luther (November 10, 1483), fomentor of the Reformation that was to split Europe asunder and leave it even today religiously divided.

But Luther's influence, it seems to me, is far greater than that usually attributed to him as father of the Protestant revolution. He was in many ways the first "modern" man and, though he did not intend it so, the inspirer of many of the great secular changes in the Western world since the sixteenth century, including democracy, capitalism and the concept of individual liberty in thought, speech and rights.

He did not intend it so because his aim at first was only to reform some of the practices of the Catholic Church, which after the fall of the Roman Empire had become the unifying institution of the West, political as well as religious. But once he had put forward in 1517 his ninety-five theses (according to legend, nailed to the door of the church in Wittenberg), he set in chain a series of events that has not ended.

Luther, himself a priest, was incensed at the sale of indulgences by the church that were supposed to ease the way of sinners through purgatory. The pope (Leo X) rejected Luther's protests. Instead of capitulating, Luther began raising other questions about church doctrine, and not in diplomatic language either. Luther was not a man of temperate words.

The outcome of this was his formal excommunication by the pope and the convocation of the Diet of Worms at which, before notables of church and state, he was given a chance to recant. Whether Luther actually said the famous words, "Here I stand, I can do no other," is uncertain, but the phrase certainly captures his attitude as he publicly defied both pope and church.

So much is history. The consequence was to split Christendom. Many of his contemporaries, secretly or otherwise, shared his view that the interpretation of God and the scriptures was a matter of personal conscience not to be dictated by authority, and to them Luther was a hero. Although his writings were proscribed, he could not be silenced. He had caught the imagination of Europe, and Christianity would never afterward be the same.

The results today need not be labored. Although Roman Catholicism is the largest Christian denomination, it no longer stands alone or unchallenged either in this country or the world. In this country, in fact, Catholics are in the minority.

Still, why should I suggest that Luther, towering religious figure though he was, was also the catalyst for the great secular changes—political, economic and social—that overtook the Western world in the past four centuries?

The essence of what Luther did was to proclaim the supremacy of the individual mind, each person's conscience, against authoritarianism; in his day that of the church. But that idea, once proclaimed, was infectious.

Barely a century later Galileo was challenging both the scriptures and the established Aristotelian orthodoxy about the nature of the universe, which Copernicus had not been able to do successfully a century earlier. In another century what we now call the Renaissance, which had begun in Luther's time, was in full flower, with artists, musicians, philosophers, challenging the orthodoxies of the Middle Ages. The revolution that wrought extends into our time.

The Reformation also unleashed other forces. In economics, for example, the church of the Middle Ages proscribed certain practices, such as the lending of money for interest; that was left to the Jews, who could perform that useful function because they were thought beyond the pale.

It was not until Adam Smith, David Ricardo and John Stuart Mill (now the "classical" economists) began to think for themselves and to speak out that modern economies with their proliferation of wealth became possible.

Without the Reformation I doubt that democracy as we know it would have been possible either, for it too depends upon challenging authoritarianism, be it of kings who rule by divine right or of tyrants who rule by force. There could have been no American Revolution without the idea that kings could be defied, that individuals had certain "unalienable rights." It is no coincidence, I think, that where the

Reformation came late, as in Latin America, the growth of democracy has been stunted. The soil was not fertile there for Edmund Burkes, Tom Paines or Thomas Jeffersons.

There is, to be sure, a certain irony in tracing so much back to Martin Luther. For Luther, while insisting upon the supremacy of his own conscience in religious matters and his right to defy the pope, did not believe in the same principles in the political realm. In politics he was conservative, what today some might call a "reactionary." Only two years after his rebellion at Worms he was defending the place of the secular government of his time in God's scheme of things, preaching the duty of civil obedience to its authority and the sinfulness of rebellion against that authority.

Indeed, in some respects Luther does not strike me as an altogether admirable man. His polemics against his enemies were violent, at times savage. His attacks on the Jews remain an embarrassment to his followers; he wanted their synagogues and their prayer books destroyed. The Nazis could and did use Luther's views to support their own purges.

Nonetheless, Martin Luther was a pivotal figure in our history—intellectual and political as well as religious. For once a man could assert he could think for himself about God, there was no way thereafter to silence other minds with other questions.

November 9, 1983

A SUNDAY CEREMONY

Last weekend was Lincoln's birthday, one of those days set aside for ceremonial celebration. Both the House and the Senate took a recess from their labors to mark the occasion, and at many places around the country there were little ceremonies to honor our Civil War president.

But one of the more unusual events to remind us of the changes that have taken place in the century since those dark days of Lincoln's presidency was in the small Southern village of Chapel Hill, North Carolina, home of the oldest state university in the country. There, in the Episcopal Chapel of the Cross, the rite of the Holy Communion was celebrated by the Reverend Dr. Pauli Murray.

It was an unusual event on several counts. For one, Dr. Murray is a woman, one among that first small group of women officially ordained as priests by the Episcopal Church. It also happens that Dr. Murray is black.

Behind that Sunday's event there also lies an interesting personal story. On December the 20th, 1854, six years before the outbreak of the Civil War, Pauli Murray's grandmother was baptized in this same Chapel Hill parish. The chapel records record that on that day five servant children belonging to a Mary Ruffin Smith were given their Christian names before the font. It was one of those little girls, Cornelia, who was Pauli Murray's grandmother.

So here was the granddaughter of a slave, one of the first women to be ordained a priest and the first black woman to be so ordained, officiating in the parish church where her slave ancestor was baptized. This in a Southern state and village in the year 1977.

That alone would have made the occasion remarkable, but that is not the whole story.

Pauli Murray was born sixty-six years ago in Baltimore where her father was a principal in the Baltimore city schools, following an educational tradition that reaches back to that third generation. Her maternal grandfather was one of the first six students at Ashmun Institute, later Lincoln University. He served in the Union army during the Civil War and then helped establish schools for Negro freedmen in Virginia and North Carolina. Her mother was an early graduate of the Hampton School of Nursing in Virginia.

After her mother's death she came back to Durham, only a few miles from Chapel Hill, where she was raised by an aunt, a teacher for many years in the Durham city schools. It was inevitable, then, that for Pauli Murray education would be both a goal for herself and an aspiration for her people.

She took her bachelor's degree from Hunter College in 1933. In 1938 she was rejected as a law student at the university in Chapel Hill because of her race. In 1940 she was rejected by the Harvard Law School because of her sex. It was not until 1950 that Harvard admitted women and 1951 that the University of North Carolina admitted blacks to its law school.

She got her law degree anyway, from Howard University in 1944. Later she earned a master's degree in law from Berkeley and was a tutor in law at Yale, where she received her doctorate in 1965.

From 1956 to 1960 she practiced law with a New York firm, but most of her years have been spent as a teacher and as a pioneer advocate of equal rights for both blacks and women, for both groups of which she was an eminent representative.

There was hardly any part of the civil rights struggle of the past quarter century in which she was not involved as legal adviser, advocate and sometimes activist. In 1940 she was arrested in Petersburg, Virginia, for resisting segregation on an interstate bus and spent several days in jail. But her major effort always was to use the law as the fulcrum for changing the ways of society, pushing on it with the persuasive powers of her pen.

Somehow amid all this activity she found time to write her biography, a small volume of poetry and an immense volume of law review articles and monographs. In interims she also taught law at Boston and Brandeis universities.

In 1973, aged sixty-two, she decided to change if not her goals at least her way of reaching them. She entered the General Theological Seminary in New York to study for Holy Orders in the Episcopal Church. She was made a deacon in 1976 and, this January in Washington Cathedral, was ordained an Episcopal priest, one of that first group of women to be officially admitted to the priesthood.

Such, then, is the story of Pauli Murray, who came back to the university community that once turned her away from its law school but also back to the parish chapel where her grandmother was baptized almost a century and a quarter ago.

For her it must have been an especially moving moment, marking as it did one more remarkable change in the ways of society and of her church which she had seen in her lifetime, and yet at the same time offering a renewal with her past.

The worshippers overflowed the pews, their ranks swollen by visitors and young people from the university. Yet a few of the parishioners, it must be said, were disturbed, wishing that their rector, the Reverend Peter James Lee, had not extended the invitation to Dr. Murray to preach and to administer the eucharist in their church.

But there was irony in this discomfort. For those who disapproved did not do so because the Reverend Dr. Murray is black; the Chapel of the Cross is now a large church with a diverse membership including blacks among those who worship there. They disapproved because the Reverend Dr. Murray is a woman. It is the ordination of women, not racial prejudice, which is now controversial in the church.

The wisdom of that change is for time to measure. Nonetheless, there was Pauli Murray, female and black, officiating at a ceremony, the Holy Communion, which has its roots in the antiquity of the church itself. It was an unusual way for a small Southern village to mark the birthday of Abraham Lincoln, and it would be hard to find a better example of continuity amid change in one simple ceremony.

February 16, 1977

THOUGHTS ON LEBANON

The first thing to be understood is that there is really no such country as Lebanon. There never has been. And it looks as though there may never be.

There is, certainly, a geographic place on the map labeled Lebanon. But as a political entity it did not even have nominal existence until it was created artificially out of five former Turkish Empire districts after World War I and placed under a French mandate.

Before that, the land once called Phoenicia had been crossed and recrossed by invading armies at least since the third century B.C. in the time of Ramses II of Egypt.

The city of Beirut where so many armies clash today, and which we speak of as the "capital" of today's Lebanon, does indeed have ancient roots, being mentioned in old tablets as early as 1362 B.C. It was destroyed by the Syrians in 140 B.C., rebuilt by the Romans in 64 B.C., under whom it flourished until it was destroyed by an earthquake and tidal wave in A.D. 551.

After that, it suffered conquest and depredations by the Egyptians (again) and by the Moslem leader Saladin at the time of the Crusades. In the sixteenth century a series of Druse emirs, as part of the Ottoman Empire, held sway over the city and over central and southern Lebanon.

In more recent times (1772) came a Russian invasion followed (1841) by another from Turks and Austrians. In 1918 the Allies conquered city and region, the British and French retaining control until 1941, when Lebanon was declared an "independent" state with Beirut as its capital, although the French did not withdraw their forces leaving Lebanon on its own until 1946.

With so many invaders crisscrossing it, it's not surprising that it acquired a polyglot population. Ethnically, the present Lebanese are a mixture of Phoenician, Greek, Byzantine, Crusader, Armenian and

Arab, into which some later European strains are added. Roughly speaking, the mountain people are predominantly Armenian, those in the lowlands descendants of Syrians, Palestinians and Arabs.

The religious groupings are equally mixed and, as we have learned, hostile to each other. Altogether there are more than a dozen recognized religions, the largest being the Maronite Christians, Greek Orthodox and Armenian Orthodox. Then there are the various Moslem sects, the Sunnites, Shiites and Druse. Taken together these Moslems may today be the majority, although there has been no official census in a half-century.

With such an ethnic and religious mixture Lebanon's history is replete with massacres beyond numbering of one group by another. Until modern times the best known was that of 1860 between the Maronite Christians and the Druse. In our day massacres are the stuff of the daily news.

Lebanon, or at least Beirut, did have its brief and shining hour after World War II. For a time Beirut was the garden spot of the Middle East with its lovely beaches and luxury hotels. Foreigners who visited it then were fortunate indeed.

But that did not, and probably could not, last. That seeming peace rested on an apportionment of parliamentary seats by religious grouping, six Christians to five Moslems. By informal agreement the president was a Maronite, the premier a Sunni Moslem, the speaker in parliament a Shiite. Though this worked for a time it was a shaky arrangement, especially as the Moslem population grew in relative numbers.

In 1958 President Eisenhower sent troops to restore order after a Syrian-inspired revolt. Yet a year later Palestinian commandos were on a rampage again, causing the Israelis to occupy south Lebanon. By 1975 civil war raged. In 1981 Syria invaded from the east. In 1982 the Israelis moved north to the edge of Beirut. Meanwhile, almost every Lebanese group and sect was fighting with every other.

So much for checkered history. Of late the turmoil has been the stuff of the nightly news and morning headlines, with U.S. Marines in the middle of it. The impulse that sent the Marines into this morass was understandable. Part of it was humanitarian, a hope that a foreign presence could stop the slaughter, and that an end to slaughter would lead to some sort of political stability, with all groups recognizing that any peace was better than endless chaos.

Part of the reason for the Marines was also recognition that Lebanon is a potential powder keg in the Middle East. With no recognized government, no dependable army, the land remains a tempting conquest for neighboring Syria, encouraged by the Soviet Union. But a Lebanon in Syrian hands would be an intolerable danger for the Israelis. And if a real war broke out there other Arab states might not be able to stay aloof.

Understandable though that is, the role of the Marines—and the troops of other countries—was doomed to futility from the beginning, for the land remains a morass. Short of taking over the country, the Marines could do nothing to keep the peace among all those factions unwilling to live in peace. Unable to retaliate, the Marines could only sit, targets for any group to shoot at or throw bombs at.

Now that the Marines have left, is there a lesson in this misadventure? If so it's the reminder that while there are places where we can help effectively, there are others in the world where the problems are beyond our reach. And learning the difference is surely the beginning of wisdom.

February 29, 1984

III

Windows on the World

CHINESE COMMUNISM'S MANY FACES

Chungking—"Very big, China."

Noel Coward meant to be amusing. But in this flip description of one China traveler lies a clue to understanding this strange, complex land.

In area it is larger than the United States. Its population is unmeasurable, something on the order of 900 million people, give or take fifty million. They embrace some ninety-three different minority races speaking a babble of tongues. Sprawling from the Pacific coast to the western borders of Tibet, it is a land historically divided by mountains, deserts, torrential and unnavigable rivers.

Nowhere does a modern visitor better get this sense of size and complexity, glimpse the magnitude of the task of its present Communist rulers in making of it a unified nation, than here in this province of Szechwan, a rich and fertile basin hidden behind towering, snowy peaks.

On the streets here one sees the faces not only of the Han Chinese but also of the Yi, the Miao, the Hui, the Chi'ang and the Tibetans. The Westerner who passed unnoticed in Peking or Shanghai finds himself quickly surrounded by curious, friendly crowds staring at him as if he were a panda in a zoo. For many years Szechwan was closed to foreigners, presumably because its independent spirit gave the Communists political troubles.

Yet because this is one of the most nearly self-sufficient of the provinces, with rich farms and busy factories in close proximity, a visitor can also see more easily than elsewhere the contrast between the way the Communists have organized culture and industry. He gets a glimpse of the pragmatism with which the Chinese Communists apply their communism.

Most of China's heavy industry, such as the sprawling steel complex here, follows the Soviet pattern. That is, the plants are owned and managed by the state with all decisions about production or capital investment being made by the central planning apparatus. The workers are simply state employees, their wages, hours and working conditions prescribed by the state.

In agriculture it is otherwise. There are a few state-owned and managed farms but most of the food and fiber are raised on communes, subdivided into production brigades and production teams with much more autonomy.

In Chinese communes the land is owned jointly by the members, not the state, much as if they were shareholders in a corporate enterprise or something like an American co-op. Individual farmers even own their own homes and are free to enlarge or improve them as their resources permit.

The basic accounting unit is the production team and the income of each member depends on the amount of the collective production. Prices are fixed but the more each team produces the greater the income rewards of the members who share the total profits.

Within fairly wide limits these communal enterprises can make their own decisions with regard to capital investment. In practice most of them retain a percentage of their gross return as a capital reserve; if they want a new tractor or other piece of equipment the decision on whether to buy it lies with the members.

In addition, each household has its own private plot on which it may grow things for its own consumption or, if it wishes, sell for its own account. Many members also engage in side activities; raising hogs is one of the more profitable and what they receive from hog sales, less their costs, is their private income over and above their communal shares. In this way some farmers earn half again as much income; a few even succeed in doubling it.

Nor is farming the only economic activity of these communes. Most if not all of them also engage in light industry manufacturing, ranging from brick making to flour milling to the manufacture of furniture.

The purpose of these activities is twofold: to increase the income of the commune members and to provide work for those who may be gradually displaced as mechanization reduces the need for strictly farm workers. It's one answer to the problem of how to keep them down on the farm.

Precise figures on these communal activities are hard to come by and always confusing but one result is clearly a kind of "creeping capitalism." There's a direct relationship between work produced and income earned. The conversation of farm managers is sprinkled with bourgeois words like profits, investments, costs and share incomes.

Another result, plain to the eye, is that by and large the so-called peasant farmers have a real standard of income higher than their factory-worker counterparts. They eat better, live more cheaply, and their homes, while generally plain and often with dirt floors, are more spacious than the tiny, crowded apartments of city dwellers.

There is talk that the leaders are groping for some way to install a similar incentive system in the state-owned heavy industries where workers have been on a straight wage basis. Already there is a graduated wage scale under which more skilled workers are paid more and managers several times the ordinary wage. Moreover, wages were increased last year and this spring a new "bonus system" was announced for many such plants.

In the Chungking steel plant the lowest paid worker gets thirty-five yuan a month. (It's futile and misleading to convert yuan into dollars; the exchange rate of 1.7 yuan per dollar is purely artificial and the whole Chinese wage and price system is on a different level.) By contrast the highest paid nonsupervisory worker gets 108 yuan, the chief engineer 240 yuan monthly, a sevenfold differential from lowest to highest. But in none of these is there any relationship between either individual wages or total payroll costs and the production efficiency of the plant.

Under the new bonus system the state would allot the plant an overall percentage bonus of total payroll if it meets or exceeds its production quota. Theoretically this would be then distributed among the workers on the basis of their individual performance in doing their jobs or in making special contributions to improved efficiency. In practice, however, the bonus has been distributed to all but about five percent of the workers, making it so far no more than a general wage increase for most, with a way of punishing a few workers denied a share.

If agriculture workers are rewarded differently it may be because organizing steel mills or shipyards on a communal basis is more complicated, but I suspect it's because the leaders recognize agriculture as their number one problem and are willing to be quite pragmatic in solving it.

China at present isn't self-sufficient in food for its 900 million people and every year there are an estimated 200,000 more mouths to feed;

by 1980 its population could be a billion. That's a staggering challenge for its rulers and it forces them to accept any means—even a little creeping capitalism—to increase production.

It was just this approach that drew so much criticism during the heyday of the "Gang of Four," shorthand for the group that wielded much power during the Cultural Revolution. This group wanted to eliminate all income-sharing among farmers and also the private plots. It wanted only "pure" communism economically and socially, pouring all China into one mold even to the extent of opposing regional or foreign cultural influences. It banned such diverse things as traditional Peking opera and modern Western music.

That effort met resistance everywhere but especially among Szechwan peasants. "If a Szechwan farmer wants to grow hogs," as one official put it, "nobody's going to stop him."

The overthrow of the "Gang of Four" by Chairman Hua led to many changes. Now people can enjoy Peking opera, regional song and dance and even concerts of Berlioz, Strauss and Tchaikovsky. Art need no longer "serve the revolution" with propaganda. And if a touch of creeping capitalism bothers the Politburo there's no sign of it.

Indeed, Chairman Hua himself uses many capitalistic terms in speaking of his plans for modernizing China. He insists "the law of value" must be applied with a strict system of "economic accounting" to all projects with the aim of "increasing profits."

None of this means the political system is any less Communistic or offers much political freedom. A Szechwan peasant on a farm or a worker in a factory still needs state permission to change his residence or his job. All it suggests is that while the present Politburo members are Communist they aren't frozen ideologues. That is, they aren't going to let Marxist ideology stop them from being practical. Which is not a bad idea for this country. After all, it's very big, China.

October 25, 1978

DECISIONS IN THE NATIONAL INTEREST

There's no doubt about it, the world around us has taken on a wild and fearful hue. It's not just that peace talks between Israel and Egypt flounder. Everywhere you look there are riots, revolutions, terrorism, wars and rumors of wars.

One day it's an Iranian mob attacking the American embassy. On another it's an Afghan mob capturing and killing our ambassador. In Italy, or in South America, businessmen must go about their daily business in armored cars against kidnappers who murder.

And there's no shortage of wars from day to day. In Africa it may be Somalia against Ethiopia or Tanzania against Uganda. In the Middle East, North Yemen versus South Yemen while Saudi Arabia mobilizes its army. In Asia, Vietnam conquers Cambodia, the Chinese invade Vietnam as the Soviets mass more troops on the Chinese border.

As one trouble spot quiets, another erupts. Not since the 1930s has the world seemed to be so full of tinderboxes a spark could ignite.

In such a world it's inevitable that men should have a sense of foreboding and that in our country we should ponder and debate what we should do.

Some complain of a weak foreign policy, others that we have no foreign policy at all. President Carter is berated for "his" failure in Iran, for not turning the Chinese away from military adventuring, for the delays in the peace treaty between Israel and Egypt. He in turn assails his critics for not recognizing the limitations of American power, for advocating reckless courses of action.

There's a grain of truth in all these complaints. There are limitations on American power. It is true that American influence has been less than it might have been because the world sees us as confused and uncertain.

But running through all the arguments is the idea that foreign policy is something that can be and should be clearly formulated and consistently applied. Something, that is, that can be concisely stated in a paragraph or two so that we, and the world, can see what it is and anticipate our actions.

That, I suspect, is a dubious idea. At any rate there have only been a few times in this century when American foreign policy could be explicitly stated, and in each case the results were unfortunate.

One was during the 1930s when President Roosevelt enunciated, and had Congress confirm, a policy of neutrality amid the war clouds over Europe. Thus explicitly stated, it emboldened Hitler. It could not, and did not, survive because changing circumstances made it no longer fit the realities of the world.

Another example was the policy of "containment" begun by President Truman. This stated our intention to resist every effort of Communist expansion everywhere, by force of arms if need be. It was an effective policy for Europe, turning back Soviet efforts to seize all Berlin. Applied everywhere it was an invitation to folly, bleeding us white in remote wars, as in Vietnam.

The difficulty with this concept of foreign policy is that the world around us changes. Former enemies become friends, former allies adversaries. Wars and revolutions break out in unexpected places, fitting no pattern. One danger must be met one way, another another.

This is, admittedly, a reality difficult to accept. It's more emotionally comfortable and intellectually satisfying to be able to say, "Here is our foreign policy; with it we know and the world knows how we will respond to new troubles anywhere." When all is not so clearly formulated there is a heavier burden on the wisdom and judgment of those who must lead the nation in response to changing circumstance.

But of course we must have a foreign policy in a different sense of that phrase. That is, a policy that our actions rest on our national interests, whatever they may be at a given moment.

If that leaves the country, and its leaders, with the excruciating task of deciding what our national interests are in a given circumstance, it is the only way—or so it seems to me—that we can find our way to right actions in the world around us.

By itself, for example, there's nothing either good or bad about signing a new SALT treaty. It could be good if in fact it diminished the arms race equally on both sides; a real détente with the Soviet Union would be in our national interest as well as theirs. But it would be injurious to our national interest to sign a treaty that reduces our military strength relative to the Soviet Union. All depends on what's in the treaty.

So also with our efforts to get a peace treaty between Egypt and Israel. Had President Carter succeeded in getting one truly acceptable to both sides, that would have been in our national interest because it would lessen one point of tension in the Middle East. That he couldn't was a disappointment. But to have a treaty forced upon either party, even if that were possible, would not have been in our interest or in the interest of peace.

A forced treaty would have been tenuous at best and it would surely have bred resentment in the country which thought itself strong-armed into signing it. Better a disappointment than an illusory success which could only breed future trouble.

In short, the trap to be avoided in both cases is in elevating the mere having of such treaties to a cardinal objective of our foreign policy. That this is what the administration appears to be doing is a more valid criticism of its conduct of foreign affairs than the general accusation that it doesn't have a "foreign policy" for all seasons.

What action would the president's critics advocate that would deal with the situation in Iran? That we should have intervened with force either to shore up the Shah or the short-lived government of Bakhtiar? Would they elevate such intervention to a "principle" of foreign policy applicable everywhere? That would make for a clear foreign policy but it could only lead into disastrous quicksands.

For it is true that there are limitations to American power; we cannot apply it everywhere to make the world as we would like it.

There is, to be sure, a certain irony in hearing a Democratic president criticized for speaking what was once a tenet of Republican critics of foreign policy under previous Democratic administrations. Yet there is, nonetheless, a possible trap also in loudly proclaiming America's role in the world as limited.

From recognizing the limitations of American power it is easy for us to slide into an attitude of resignation, forgetting there is much we can do to influence events if not control them. It can become an excuse for non-action. And an attitude so proclaimed can tempt other nations to ignore us.

Yet they cannot ignore us if we choose not to be ignored. We do, after all, hold some cards in negotiating with the Soviet Union. We are not helpless in bringing our influence to bear on events in the Middle East in general or in such places as Iran in particular.

The problem is one of deciding what is possible where and what is not; of deciding when risks are justified and when they are not. Because it would be foolhardy to intervene in a war between Tanzania and Uganda doesn't mean we should shy from using our power, including military power, where our national interest is overwhelming, as it might well be from war or chaos in the Middle East. Each circumstance demands its own judgment.

There's no gainsaying, however, that this is a problem yielding to no facile solutions. It means that we must make many *ad hoc* decisions, always with the terrifying realization that we may be wrong, doing too much or too little. It's a problem to challenge to the utmost the statesmanship of our leaders and the resolution of us all.

We would all wish it otherwise. Would that the world were different, or that we could find some simple, one-paragraph formula on which to rest a foreign policy that would carry us safely through its dangers. But the world is what it is. Being so, we can only strive with fortitude to manage as best we may amid its wild and fearful hue.

March 14, 1979

THROUGH THE LOOKING GLASS

O ne of the secrets of successful generals or statesmen is their ability to turn the map upside down, or spin the globe, and view the political or military terrain from the other side.

Whether in war or peace we are always conscious of our own troubles or deficiencies, as well we should be. To ignore them can lead to uncon-cern or over-confidence, either of which can be fatal in the face of de-termined adversaries. But there is some danger too in seeing only what is reflected in our own mirror.

In any event it's an interesting exercise, and one not without its uses, to spin the globe and try to imagine how the current situation may look to the men in the Politburo.

Begin with the Soviet position in Afghanistan. At this remove it is, admittedly, difficult to gauge. The Soviets say everything is going smoothly, their military control of the country has stabilized and for that reason they are able to withdraw some several thousand troops.

Yet from other sources there are persistent reports that the Soviets are in deep trouble, militarily and politically. Guerrilla resistance is re-ported growing. Comparisons are drawn with our difficulties in Viet-nam and the word "quagmire" keeps cropping up as descriptive of the situation.

If that's the case, then the withdrawal may be tactical shuttling only. It would make military sense for the Soviets to alter the composition of their forces, with less reliance on those designed for "set" battles and more emphasis on mobile troops to cope better with guerrillas.

Which of these views is closer to the truth I certainly don't know. And given the handicaps we've laid on the CIA it's possible President Carter doesn't know either.

What we do know, though, is that the Politburo decided to an-nounce a partial withdrawal, a gesture it heretofore refused, and that it elected to make the announcement in the midst of the summit meeting of Western heads-of-government. That alone is worth pondering.

When the Afghanistan adventure began the Soviet attitude was that it was no one's business but their own and that, anyway, they didn't give a fig for world opinion. They snorted, at least metaphorically, at foreign criticism and at such feeble gestures as the effort to boycott the Moscow Olympics.

That disdain was justified in the sense that no one took arms to push them out of Afghanistan. Even the Olympic boycott was only partially successful, a sort of mild rap on the knuckles. But if you were a member of the Politburo, what else would you see?

Well, for one thing Afghanistan caused President Carter to be born again in his attitude toward the Soviet Union. He decided among other things to enlarge his proposed military budget—not by much, to be sure, but enough to mark a changed attitude. The American Congress was aroused to consider increasing the defense budget further and to lay the groundwork for re-instituting the draft.

The rumbles started by Afghanistan weren't limited to this country. The NATO nations also decided to strengthen their forces in Western Europe—again not by much but even that little was more than would have been done before Afghanistan.

At the Venice summit meeting the one thing the Western leaders managed to agree upon was opposition to the Afghanistan occupation. If the Soviets hoped to defuse that with their announcement of a partial withdrawal they were disappointed. The government heads unanimously agreed they would be satisfied only with a total withdrawal.

As if all this weren't annoying enough to the Russians there have been surprising mumbles of disapproval from European Communist parties. Their criticism may have been only for show, to suggest their independence from Moscow. It's evidence all the same how these local Communist leaders read public sentiment in their own countries.

And while the military situation in Afghanistan may or may not be a quagmire, it certainly hasn't developed according to Kremlin plans or expectations. In short, to anyone sitting in the Politburo it must seem a time of troubles.

Of those troubles, I should think, the most disturbing one might not be the military situation in Afghanistan itself. With an army of 3.6 million men the Soviets have ample power to crush the country if they wish to pay the price, which would surely include keeping an army of occupation there indefinitely. More disturbing could be the political cost of launching that adventure in the first place.

One of the main Soviet strengths these many years has been their ability to beguile peace-loving people about their peaceful intentions—including by his own admission President Carter. Behind that peaceful facade they have been able to build up an enormous military power without alarming the rest of the world to man the defenses.

Coupled with that of late has been the impression that the Communist ideology has an irresistible appeal to "Third World" countries and that the Kremlin masters themselves are "ten feet tall"—that is, they don't fumble, bumble and blunder the way Western leaders do, especially American ones.

Those images are now shattered. The Afghans proved immune to Communist blandishments. Their ragtail tribesmen proved resistant to Red Army might. A once-sleeping West has been awakened. Staying, the Soviets face unending woes; withdrawing, they expose a blunder.

We have our troubles, indeed we do. But all doesn't look serene for the Kremlin when you look from the other side of the looking glass.

July 2, 1980

OUT OF AFRICA (I)

Africa is the second largest continent. Stretching some five thousand miles from the northern bulge to the southern tip which separates the Atlantic and Indian oceans, it occupies one-fifth of the earth's land surface.

But size is not what most impresses a traveler from Capetown to Cairo. Africa's impact comes from the feeling of its antiquity, from the extreme contrasts in its geography, from the multiplicity of its ethnic groups, from the economic, social and political disparities among its parts.

So a traveler is bound to bring out of Africa a mixture of impressions about its past and present and a host of unanswered questions about its future.

Anthropologists seem agreed it was in central Africa that our species first came down from the trees to walk upright, untold millennia ago. It was in northern Africa, mainly in the land of Egypt, that there sprang up six or seven thousand years ago the oldest civilization of which we have a continuous record. The relics of it are still there to astound tourists.

But as a once-impenetrable barrier between Egypt and the rest of Africa there lies the world's greatest desert, the Sahara, which fills a quarter of the continent. Below it is a different land of jungles, mountains and savanna more hospitable to other animals than to humans. In this part of Africa there was only a rudimentary stone age, no bronze age at all. The people of the south never discovered the principle of the wheel.

Thus for most of history the rest of the world paid great attention to northern Africa, none to its southern parts until the age of European exploration. Romans and Carthaginians fought over what is now Tunisia. Egypt was a target of conquest for the Macedonians, the Romans, the Moslems, the French and British, each of whom left their imprint. The rest, primitive and sparsely populated, dozed for centuries.

The result is noticeable to the modern traveler. Egypt remains a focal point of world interest, as daily headlines tell us. From time to time the world has been forced to take heed of Libya or Ethiopia as they became fields for warring armies or centers of geopolitical struggles.

Only in more recent times have Americans or Europeans had much interest in the area south of the Sahara and then only when some disturbance compelled it. The average American knows little and ordinarily cares not much what happens in Chad or Upper Volta, the Cameroon or the Congo. It's when the Mau Mau erupts in Kenya, an Idi Amin goes mad in Uganda or white rule topples in Rhodesia that reporters descend in numbers and force our attention.

There are many reasons for this. One is that the southern continent is broken into many small countries more the result of history's accidents than anything else. Another is that while most of the people are black they are not really homogenous. There's only a remote kinship among the Pygmy, the Zulu, the Masai, the Ashanti, the Bushman, the Falani, the Ibo, and much hostility between them.

Time and again as these countries became independent the aftermath was intertribal warfare, as happened in Nigeria when the Ibo fought for a separate state of Biafra. Few of these new countries— Kenya is a possible exception—give confidence in their future social and political stability. Even the early promise of Zimbabwe, the former Rhodesia, is fading as personal and tribal rivalries tear at its fabric.

A related reason is that when the colonial powers arrived they came to exploit, not to develop. Many people were sold into slavery. The land's agricultural products (palm oil, cocoa, cotton, rubber), its mineral resources (copper, gold, diamonds, chromium, cobalt) were raw material for factories elsewhere.

Politically the sub-Sahara remained the domain of conquerors. Socially it stayed mired in tribal culture. Economically the industrial revolution passed it by.

All that is now changing. Everywhere a traveler can feel a new ferment, although he cannot be sure of the outcome. Egypt is advancing industrially and should advance further with the coming of peace between it and Israel, begun by Sadat and continued by his successor. Economic troubles remain for it is an over-populated land, it still lacks good relations with its Arab neighbors, and all this could beget political problems. But its future is brighter than it has been for many years.

Then at the other end of the continent is the anomaly of South Africa. It is highly industrialized, prosperous despite the sanctions that have been laid on it by many countries, because its natural resources make it self-sufficient in nearly everything but oil. To a visitor it appears on the surface much like any modern Western nation.

But South Africa is the last of the white-ruled countries, with an overwhelming black majority denied much of that economic prosperity, and under the policy of apartheid deprived of all political participation, having neither the right to vote nor to live and work where it will. This creates enormous pressures, internally as many blacks understandably grow militant, externally as the revolutions that overtook Kenya and Rhodesia press down on it through Botswana and Namibia.

Here too a visitor feels that change is inevitable. The question is whether it will come in an orderly fashion without destroying the country politically and economically, or whether it will take the form of another explosion.

On the answer depends not only the future of South Africa itself but much of the future of the whole southern continent. For that reason it's a question that spurs a visitor to special thoughts.

May 5, 1982

OUT OF AFRICA (II)

In the Republic of South Africa last year eight Coloured people became black, 558 Coloured became white, fifteen whites suddenly found themselves Coloured while seven whites became Chinese. These were part of some 700 "racial re-classifications" by the Department of Internal Affairs.

There's a touch of absurdity to these metamorphoses but there's nothing funny about it to those involved, even for the blacks and Coloureds who may have welcomed their change in status. For in South Africa racial classification is a serious business, determining who can vote, where one must live and who can cohabit with whom.

This is the consequence of the policy of apartheid, a system of racial discrimination more extreme and more dehumanizing than the segregation practiced in the American South before the 1950s. The separation of the races in social association, in living areas, in access to the ballot, is not a matter of custom but of strict laws rigidly enforced.

The practice of apartheid is also an ulcer that suppurates below the otherwise bright surface of South Africa. This country is far and away the loveliest, most modern, most technologically advanced and most prosperous of any on the whole continent. It has, at least for the time being, the most stable government, operating for all but the disfranchised as a parliamentary democracy.

Thus for the casual tourist—last year there were 700,000 of them, about half from Europe or America—South Africa appears as an oasis of calm in a disturbed continent.

In North Africa Libya is run by an unpredictable madman, Egypt is beset by all manner of economic woes. South of the Sahara, east or west, the black-run countries stand on the edge of turmoil if they are not already entangled in it.

Kenya is wracked by inflation, a severe balance of payments problem, unemployment and charges of corruption. Uganda is worse off, with Idi Amin's torture chambers back at work. The corruption bug is rife too in Sierra Leone. Ghana, the first black nation to win independence, is sinking into a quagmire. Nigeria has been plagued by strikes that shut off water and electricity, bringing industry and business to a halt.

There were once bright hopes for black rule in Zimbabwe (the former Rhodesia) but they have been at least tarnished. The coalition of Robert Mugabe and Joshua Nkomo has sundered. Tribal rivalries have flared. Remaining whites have lost all influence, many have fled. Mugabe is creating a one-party government with a strong Marxist orientation.

That leaves South Africa. In part its success rests on its natural resources; it's 95 percent self-sufficient, mainly lacking oil, and most of its energy needs can be met by coal. Its currency is relatively stable and despite the decline in gold and diamond prices, it offers a sharp economic contrast with the rest of Africa.

But a part of this success is obviously due to the influence of its ruling European minority, mostly those of Dutch or English descent. They provide the technical sophistication, the managerial skills for industry and government that have made the country prosper. The black (and Coloured) majority has been under-educated, many are unskilled, and all are without experience in democratic self-government.

So it's understandable if the European minority is frightened by the prospect of a sudden one man—one vote political system for which world opinion is pressuring it. The governing Europeans would be inundated, with very likely disastrous results for everyone.

Yet a visitor who looks beneath the placid surface cannot escape the feeling that change is both necessary and inevitable. The black majority cannot, and should not, be kept submerged by apartheid. The problem is how to end that system, to let the blacks share economic and political life in such a way as to smooth change. Otherwise South Africa will surely in time succumb to the relentless pressure of the black movement that has swept the rest of Africa south of the Sahara.

In fact, much has changed recently. There are more educational and economic opportunities in South Africa for blacks and Coloureds than a few years ago. A number now hold skilled jobs in industry and business, especially in international companies, a few even in supervisory positions. The government itself has done much to improve housing and other living conditions, though much remains to be done.

But of political liberty, of a voice in the conduct of the country's affairs, this submerged majority has none. And this want feeds the running sore beneath the surface.

Black militancy is growing, especially within the presently repressed black unions. For the moment the emphasis is mainly economic, improving jobs and wages and altering the sometimes feudal system of employment. But along with it is an undercurrent of political militancy that threatens one day an upheaval.

At least some white Afrikaners realize this, and there is a stirring among the ruling class for some form of change. They seek an end to the crueler forms of apartheid, an increase in education and training to prepare blacks gradually for a larger role in society. Even a form of "shared power" in the political arena is talked about.

But die-hard opposition to any change remains strong, so a passing visitor cannot foresee the outcome. But he leaves persuaded that much of the future of the southern continent hangs on what happens in South Africa, and that in turn depends on how South Africa resolves its racial problem.

May 12, 1982

EUROPE: A DURABLE DREAM

For years after we had adopted our national Constitution, and after the first Congress under it had met in 1789, the inhabitants of the former colonies still regarded themselves as first of all Marylanders or Massachusetts men. Only secondarily did they feel they were "Americans."

Indeed, as late as 1861 Robert E. Lee resigned from the Army, which he had served for thirty-six years, not because he favored the secession by Virginia but because he felt he had to offer his services "in the defense of my native state."

This bit of history comes to mind as I return from Europe with the feeling that despite the years it has been talked of, the supra-national European Community remains a dream unfulfilled.

That remembered history is a reminder of how strong is people's sense of place, how difficult it is to put aside accumulated loyalties, acquired over generations, in the name of some larger abstraction.

It is also a reminder, though, that given time and the right circumstances it can be done. Were that not so, there would be no United States in any meaningful sense stretching from coast to coast across a continent. So though I wrote about the failure so far of the vision of creating in Western Europe a single political entity overriding national boundaries, I am not as gloomy about the future of the European Community as I may have seemed.

It took us a long time to create a meaningful United States, and that not until a fearsome civil war, even though we had the advantage of a common language among the erstwhile sovereign states as well as a common political and cultural heritage from our former mother country. None of this exists in Europe.

It's not easy even to count the number of languages in Europe. That can't be done by just counting the sovereign countries, for many stubbornly retain provincial languages: the Belgians, for example, or the

Spanish. And these sublingual groups are still sources of friction, making governing difficult. The Welsh and the Scots still cause problems in so small a country as Britain.

The cultural differences are as great. The English and the Italians are different peoples in history and so in manners, customs and ways of viewing the world. The Germans and the French have not only long memories of mutual hostility but very different ideas about the nature and function of government.

Yet for all of that, you need only look at the map to see that these countries—at least those west of the Iron Curtain—ought to share a common political and economic interest; there ought to be more to unite them than to divide them. Conquerors, from Napoleon to Hitler, have thought this. The tragedy of Europe is that they tried to unite it by force of arms.

One result of those wars, especially the last one, is that men of peace had the same vision and sought it by peaceful means, if for no other reason than to avoid the incessant warring that has plagued Europe for centuries. What is surprising is how far that vision has come.

It's barely thirty-five years since the first International Committee for European Unity met in The Hague with sixteen countries sending representatives, including Winston Churchill, who had earlier called for a United States of Europe. In 1949 ten countries created the Council of Europe, which was to include a parliamentary assembly, though its powers were to be only "consultative." From this small beginning came first the European Economic Community and then the European Community, which was to be both political and economic.

By 1979 it was possible to hold direct elections in nine member countries of representatives to a parliament of Europe, something that a generation earlier would have been impossible. A small note: In the U.S. it took 120 years before senators were elected by the voters instead of being representatives of the individual states chosen by their respective legislatures.

It's true enough that this European parliament has very limited powers, as do the executive officials of the EC in Brussels. Any increase in powers would require the approval of the Council of Ministers and ratification by each national government. No one should expect that any time soon.

For one reason, nationalism is by no means gone from Europe; in the guise of "states' rights" it hasn't totally disappeared in the U.S.

What exists now in Europe is a loose confederation of sovereign countries, none of which is at present willing to yield more powers to any kind of central government.

For another reason the economies of the member countries vary widely as do the consequent problems. It probably wouldn't be possible for any "central" government to set agricultural, industrial, fiscal or monetary policies that would fit the whole community, even if there were such authority.

So it's true that the idea of "Europe" as a unified entity remains an unfulfilled dream. The recent currency turmoil, resolved only by France and West Germany going their separate ways, is illustrative of the difficulties of arriving at a common policy, as are the differences among the members on the defense of Western Europe.

Yet what also need to be remarked upon, I think, are not only the shortcomings of the European Community as a viable instrument of unity but also the accomplishments of the past quarter century. The day will come, however far off it may be, when an Italian, a German or a Frenchman will say of himself, "I am a European."

April 27, 1983

AMERICA'S CRITICS ABROAD

An American in Europe—if he does more than visit cathedrals and museums—will hear and read of a lot of criticism of his country. We are, so it's said, badly governed and so responsible for much of Europe's troubles, and even those of the whole world.

Our own recent economic troubles, for example, are called a major cause of Europe's troubles. Of late our monetary policy, which put the brakes on inflation, has supposedly resulted in the dollar being "overvalued," to the disruption of world trade, although no one explains how he knows what its value ought to be.

Our foreign policy zigs and zags to the consternation of foreign ministries. They can't tell, they say, what our policy is toward the Soviet Union, whether on disarmament or trade. And what in the world are we trying to do in Latin America, repeat Vietnam?

Overall, there's a wonderment that we get along as well as we do.

But relax. The complaints are perennial. And no matter what we do, or who governs us, I suspect the complaints will be undiminished.

I recall a dinner in Paris a decade ago. This was when we were still in the throes of Watergate, which was inexplicable to Europeans; the dollar had just been cut loose from gold and was thought, not surprisingly, to be a "weak" currency, a view that increased in subsequent years. The dollar sagged on world markets with all sorts of accompanying ills.

Most of those present at that dinner were French, although there was a West German businessman and an English journalist. Through the dinner all I heard was disparagement of the governance of my country.

Finally, I thought to pose a question. Take any reasonable period of time, long enough to even out the peaks and valleys of history. Say, a half-century, or two generations. In that time, I asked, what nation would the guests name as being better governed?

Germany? Certainly not. At the time the western half of it seemed to be reasonably governed, but that blessing came only after Germany had had the Kaiser, the Weimar Republic and Hitler in the years preceding.

France? Hardly. It was then in the midst of its Fifth Republic, the Fourth having collapsed in the aftermath of World War II—which was itself not exactly testimony to good governance.

Italy? Ridiculous. It was then on its seventh president since 1948 and nobody could count the numbers of premiers that had gone through the revolving doors of government.

Britain? Still then the "sick man" of Europe, for all that the voters had just thrown out the Labour government in disgust. Many industries had been nationalized and later de-nationalized to the confusion of everybody. It was beset by strikes, many of them "wildcats"; its trade was languishing as was its currency.

So the conversation went around the table. No one offered any country in Latin America. Only one mention was made of the Soviet Union, which had been forced to resume its purge trials because of unrest among dissident intellectuals. What the table-talk came down to, as I recall, was Sweden and Switzerland as possible candidates.

The same question, I think, might be posed today, and the longer the period used for discussion the harder it would be to find a nation that could lay claim to have been consistently better governed than the U.S. over the years. Even Sweden has lately had its political troubles.

This doesn't mean that much of the criticism of the U.S., then and now, isn't valid. We've had our troubles, indeed we have, from bad government policies. The inflation we recently suffered can't be blamed on anything except poor government, beginning with President Johnson and his attempt to have the government provide both guns and butter. Nor do we have a very consistent record in our dealings with the rest of the world, including the Soviet Union. Our policies toward our Latin neighbors haven't been a resounding success, either.

As for the present, it's perfectly true that President Reagan sometimes perplexes both political friends and foes, and the rest of the country as well. Domestically the government has swung from cutting taxes to raising them, from promises of less government spending to bigger budgets with larger deficits.

Nor should we forget that our voters too have a way of zigging and zagging in their choice of governors. Since 1973 they've swung from

Richard Nixon, reelected in a landslide, to an enigmatic Jimmy Carter followed by a relative conservative, Ronald Reagan.

So it isn't possible to hold up the U.S. as a peerless example of good government—too many blemishes from our long mistreatment of blacks or the incredible mismanagement of Vietnam, not to mention the wild swings in domestic economic policy.

Except for one thing. The last real breakdown in our governing system occurred more than a hundred years ago. Since 1865 we've survived five wars and the greatest depression in history, not to mention innumerable social upheavals, with our system of governance intact. If, from time to time, we have had poor governing, we have survived that too.

Moreover, it's hard to think of any country over that time that can claim to have been better governed, taking the bad with the good, than our own. Not Germany nor France nor Britain nor Belgium nor Russia nor China.

That's about the only answer you can give when your European friends castigate us. But it's not, I think, a bad answer.

May 4, 1983

'WHEREVER' IS A BIG PLACE

When President Truman announced what came to be called the Truman Doctrine—to resist all aggression however far from our shores—a few journalists (including Walter Lippmann and the then editor of *The Wall Street Journal*) weren't the only ones to see it as a major change in U.S. foreign policy. As a reader has reminded me, so did Mr. Truman himself.

In the second volume of his memoirs, Mr. Truman writes: "This was, I believe, the turning point in America's foreign policy, which now declared that wherever aggression, direct or indirect, threatened, the security of the United States was involved."

Mr. Truman was correct; it was a turning point. After the struggle of World War II, the country had demanded the quick dismantlement of our military power, hoping victory would bring peace, and longing to return to the policy long ago preached by President Washington, the avoidance of foreign entanglements. The country dreamed, once again, of isolation from the world's woes.

The Soviet Union, by becoming a new threatening world power, changed the nation's mood, and Mr. Truman responded by changing American foreign policy. Greece and Turkey, small and distant countries threatened by the Soviets, became part of our defense frontiers.

The key word in President Truman's summary is "wherever." For that meant that our security interests would be not only in Europe, as they appeared in 1947, but in then unimagined places threatened by aggression "direct or indirect."

In time that policy would lead us into war in Korea and, as this view was adopted by Mr. Truman's successors, later in Vietnam.

Today, nearly forty years later, this sweeping view of the U.S. responsibility in the world accounts for our military involvement in Lebanon, whether or not President Reagan—or his critics—acknowledges the origin of his foreign policy.

Nor is Lebanon the only place where today we have foreign "entanglements," military or otherwise. Aggression, "direct or indirect," can be found all over the globe.

A glance at that globe can be startling. Lebanon with U.S. Marines, aircraft carrier, battleship and destroyers is but a small part of our total military commitment. Altogether, our forces are deployed from the Caribbean to the far Pacific Ocean.

The largest force remains that in Europe, seed ground for both the great world wars. There we have approximately 200,000 Army troops, or nearly 40 percent of our total Army. In addition, there are some 2,500 Marines and nearly a thousand combat aircraft. In the surrounding waters, we keep a carrier group and an amphibious unit manned by about 45,000 Navy personnel.

Some of this naval force, including the antiquated battleship, is now off the shores of Lebanon trying to support the morale, if nothing else, of the hunkered-down Marines.

Far away, in the Indian and Pacific oceans, we keep five or six aircraft carriers, about forty submarines and fourscore other combat ships including another amphibious unit.

In Japan, there are 24,000 Marines more or less; 2,500 Army troops and a hundred-plus combat aircraft. North of there, in Korea, we keep another hundred aircraft and almost 30,000 soldiers, all "just in case." Southward, in the Philippines, is our main naval base at Subic Bay, manned by 5,000 sailors, together with 8,000 airmen and half-a-hundred aircraft.

Closer to home, we have the Atlantic fleet of about 150 combat ships (seven carriers) to keep an eye on Castro's Cuba and to protect the Panama Canal and Caribbean islands such as Grenada. Then we must count Central America, where we supply arms and advisers in El Salvador and Honduras.

If you take each of these places separately, it is difficult to argue any one of them isn't important to our national interest. Each is a potential tinderbox that could at any time explode into a wider conflagration. The problem is much like that of the government's budget, where every spending item can be defended as reasonable, even necessary. It's when you add up all those spending items that the total augurs trouble.

So it is with these world-wide commitments. To meet them, we have a relatively small army (smaller than Russia's or China's), a navy not much more than half the Soviet Union's in key combat vessels, fewer tanks and aircraft. We have no ready means, as we had in both world wars, to quickly expand our military strength. The defense budget already lays a heavy burden; we have no effective military draft.

Meanwhile, ironically, the foe that is the ostensible cause of all these commitments, the Soviet Union, has itself avoided direct military involvement in any of these places. No Soviet troops fought in Korea. None fought in Vietnam. None are fighting now in Lebanon. The only Soviet fighting is in Afghanistan, the one place where we are not resisting aggression even though there is nothing "indirect" about it.

It's no wonder then, I think, that the American public grows uneasy. Right now, that uneasiness justifiably centers on Lebanon, a country in chaos where our forces are exposed with no rational expectations of achieving any military objective any military staff could define on paper. No wonder the American people would like to see our Marines out of there.

But the real problem for President Reagan and the country transcends Lebanon. Simply put, it is how much of the world order can the U.S. carry on its shoulders. What are the limits on our strength? Whatever anyone may think, "wherever" is a very big place indeed.

January 11, 1984

IV

Of Peace and War

FORTY YEARS AFTER

That Sunday may have been a day to live in infamy but its lesson doesn't seem to linger in memory even among some old enough to remember.

For the lesson of Pearl Harbor, when the bombs rained down killing thousands of unwarned Americans, should be a perpetual reminder of the dangers that complacency hides in a perilous world. The infamy of that day lies not upon the Japanese alone. All among us who looked at the world but would not see, and they were legion, must share it. Had we not been blinded by wishful thinking it would not have happened.

Only a few months before, Congress had very nearly ended the draft on the ground that it wasn't necessary; it passed by a single vote in the House. That spring and summer the Navy still had ancient destroyers at sea with no sound gear to seek out submarines and no weapons to hunt them down if they were found. On land young recruits marched with brooms as pretend rifles and drove trucks as pretend tanks. This though war had been raging for two years in Europe, where Hitler's armies had conquered nearly all but the island Britain.

But the lesson of Pearl Harbor was not for Americans only. To much of the Western world—to the Belgians, to the Dutch, to the French, to the British—the American disaster was just one more incident in a global war. Indeed, many of them welcomed it, in the words of Winston Churchill, with "the greatest joy." The United States had at last been rudely awakened and "there was no more doubt about the end."

Those same Belgians, Dutch, French and British, however, had earlier had a like rude awakening themselves. Had they not likewise been blinded by wishful thinking history would not have repeated itself.

Of that first World War, then being repeated, my own memories are dim. Reading about it I've always been surprised that people and their leaders could not see, or would not believe, that it could come until the guns of August sounded. Kaiser Wilhelm and his ministers had made no secret of their aggressive intent, yet their intended victims did nothing to discourage them from their ambitions.

In the 1930s neither Hitler nor Tojo hid his ambitions either. But to remember Pearl Harbor is to remember how my generation told itself war was made only by armaments makers, whom we would abolish. How in Britain our contemporaries swore nevermore "to fight for king and country." How the Belgians and Dutch believed they would be spared. How even after war had come we here thought we could stand aside.

So it was that global war came a second time. Poland, Belgium, Holland, France, Norway, Denmark and the Balkans were overrun, Britain left in lonely peril. On that fateful Sunday we found ourselves once more embroiled.

As it happened, the Japanese did not swallow all of Asia, the Nazis engulf all of Europe. Millions, once awakened, died to stop them. And lest we forget, none of those millions thought it better to be under the heels of conquerors than to be dead.

Will there be a third time? Of that I cannot say. But I hope I will be forgiven my shock at hearing the children of those dead chanting that it were better to be Red than dead. Yes, in the very lands their fathers died to keep free. And even, sadly, some among ourselves.

My feelings are not for want of sympathy for those who cry this. The peoples of Europe have every right to feel bitter that having aroused themselves to twice throw off the yokes of barbarism, they now find half of Europe under another, with the rest of Europe once more threatened. It was not the war of my time that was lost but the peace. And those who made that peace have much to answer for.

How many times can people arouse themselves against such perils without risk of exhausting both strength and spirit?

I also share the fears of those who look with horror on the specter of nuclear war. Any who do not are fools. Hiroshima I never saw, but after one look at what a very primitive bomb did to Nagasaki I need no one to tell me about the new winds of war. They will blow such destruction as men have never known.

I would, in fact, add my own voice to those crying "ban the bomb" if banning it were possible. The agony is that knowledge once gained can never be buried or put out of man's mind. The nuclear bomb will not go back into the box.

But what those who parade under that banner really ask is that the civilized world, because it is civilized, ban the bomb unilaterally. They know full well the Soviet Union will not do so. And that is madness. It would leave the civilized world defenseless before its enemies.

Only the blind cannot see what kind of world lies behind that Iron Curtain. The Soviet Union itself no more disguises its ambitions to extend that world than those would-be conquerors before it. Year by year it has multiplied its array of weapons while we and the rest of the world looked on complacently. If war today were only a duel of guns, planes and tanks the Soviet Union could overrun Western Europe more easily than Hitler's legions. If the Soviets are deterred, the deterrent is that same nuclear arsenal.

The nuclear threat, in all truth, is a terrible thing to think of. If we can diminish it let us by all means do so. But the abject surrender of the world to a new barbarism is also a frightful thing to contemplate.

This year December 7 fell upon a Monday. Among my generation there were a few quiet ceremonies to mark it. But how many others recalled its warning against complacency, its reminder that civilization stands always precarious unless people will hazard their lives to preserve it?

December 9, 1981

WAR AT SEA

A lone torpedo from beneath the sea and down goes a cruiser. A single guided missile from 20 miles away and down goes a destroyer.

These weren't the only naval casualties in that distant fighting between Britain and Argentina over the Falklands. But neither came in the midst of a general engagement where losses are expected. So they dramatized as nothing else could the vulnerability of surface ships at sea in a modern war.

The result has been a battle of words among those who must think about future wars at sea—military men, political leaders and all concerned about the nation's defenses—that continues long after the Falkland struggle was resolved.

For those two sinkings came at a time when the Reagan administration and its naval advisers are preparing to resuscitate old battleships and spend much of the funds for the Navy on a few huge carriers rather than on a more numerous and diversified fleet of smaller vessels. If nothing else, the loss of these two ships in a matter of moments ought to give everyone pause.

Heretofore any questioning of the "big ship" strategy has brought outraged cries from admirals, spokesmen for the Navy League and others who feel that big ships should constitute the backbone of future fleets. It's been charged that any who question that strategy are really hostile to big Navy spending in general and would have us defenseless on the sea.

Not any more. Elmo Zumwalt and Stansfield Turner, retired four-star admirals both, are no foes of the Navy or a large budget for it. One is a former chief of naval operations, the other former president of the Naval War College as well as director of the CIA.

Admiral Zumwalt says that if he still had a voice in planning he would build "many and smaller ships" for the same money that will be spent on the big carriers and their supporting forces.

Admiral Turner, in a thoughtful article in *Newsweek*, pleads for more ships (including carriers) which by their numbers are less vulnerable to being put out of action than a few, however well armored.

"Dispersing our sea-based airpower as widely as possible," he says, "prevents a crippled carrier from tying up too many aircraft and makes it more likely that a carrier will be there where it is needed."

Neither admiral—nor any other thoughtful person, I think—supposes that surface ships will disappear from the sea in wartime. They cannot as long as we must be prepared to deploy and support military forces over wide areas of the world. Neither submarines nor airplanes can at present supply the huge tonnages of men, arms and materiel that surface ships can carry to distant battlefields, much less maintain the flow of food and other civilian goods that is equally necessary in wartime.

For any who have forgotten the example of World War II, the lesson was shown again in the logistics required to support the British forces in the Falklands thousands of miles from home.

To protect those supply ships as well as to deploy military power to far-off battles requires also surface warships—destroyers, cruisers, carriers, amphibious assault ships—and many of them. So the argument is not over "whether" surface warships but what kind.

Advocates of the battleship and the huge carrier contend that the modern larger ships can be better armored, supplied with more compartmentation and more sophisticated damage control equipment. That makes them, so runs the argument, less vulnerable than the *Sheffield*, a destroyer, or the *General Belgrano*, a cruiser of World War II vintage.

This is certainly true. Nimitz-class carriers as well as the recycled battleships can take much more punishment than smaller ships before sinking or being put out of action. But that is only part of the story.

No admiral in his right mind would send a battleship or a carrier to cruise the sea alone; none did so even in World War II. For neither is invulnerable. Even a super-carrier, as Admiral Turner notes, has many extremely vulnerable points—aviation fuel lines, bombs and planes loaded with fuel on the flight deck—which cannot be hidden behind defensive shielding.

A carrier task force must be surrounded by a veritable armada of support ships, the larger and more expensive the carrier the larger the necessary armada. And today the danger comes not alone from enemy planes that might be fought off or from slow-speed submarines with short-range torpedoes. The danger now is from fast homing torpedoes and guided missiles launched from far away. Both can carry tactical atomic warheads that could finish off the largest ship afloat.

The simple, basic truth is that modern technology has altered the face of war, at sea as well as on land. This requires that admirals and generals rethink not only tactics but fundamental strategy, and that in turn requires a reexamination of war's weapons, from tanks to ships.

It's true enough that this is not a task within the competence of the ordinary citizen. It is also true, though, that it is the ordinary citizen who will pay for miscalculation by the military, pay in sweat and perhaps ultimately in blood.

So it behooves us to pay attention to the argument and to listen carefully to those with military experience who have been set free to say what they think without being any longer required to defend "official" doctrine. Admirals Zumwalt and Turner might just be right.

And who's right could make a lot of difference to those in future wars going down to the sea in ships.

June 2, 1982

THE PROMETHEAN GIFT

I never saw Hiroshima. But in the autumn of 1945, I was among the first naval group to visit Nagasaki to bring out our prisoners of war held by the Japanese.

In Nagasaki harbor, all seemed peaceful and serene and we were greeted by the Japanese as if the war had never been. It wasn't until after a brief drive from the harbor, rounding a curve to come upon what was left of the city, that we could see what man had wrought. You knew in an instant that the world, in war or in peace, would never again be the same.

The shock was not merely from the devastation. There had been as much of that in Coventry or in Hamburg from the firebombs that rained down upon them, as many dead or dying. What stunned was that all this came to Nagasaki from a single bomb from a single plane and that it happened not in hours but in an instant. And this, as we were to learn later, was from a very primitive atom bomb.

So better than most of those parading now in ban-the-bomb marches, I have glimpsed what a holocaust a nuclear war could be. Those who lightly dismiss these anguished cries are fools. I would myself march to put the atom bomb back into the box whence it came if that were possible.

But most of those chanting their slogans in the streets of Europe, and some in our own country, are foolish in a different fashion.

For one thing, only the deluded can expect the jinni of nuclear knowledge to somehow be made to disappear, leaving the world as it was before. There is no way to unlearn the knowledge that the energy locked in matter equals its mass times the velocity of light squared. If Einstein had not seen it, another would have. Nor is it possible to secrete the technology to convert this formula into terrible weapons.

That simple formula is now the property of all mankind, for an enduring truth is that knowledge once gained is never lost. Already the technology for converting mass to energy has proliferated around the world. Any one of many nations can, if one chooses, do today what none could do forty years ago.

Moreover, that knowledge is not all evil. Like the Prometheus of the legend who stole the secret of fire from the gods, Einstein's gift can be blessing as well as curse as we learn to put it to use in ways from providing energy to curing the sick with nuclear medicine.

But those now parading to "ban the bomb" are misguided in another way. What they ask, whatever they say, is that the Western world—mainly the United States—abolish its nuclear weapons unilaterally. There are no such parades in the Soviet Union and no one expects the chants in the West to be heeded in the Kremlin.

This is the dilemma. If the Soviet Union were not what it is, the world would not fear a nuclear holocaust. There was no such fear in the brief time when the United States alone held the secrets. We even proposed to the Soviet Union, and the world, that the knowledge of the bomb be locked up. That proposal failed against the intransigence of the Soviet Union. So has every proposal since then to restrain the making of atomic weapons.

There are those, I know, who think it "better Red than dead" and would willingly leave themselves defenseless before the Soviet Union. For them there is nothing worth dying for, not for country, not for liberty nor freedom, not even for the preservation of civilization. What is the good of that, they ask, if the price is death and destruction?

That cry falls strangely on my ears, especially when it is heard in Europe. For those who chant it owe their freedom to march to their fathers who believed resistance to tyranny was worth fighting for, even dying for. There could have been peace a generation ago if they had thought it better to be conquered than dead. But the fields of Europe are dotted with the graves of those—many of them American—who did not think so.

Do we, the living, owe them no debt? And do we pay it by holding life alone so precious we will not risk it for any cause? Certainly there are men and women today in Poland, in Czechoslovakia, in Hungary, in Israel and in many other places, who value other things more than life.

I do not for one moment deny that an atomic war, should one come, would be more terrible than any war the world has ever seen. The fire and brimstone would be unimaginable. But civilization, like mankind itself, has always stood on that razor's edge between preservation and destruction.

Over the millennia the original Promethean fire, whether from heaven's thunderbolts or the willful acts of man, has wrought destruction everywhere, consuming homes, towns, cities in deadly conflagrations. There have been times before when men thought the end of the world would come. Yet up to now men have not surrendered, knowing they could not, if they would, give back that secret of destruction.

Therein lies the true anguish of the nuclear age. Live with it we must. We have no other choice. Its secrets, too, cannot be returned to some hidden place.

And live with it we can. But not by foolishly leaving its powers in malevolent hands alone. The only thing that will restrain the Soviet Union, and perhaps lead it to a true nuclear arms agreement, is the fear that it also will not escape atomic terror if it is unleashed.

June 16, 1982

APPRAISING VICTORIES

"'Twas a famous victory," observed Little Peterkin's grandfather, Old Kaspar. "But what good came of it at last?" the boy asked. And the old man answered, "That I cannot tell."

The question and the uncertain answer were put in the characters' mouths by the English poet Robert Southey after the battle of Blenheim in 1704, in which the French were defeated (for the first time in fifty years) by Winston Churchill's most famous ancestor, the Duke of Marlborough.

It's a question that has recurred repeatedly after many another famous victory. Quite often on its morrow the answer seems self-evident, as it did after the Allied defeat of Nazi Germany. For there, surely, we saved Europe from remaining prostrate under an iron boot. How were we to know then that the aftermath would be half of Europe lying prostrate behind an iron curtain?

Half of Europe saved, it's true, is better than leaving all of it conquered by tyranny. But as it turned out the result was not quite as splendid as we thought in that summer of 1945. The world is still haunted by what was made afterwards of the peace that victory bought so dearly.

The point of Little Peterkin's question, like my own recalling it, is not to disparage victory. Rather, it's simply to remind ourselves that it takes time to take its measure.

That's a useful reminder, I think, on the morrow of two splendid victories, that of the British in the Falkland Islands and that of the Israelis in Lebanon. Without in the least detracting from the triumphs of either or denying what, in both cases, was accomplished, it's worth remembering that we still must wait a space of time before the consequences can be fully appraised.

The immediate result of that little war in the Falklands is clear enough. For once, anyway, an aggressor got his comeuppance. The military junta in Argentina did not get away with its effort to alter the political map by armed force, thanks to a determined—and unexpected—response from Britain.

We haven't seen much of that kind of response to aggression since the United States responded to it in Korea and Vietnam, and in neither of those instances was there a splendid victory for our side. Korea can at best be put down as a draw. Vietnam was a defeat, one that proved costly for both us and the people of Southeast Asia.

Elsewhere aggression has been met with nothing more than words, as when the Soviet Union decided to include Afghanistan in its empire or when its tanks rolled into Hungary.

But it was a costly victory for the British. We can all only hope that, the battle being so decisive, peace will return to the area and that the bitterness will not long linger. If it should, if the Argentine junta feels it can redeem its injured pride only by continuing its hostile stance, then we will have another area of simmering trouble to add to those already dotting the world.

One of those, of course, has been the Middle East, where Israel has led a precarious existence and poor Lebanon has had hardly any existence at all except as a continuing battlefield. Now Israel has conquered Lebanon in a dazzling display of arms. Both the PLO and the Syrians, who between them have torn Lebanon apart, have been routed.

The fruits of that victory, however, remain uncertain. Part of the uncertainty is what the Israelis will do. Having defeated their enemies, what next? Withdrawal would leave once more a political vacuum to be filled again by the same forces Israel fought to expel. To remain would leave Lebanon an occupied country, not a good prospect for enduring peace.

Some of the uncertainty is not within the power of Israel to remove. It has aggressively crushed any military threat to its northern borders. It has not ended the Palestinian dream of a homeland from which the militant PLO draws its strength. On the contrary, it could strengthen the PLO politically. The making of martyrs is never conducive to tranquility.

Another uncertainty is the long-term reaction among Arab countries. The Syrians have certainly learned to respect Israeli arms, as did the Jordanians and Egyptians before them. It by no means follows that fear of arms will reduce the hostility of the Arab world toward Israel. That could indeed become more virulent.

Another price Israel has paid for its victory is the loss of sympathy among many nations. Some 100 delegations at the U.N. refused to listen to a speech by Prime Minister Begin. Even the United States, Israel's most faithful friend, has been disturbed. To put the world's goodwill at risk is not a trivial matter for Israel.

In both the Falklands and Lebanon the victors felt they had to do what they did because of the consequences of not doing it. Both succeeded brilliantly. Argentina was driven from the Falklands. Lebanon has ceased, at least for the time being, to be a sanctuary from which Israel's enemies could with impunity do it injury.

Yet in both the Falklands and in Lebanon the full measure of victory has yet to be taken. Nor will it, I think, soon be known.

If it's any comfort to Britain or Israel, that question posed by Little Peterkin was finally answered. Although the battle of Blenheim seemed to settle nothing at the moment, history sees Marlborough's victory as a turning point in the years of war over the Spanish succession that had torn Europe apart.

As to what good will come at last from these two splendid victories—well, that I cannot tell.

June 30, 1982

THE DRAGON'S TEETH

If there were ever any doubt about man's enduring inhumanity to man—regardless of race or religion—it's been dispelled on the Mediterranean shores of the Middle East.

It was the followers of Mohammed who shelled peaceful settlements and blew up buses loaded with schoolchildren, driving the Israelis to send an army to halt them.

It was the sons of Abraham who invaded Lebanon destroying all in their path and leveling the city of Beirut under the guise of saving it.

It was the disciples of Jesus of Nazareth who lined up their fellow creatures and slaughtered them, a thousand all in a row.

In such a tangle of violence, it's impossible to mete out justly the responsibility for so much death and destruction rooted in ancient animosities. We will probably never know to what extent, if any, Jewish soldiers are answerable for the holocaust of Palestinians. The ultimate cause is something too deeply imbedded in the human soul. Of all the animals, we learn anew, only man is vile.

What can be said is that the Begin government—and as always we should distinguish between a people and their government—unleashed with its invasion of Lebanon terrible forces it could not control and of which no man can take the measure.

In the phrase attributed to Talleyrand, it was worse than a crime, it was a blunder. The cost of that blunder to Israel is for now incalculable. It will not be inconsequential. That invasion, and all that followed from it, has cost Israel the good will of the world. Mr. Begin has made his country appear a ruthless bully.

That appearance has not escaped his own countrymen. Heretofore the political divisions within Israel were on domestic issues. Now for the first time, there is a deep cleavage within the country over the use of its military strength. Army officers and cabinet officials have resigned in protest. Crowds in the street demonstrate disapproval. The opposition party has become vocal.

Nor are the outcries in Israel alone. In the United States, Israel's most faithful ally since the day of its birth, the voices of censure rise. President Reagan has publicly expressed outrage. In newspapers and other organs of opinion the criticism is almost unanimous, much of it coming from those long unwavering in their support of Israel.

The vocal critics of Prime Minister Begin include many within the American Jewish community. That community, once solidly steadfast in its devotion to this homeland for its people, is split asunder.

If its public criticism has been muted, mainly taking the form of support for President Reagan's peace proposal, not so with private Jewish voices at social gatherings and in synagogues. As one producer of a Jewish radio program puts it, "There is reaction to what seem to be insupportable actions Israel has taken." Albert Vorspan, vice-president of the Union of American Hebrew Congregations, thinks Mr. Begin's "West Bank policy is crazy."

This has led Norman Podhoretz, editor of *Commentary* magazine, to label all criticisms of Israel as "anti-Semitic even when they are mouthed by Jews." That is the kind of angry remark neither Israel nor American Jews can afford because it seems to say the Israeli government must be supported no matter what it does. If that ever becomes perceived by the American public as the attitude of its Jewish citizens, then—and only then—do we really stand in danger of anti-Semitism.

In any event it's clear that the Begin government's conquest of Lebanon, and the manner of achieving it, has been a costly one for Israel. It has put at risk what was heretofore Israel's greatest strength, the sympathy and decent respect of civilized mankind.

What is far from clear is how Mr. Begin can extricate his country from the mire into which he has plunged it. President Reagan says that Israel should withdraw its forces. But it may be too late for that. Lebanon, once a lovely country, has long been in disarray; now Israel, departing, will leave chaos in its wake.

It's dubious whether an international force, including the U.S., can restore tranquility much less achieve political cooperation among Lebanon's hostile groups. We may be plunging into the same mire. Even if such an international force succeeds, the credit will go to it and not the Israelis. Israel will get only the blame for everything that goes wrong.

The resignation of Mr. Begin and his belligerent defense minister might help. At least a new government would not carry the burden of responsibility for its predecessor's actions; it could offer a different face to the world.

The full-scale judicial inquiry into Israel's conduct during the massacre, announced by Mr. Begin, may go some way to temper the past week's anguish.

But that won't wash away the tragedy that has befallen this tiny country which so long held the regard of the non-Arab world. For that tragedy, Menachem Begin bears the burden. His blunder, not unknown in history, was to launch a war without considering what would confront him if he won it. Having conquered Lebanon, what would he do with it?

That brings to mind the remark of the Duke of Wellington that nothing is so melancholy as a battle lost except a battle won. That the Israeli arms won a brilliant victory there is no doubt. Its soldiers can be proud of their bravery and their skill. But what was won was a Cadmean victory, so named after the Phoenician hero who slew a dragon only to find that from the dragon's teeth there arose new enemies to confront him.

Prime Minister Begin slew the dragon that was the PLO in Lebanon. But from the bloody fields left by his conquering armies, there have sprung new woes undreamed of for his tormented country.

September 29, 1982

THOSE WHO WERE THERE

"And gentlemen in England now abed shall think themselves ac-curs'd they were not here."

My father understood what Henry the Fifth meant on the morning of Agincourt. Exempted in World War I because he was married with a newborn son and was needed to manage a family business, he after-wards regretted he was not there. Especially when old friends talked of the Argonne Forest or Château-Thierry.

There were some of my war, too, who were not there, and I have heard their silence when those who came home safe from Normandy or Okinawa spoke those names, as familiar in their mouths as house-hold words.

It was remembrance of that which made me say, some years ago, the day would come when those in Vietnam would strip their sleeves to show their scars, while others stood silent outside the band of brothers.

That was not my most acclaimed remark. For those who slept abed those years, many of whom had fled to Canada that they might, there was only scorn for those who went to fight in far-off paddy fields. Those who were there have been the silent ones. They felt they had to apologize, in shame, and try to hide those years lest they be put down as fools or knaves.

So I thought myself mistaken. For once, it seemed, there would be no pride among those who bore our arms, no honor for them among those who sent them off to war, no vigil feast for those who went and never came home again.

Today I am not so sure I was mistaken. We can see today some first, faint signs that shame has turned to pride and scorn to shame. The country may not have changed its mind about that fruitless war. What is changing is its view of those who were there and of those who weren't.

The first sign was that monument in Washington. When it was spoken of there was much controversy. It was not one of those heroic monuments, like the raising of the flag on Mount Suribachi. Simply a long plain slab on which are named those who died in Vietnam.

Yet when it was unveiled people came in endless lines seeking the name of friend or brother, son or father. When they found one they wept openly that at last he was enrolled with honor. Many who watched on television wept also to see them weep. It was as if the whole nation felt the need to pay homage to those who did what was asked of them and paid the price.

That is not the only sign. When, shortly after Vietnam, James Fallows wrote in *The Washington Monthly* of his "sense of shame" at having tricked his way out of the draft, hardly anyone paid much attention. Those who did likewise put down the confession as an aberration. So did those who had answered the call to arms. He seemed to speak for none but himself.

Since then newspapers all over the country have carried stories of those home from Vietnam and how they fared. Editorial writers, and even the president of the United States, have apologized for our shoddy treatment of them. We have at last passed laws to give them some of the rewards that went to those of World War II.

Now in *Esquire*, a magazine that prides itself on keeping in touch with intellectual fashions as well as fads, there is an interesting report by Christopher Buckley, himself one who shouted with glee when he flunked the medical examination for the Vietnam War and now regrets it.

But there is more to Mr. Buckley's report. He interviewed many who went and many who didn't. Some of what he found among them is surprising.

Some were friends who served in Vietnam. They saw death up close every day, yet today they are married, happy, secure and "they don't have nightmares and they don't shoot up gas stations with M-16s." Mr. Buckley confesses some envy of them, for they were "weighed in the scales and weren't found wanting."

Nor, he says, is he alone in envy of those who were there. "Until recently" he'd never heard anyone admit to guilt or shame over not having gone to Vietnam. Now he has. He quotes a friend who wrote him a fourteen-page letter from Paris filled with something like regret "about what not going meant to him." Another confessed he was now disappointed that he hadn't been gassed or wounded there because "then it would be my war too."

I doubt that James Fallows, Christopher Buckley or their now regretful friends speak for all of those who dodged that war, tearing up draft cards, fleeing the country.

There were, roughly, fifty-three million who came of age during those years, of which some nine million served in the armed forces. Of these about three million actually went to Indochina. Of the remainder, according to a survey by the Veterans Administration, only 3.5 percent will say that missing the war had a "negative impact" on their lives.

Most, then, are still content with themselves that they were not there. And I suspect that most who were there wished they hadn't been. Most of us who served in World War II also wished we hadn't had to do it. Few there are who eagerly go to any war. Few of us can feel like Navy Capt. Jeremiah Denton, returning from years as a prisoner of war in North Vietnam, who said he was "happy . . . to serve our country in difficult circumstances."

Happy? Difficult circumstances? How oddly those words fall upon our ears remembering that agony for our country.

And yet . . .

The day will come, I no longer have any doubt, when those few who were there those years ago will gather their wives and walking canes, as old soldiers have always done, to talk of how it was.

When that day comes all the others will be excluded from that band of brothers.

September 14, 1983

A MATTER OF WORDS

At his first press conference after sending American troops to fight in Korea, President Truman said, "We are not at war." Then some reporter, nameless to me, asked if it could be called "a police action." Mr. Truman replied, "Yes, that's exactly what it amounts to."

And so a sort of 1984 "newspeak" phrase entered our political vocabulary, for that's what the Korean War was long called in Washington's official language—just a police action.

The memory of that returned to mind as U.S. Marines found themselves (once again) in Lebanon. Officially they are there on a "peacekeeping" mission, although they aren't allowed to do anything to achieve or enforce peace in that war-wracked land. To President Reagan, they haven't even been in a "hostile" situation although some have been killed by shell-fire and more have been wounded. They can only hope that the latest cease-fire will hold, something none of the two hundred previous cease-fires has done.

That situation in turn brings to mind a passage from Aldous Huxley. It isn't from his most famous novel, which gave new currency to the phrase "Brave New World," but from a later, long essay on "Words and Their Meanings."

Words are magical, he wrote, in the way they affect the minds of those who use them. "A mere matter of words," we say contemptuously, he noted, while forgetting that words have power to mold men's thinking, to canalize their feelings. "Conduct and character," Huxley said, "are largely determined by the nature of the words we currently use to discuss ourselves and the world around us."

Of course presidents aren't the only ones who sometimes prefer to call a spade by some other name. Advertising copywriters are adept at it. They don't ask you to buy plain soap but a soft, gentle, luxurious cleanser, those being appealing words. But politicians have always known the power of words to affect our view of things.

Mr. Truman had a reason to avoid the word "war." Had he used it for the fighting in Korea he would have armed his critics, for our Constitution plainly gives the power "to declare war" to Congress and Mr. Truman was acting on his own. That might make his action seem "unconstitutional," which is a "snarl word" in our political vocabulary.

President Reagan had a similar problem in Lebanon because of the War Powers Act, passed by Congress, which limits the president's power to keep our troops in hostile or combat situations. The constitutionality of that act is debatable, but Mr. Reagan thought it better to avoid calling the situation of the Marines by its right name until he could work out a compromise with his congressional critics. Sometimes it's better to avoid political issues than to force a confrontation.

I don't know how the Supreme Court would decide the constitutionality of the War Powers Act, but I don't share the view that it's a bad thing for the president to have to go to Congress for support when he sends American soldiers to be shot at.

Much of our trouble in Korea, and more so later in Vietnam, grew out of the fact that they began as unilateral actions by presidents. In neither case did the Congress "declare war" but you have to wrench the language to say they weren't wars.

In the end it was the want of public support that proved our undoing in both cases. I won't pretend that congressional approval necessarily represents public approval. It is, though, the best institution we have for representing it. Congressmen, whatever their faults, do try to reflect the sentiments of their constituents because failure to do so can be costly at the voting booth, and representatives at least are answerable every two years.

I'm aware that, constitutionally, the president is commander-in-chief of the armed forces and so responsible for their deployment after they "are called into service." I share the view that since we live in a parlous world the president must sometimes be free to act decisively in the use of the armed forces. And sometimes quickly, not only if the nation is attacked but in other circumstances where there's no time for long, quarrelsome debate. President Eisenhower's prompt action in sending Marines to Lebanon the first time (in 1958) headed off for the time being the chaos that later engulfed that unhappy land.

But Mr. Eisenhower did not keep them there, nor should he have by his own decision. When time permits public discussion on military action, it is advisable for a president to act only with public support.

Ours is not a "presidential government." Those who wish it were (and there are some) wish it only when they approve of his actions. Otherwise, they too are grateful for the checks and balances so carefully provided in our Constitution.

It may or may not be wise now for the Marines to be in Lebanon. The Congress might have made a grave mistake to force their recall; Congress itself is not always wise. But Senator Goldwater (that erstwhile "hawk," remember?) and others thought they should be recalled. Not to give such voices a chance to be weighed and counted is perilous in a free society.

Those beleaguered Marines needed the support not only of a battleship but of both the policy-deciding arms of the nation, the Congress as well as the president. So President Reagan acted prudently when he sought congressional approval and didn't insist upon his authority to act without it. At the very least, he is not now left standing all alone.

It's no "mere matter of words" whether a Korea is called a "war" or whether our Marines are now in "combat." We should have learned what woes await when our arms are used without the political support of the whole nation.

October 12, 1983

MILITARY MEN AND MATTERS

One of the mysteries of World War II to some people—it certainly must have puzzled Presidents Kennedy, Johnson and Carter—is how we ever defeated the Germans, Italians and Japanese.

For in that long-ago war the conduct of the fighting was left entirely to military men. Roosevelt and Churchill made some basic strategy decisions, about invading North Africa and when to launch the reconquest of Europe, for example. But such decisions made, the how-to-do-it was left to Eisenhower, Nimitz, Bradley, Spruance and other commanders on the spot.

Even the military headquarters in Washington and London were chary about interfering with the tactics of distant operations. Admiral King in Washington did once try to dissuade Admiral Nimitz from the dispositions he planned for what became the Battle of Midway but, fortunately, Nimitz was not ordered to change them.

Partly, this restraint arose from the communications then existing, slow and not too reliable. In greater part the restraint followed from long existing military traditions developed by experience over centuries of warfare.

With the development of modern, sophisticated communications this practice changed. During the Cuban missile crisis President Kennedy could talk on the telephone to naval commanders as easily as calling a cabinet officer, and did so. During Vietnam President Johnson was on the phone day and night telling the commanders when to fly sorties, when to stop and other operational details. President Carter involved himself in the nitty-gritty details of the disastrous Iran-hostage rescue attempt and personally issued the order to abort it.

Now, so Gerald Seib reports in *The Wall Street Journal*, the Reagan administration is following a different policy, or rather the old one resurrected. For the invasion of Grenada (call it what you will) the military was given the objectives it was to obtain. Then the achieving of them was left to the military commanders.

The result, as we know, were a few snafus and we will doubtless hear of more. We bombed a hospital by mistake; some American soldiers got killed by "friendly fire." There were also some tactical errors, such as inadequate coordination between the forces landing on the north and south sides of the island. No doubt this will bring criticism of the Reagan-Weinberger policy of hands off the military during the battle.

But that criticism is likely to come only from those who never fought a war or have studied none. For snafus are inevitable in anything as turbulent and confused as a battlefield. In our Civil War one of the Confederacy's greatest generals, Stonewall Jackson, was killed by his own troops. Even Eisenhower was caught unprepared for the Battle of the Bulge.

Nonetheless, the professional military men made some very sound decisions at Grenada given the short time they had to prepare. For one, they avoided a common error of civilian planners, which is in applying force to use too little too late. The military nearly doubled the size of the landing force previously planned.

This is in accord with an old military maxim: If you think a company can do the job, send a battalion; if you think it will require a battalion, send a regiment. This proved sound at Grenada because, as so often in battles, prior intelligence of hostile forces proved to be inadequate.

Moreover, once the fighting started the military did the job with neatness and dispatch, any little snafus notwithstanding.

The wisdom of leaving military operations to military men has been shown over and over. In World War II a sea commander might be ordered to go there and do such. How he got there and how he did what was needed was his responsibility. This principle applied all the way down the line of command. A company captain might be told to hold a certain line or to take a certain hill. Even a general back at headquarters didn't tell the captain how to do it. After all, the captain was there, the general wasn't.

There are some things, of course, that shouldn't be left to military men. A wise subordination of the military to civilian authority means it is not up to generals to decide whether to send troops to Grenada— or Lebanon or anywhere. They ought to be consulted, certainly, on the do-ability of the decision; if a general says sending troops to Lebanon is risky he ought to be listened to carefully. But the decision made, the general's task is to carry it out.

It's after the decision that the operational responsibility should fall to the generals or admirals, not civilians in Washington. It's fashionable in some quarters to denigrate the "military mind," and it's true soldiers sometimes have a narrow political view. That's why military governments, known in many countries, usually make a mess of a country. It doesn't follow, though, that military minds are incompetent on military matters.

After all, a general or admiral has spent a lifetime learning his craft. He's studied past battles back to Thermopylae. Perhaps he knows little about economics; he knows far more about tactics and logistics than any civilian. He makes mistakes, certainly, but they are fewer and less fateful than those of politicians turned amateur commanders.

So we ought to welcome the return of purely military responsibility to military men. To do otherwise on a battlefield makes as much sense as allowing a hospital administrator to tell a trained surgeon how to do a coronary bypass.

November 23, 1983

V

Of Politics

THE PUBLIC MORALITY:
AFTERTHOUGHTS ON WATERGATE

The scandals of the Watergate affair do not, technically speaking, embrace the scandal of former Vice-President Spiro Agnew, which ended in his resignation as a convicted felon. Mr. Agnew, so far as we know, had nothing to do either with the break-in of the Democratic headquarters at the Watergate complex or with its related events, including the subsequent efforts of a cover-up; indeed, for a time it appeared that alone among high administration officials, Mr. Agnew would be left free of scandal, thanks to the fact that he was deliberately kept outside the White House inner circle. Conversely, none of those involved in Watergate were responsible for Mr. Agnew's troubles; they were of his own making. Moreover, the two affairs were different in kind. Mr. Agnew's was a simple case of bribery and kickbacks, an all-too-familiar felonious behavior among public officials. What has come to be subsumed under the single word Watergate was of another order, an attempt to use governmental power to subvert the political process in the broadest sense of that term.

Nonetheless, the two affairs are related, and not merely in that they were coincident public scandals. In at least one respect, as we shall see, they had a common denominator in the rationalizations by those involved for what they did. In addition the Watergate participants, self-righteous in their freedom from personal greed, reflected moral views more widespread than we care to acknowledge. Neither, therefore, can be treated as isolated incidents of aberrant behavior, or so it seems to me. They are worth examining in a broader context than simply as political scandals because of what they suggest about the state of our public morals.

The scandal of Spiro Agnew is that he is our first vice-president to resign from office with an admission of a felony, income tax evasion. He is not, however, the first vice-president to lie under suspicion of illegal activities involving bribes and kickbacks of the sort the Justice Department also alleged against him. Vice-President John Calhoun in the second Adams administration and Vice-President Schuyler Colfax in the scandal-ridden Grant administration lay under like suspicions. In the Colfax case a special investigating committee looking into alleged bribes came to no conclusion one way or another and the House dropped impeachment proceedings. Calhoun, charged with war profiteering, asked for and received a congressional investigation which found no cause for prosecution.[1]

Nor is Mr. Agnew the first public official of modern times—including cabinet officers, governors, judges and members of Congress—to be caught in the coils of the law. Apart from those convicted, he is not the first, or only, public official to accept "gifts" from those doing business with the government; that is, he did not invent the system of payoffs from contractors when he became Baltimore County executive and, later, governor of Maryland.

Indeed, in his postresignation apologia, Mr. Agnew made much of the fact that he found it "customary" for engineers and contractors to make substantial payments to state officials in return for, or at least in parallel with, state contracts. The Justice Department conceded as much; the net that caught Mr. Agnew also entangled predecessors and successors. And nobody familiar with politics, especially state government politics, will deny the prevalence of the custom, not only in Maryland but almost everywhere. A cynic might say that this sort of thing is as American as apple pie.

Those involved in the Watergate affair didn't invent either political dirty tricks or the wholesale sowing of campaign millions. Campaign spying and campaign tricks, including forged documents to use against opponents, are as old as politics. Two famous examples come readily to mind: the smearing of Al Smith with fake photographs and the smearing of Herbert Hoover by rearranging phrases out of his speeches to make it appear he had said things he didn't say. More recently a "missile gap" was invented for the 1960 campaign, and in that election there is a suspicion that votes were actually stolen in Texas and Illinois; nor was the 1964 campaign against Barry Goldwater a model of propriety. As for wiretapping and covert surveillance by those in authority

[1]Calhoun did later resign, the only vice-president to have done so prior to Spiro Agnew, but this was unrelated to the investigation. He resigned to become senator from South Carolina.

against their political enemies, real or imagined, previous administrations have used them to keep tabs on certain people, ranging from Jimmy Hoffa to Martin Luther King.

So to a certain extent it is true—and might as well be conceded—that there is a touch of applying ex post facto ethical standards in the public condemnation of Mr. Agnew and the Watergate crew, as well as with the indignation over President Nixon's finances. That is, they are being held accountable for conduct that in the past has been too much tolerated or at least cynically shrugged off. The peculiar record of James Curley did not stop voters from repeatedly reelecting him mayor of Boston, congressman and governor. The use of Kennedy family money in wholesale lots to win the West Virginia primary from Hubert Humphrey was widely reported at the time; it had little effect on the political fortunes of John Kennedy. It was well known that Dwight Eisenhower and Lyndon Johnson spent most of their careers on small government salaries and nonetheless ended up quite well-to-do, Johnson in the millionaire class. There was no great indignation over Eisenhower's Gettysburg farm or Johnson's Texas ranch, both of which cost taxpayers for "security" and other improvements, nor was there a public outcry for a look at their tax returns or an accounting of their private finances.

Let there be no misunderstanding. To recall these past examples is not in any way to excuse Mr. Agnew, the Committee to Reelect the President or those involved at the White House for their conduct. It does, however, suggest something about the public attitude toward past conduct of those in public office, including profiteering from office. It suggests an acceptance of much of it, or at least an apathy toward it. And that surely says something about the state of our public morality.

To all this the Watergate affair and its related matters add an extra dimension and pose an extra puzzle. The Agnew scandal was a case of simple greed, the inability to resist the temptation of sticky fingers, perhaps made more tawdry by the fact that the sums involved were picayune. In the Watergate affair, so far as we now know, nobody stole any money.[2] With all those millions of campaign dollars floating around, and with the laxest sort of accountability procedures in effect, none of it stuck to anybody's fingers. Nobody even stuffed a ballot box,

[2] On the evidence as of February 25, 1974.

that other familiar political sport. That is, the element of greed seems to have been totally lacking. As political scandals go, that has made it an unusual one indeed.

The first puzzle this raises is why it all happened. Agnew's transgressions are at least understandable. But how could men who were not motivated by personal gain come to do such things? What motivated them? What rationalizations could they use to justify their conduct?

It would be comforting if we could answer these questions simply by saying they were all bad men, devoid of ordinary moral sense, who by unhappy fortune happened to come to political power at a particular time. The comfort in this would be that if after all the culprits are identified, the appropriate ones jailed or otherwise punished and the president removed from office, then we could dismiss the whole affair as a passing aberration.

It is not, I think, so simple. At any rate, by the light by which we usually judge men, none of these could be called evil men. On the contrary, they seem to have been men of the utmost probity in their personal lives, men whom any of us—before all this happened—would have been glad to have as friends and neighbors. One of them had spent a lifetime in the law, another many years handling other people's money, with never a moment of distrust for either. Among the others there were men who were free even of the small frailties of men in their personal behavior. All, so far as anyone could see beforehand, were men who loved their country and wished to serve it well.

So when we look for the moral fault that led them to such dreadful deeds, the only one I can see that could fit them all is the moral confusion between means and ends. They began, I am sure, with what they thought were worthy ends and then, thinking so, came to think these worthy ends justified the means they used. At least one witness before the Senate Watergate Committee made this rationalization explicit. Consider this colloquy between John Mitchell and Senator Talmadge.

Senator Talmadge: "Am I to understand . . . that you placed the expediency of the next election above your responsibilities as an intimate to advise the President of the peril that surrounded him? Here was the deputy campaign director involved, here were his two closest associates in his office involved, all around him were people involved in crime, perjury, accessory after the fact, and you deliberately refused to tell him that. Would you state that the expediency of the election was more important than that?"

Mr. Mitchell: "Senator, I think you have put it exactly correct. In my mind the re-election of Richard Nixon, compared with what was available on the other side, was so much more important that I put it in just that context."[3]

It would be hard to find a clearer statement of the viewpoint that the end justifies the means.

We confront, then, two moral questions raised by our year of scandal in Washington. One is how much does the prevalence of the behavior excuse a behavior; the other is to what extent does the worthiness of an objective justify the means to achieve it. And again it would be comforting if we could treat the answers given by these particular people, which we all deplore, as being due only to their own moral blindness; we could all then go our own self-righteous ways in peace.

Yet let us look at this attitude that the prevalence of behavior excuses that behavior, and choose an example as far removed as possible from politics. For centuries both theology and philosophy held up certain ethical standards in regard to our sexual behavior. The Seventh Commandment says thou shalt not commit adultery; the Tenth says thou shalt not even covet thy neighbor's wife. Now for all these centuries nobody ever pretended that people, weak creatures that they are, always lived by those commandments. Nonetheless, the standards were there for good men to repair to. Then along came Kinsey and his followers who surveyed us in detail and showed in detail how far our actual behavior differed from the moral adjurations. From this came the view that since "everybody's" private actions transgressed the professed morality, then there was no reason to uphold the morality.

This attitude is widespread. In a carefully controlled study of college students' attitudes toward cheating, conducted by Charles R. Tittle and Alan R. Rowe at Florida Atlantic University, it was found that the threat of sanctions (disciplinary action) did have some effect on reducing cheating on examinations but that moral appeals had none whatever. In fact, after morality was mentioned to the students as a reason for not cribbing—but after the threat of sanctions was removed—cheating *increased* in each of the student groups studied. There was no discernible sense of guilt on the part of those who cheated nor, apparently, any peer-group disapproval. Tittle and Rowe concluded that "the moral appeal was simply irrelevant."

[3] As quoted in *Watergate: Chronology of a Crisis*, published by *Congressional Quarterly*.

These are only two of many examples. The new behavioral scientists tell us not what we ought to do, as the moral philosophers did, but what "everybody" is actually doing. The catchphrase is "do your own thing," which means in effect to reject the very concept of behavioral value judgments. Of course the older moralists, whether theologians or philosophers, recognized the inability of fallible human beings to live up to ideal standards, but the new morality says that because people do not live up to them, the standards have no value. So if Mr. Agnew and those involved in Watergate succumbed to the idea that the prevalence of kickbacks or dirty tricks somehow excused their own behavior—and mournfully asked, why pick on us?—we ought to concede that they are not alone.

When we turn to that other rationalization for the White House plumbers and the like—the justification of means by the ends sought—we plunge deeper into a metaphysical thicket. For we must recognize that ends do justify means; in fact, if the ends sought do not justify the means, what does? We even have to recognize that a worthy end may at least excuse unworthy acts, as when, to protect his family, a man kills an intruder. The question needs to be restated: Does a worthy end justify *any* means? Can an action, no matter what, be justified by saying it was done for a worthy aim?

The answer of the Messrs. Mitchell, Haldeman, Erlichman and company was, for the most part, "yes," although there surely must have been someplace where they too would have drawn the line. First of all, they identified the good of the country with the reelection of Richard Nixon, given what they saw as the choice between that and the ideas seemingly represented by George McGovern; this was, incidentally, a judgment shared by the electorate. But they were motivated by more than just winning the election, which Mr. Nixon would have done anyway. In fact, much of what they did antedated the 1972 campaign or was unrelated to it, as for instance the break-in at the office of Daniel Ellsberg's psychiatrist. When the Nixon administration came to office, the country had been through a decade of disorder, turmoil and violence. Two political assassinations had followed that of President Kennedy; there had been some three thousand bombings, large and small, some fifty thousand bombing threats sufficient to cause the evacuation of buildings. Government documents had been stolen, and security leaks were epidemic. From the bastion of the White House the country seemed to have a wild and frightful hue. To take arms against all this was, they thought, to do a service for their country.

Thinking so, they turned to the most extraordinary means. They stooped to common burglary. They spied by wiretapping and other methods, not only on their enemies but even on each other, creating in the process what amounted to a private secret police. They forged documents for their own purposes. The catalogue is almost endless. They not only skirted the law, they flouted it, and then some of them compounded the felonies by perjury in an effort to cover up. All, of course, in the name of what they believed to be a good cause.

It has been a sorry spectacle. But not the least disturbing thing about it is the gnawing thought that the attitude that it represents may be a reflection of the current public morality. In any event there is an unhappy resemblance between that attitude of the Watergate conspirators and the attitude of many among us toward the relationship of means to ends.

We see it on one level when disgruntled truck drivers block the public thoroughfares, and resort to violence against their noncooperating fellows, to gain what is to them a worthy objective, a change in the fuel-rationing rules. We see it on another level when those presumably more sophisticated, and to whom the community might be expected to look for guidance, find their own worthy causes and then turn to the most extraordinary means for winning them. Ending the Vietnam War was certainly such a worthy aim; many would also put the ending of the draft in that category. Being considered worthy, these aims justified in the minds of many academicians, journalistic commentators and other intellectuals such means as breaking and entering draft offices to burn draft cards, riots and disorder in the streets and, at times, real physical violence to gain their ends. Not long ago a mathematics research center at the University of Wisconsin was blown up and a faculty member killed in protest against the practice of doing military research in universities. Subsequently many reputable people joined in a defense committee for the accused, and their argument was not that the police had arrested the wrong culprits but that the culprits, whoever they are, should be acquitted of dynamiting and manslaughter because they acted sincerely in a good cause. Although no one denies that the Pentagon Papers were stolen, the act has been widely condoned on the grounds of a "higher patriotism." In many quarters lawlessness in pursuit of virtue has become eminently respectable.

The sum of it is that in the current morality one man's crime is another man's worthy cause. Crime we have always had with us, including malfeasance of office; amoral behavior is a human constant. The present peculiarity is in the rationalization for it. Somewhere along the line there has been an erosion of our sense of right and wrong; that is, we have lost our belief that certain actions are wrong simply because they are wrong, whether or not they violate civil statutes. The preachment has been that morality is relative, that ethics depend upon the situation. It is not wrong to steal, to commit adultery, to bear false witness, in and of themselves—it all depends. If bearing false witness results in convicting a man who is in fact guilty, then is not justice done in the end? If crime is done from sincere motives or with good provocation, should we not absolve it? It is not that we do not live up to professed moral values; the latter-day concept is that there *are* no fixed, permanent moral values for anyone to profess.

Were I a theologian I would say that we have lost our sense of sin, that we no longer believe in the existence of evil. If some men pour gasoline on a woman passing by, we must not judge the act evil however much we deplore it. We must consider what life circumstances led to this behavior and the worthiness of the social protest their act proclaims.

Perhaps here I should repeat: In all of this there is no condoning those involved in what has come to be known as Watergate. In the name of serving their country, they have done their country a great injury. But I find it more than an odd coincidence that the Watergate scandal and the Agnew scandal should come upon us at the same time. I have the fearful thought that the morality of these men reflects, as in a magnified mirror, blemishes on the public morality. When we have abroad the idea that the prevalence of behavior excuses behavior, and that worthy aims justify any means, why should we be totally surprised when a high official takes a few customary kickbacks or other high officials think preserving the public tranquility justifies burglary, forgery, spying and perjury?

In a recent issue of *The American Scholar* Howard Stein spoke of our "silent complicity" in Watergate, using Freudian psychology to suggest that much of what was done responded to a deep public desire. Complicity may be too strong a word, for it implies the active accomplice; like Edmund Burke, I know no way to indict a whole people. But in the sense that public attitudes form the climate for the conduct of public office his comment is perceptive. To the old adage that people get the kind of government they deserve, it could be added that they also get the kind of public morality they ask for.

To state the matter in political rather than moral terms, what has been diminished is our traditional belief in due process as a political imperative. Our Constitution, and most especially our Bill of Rights, deals not with what is to be done but how it is to be done; it rests upon the principle that the means of achieving something must be as proper as the aim sought. The needs of society demand that criminals be brought to court, that domestic tranquility be assured, that the people's grievances be corrected. But the police are restrained in the means of achieving tranquility, and even the people are restrained in their manner of expressing grievances; the Constitution sets forth due procedure for achieving each of these aims. When that due procedure is flouted, whether by individual citizens or by their chosen officials, then it is the substance and not merely the forms of democracy that are assailed. It is in this way that the public morality touches the public polity. When this is lost sight of by either the public generally or its public servants, then the political process is subverted.

There remains now the question of whether our year of scandals has in it any compensation for the year of agony. I can only answer by observing that there are cycles in the public morality, as there are in moral preachments. After every period of social disturbance there is a renewed search for those fixed standards to which good men can repair. It is interesting, and perhaps not just coincidental, that there is now going on a sort of introspective public soul-searching, or at least questioning, about such things as permissive child rearing and its effects on adult behavior. In the pulpit, in the press and in thoughtful journals of opinion our value system—or lack of it—is being reexamined.

However that may be, the saving grace in the current scandals, for all that it sounds like an inappropriate phrase, is that they were so flagrant. While we have had dishonest officials exposed and convicted, never one so high as a vice-president. While it is true that each separate action of the Watergate perpetrators has an antecedent example, never has so much been done by so many. Scandals have been piled upon scandals, until they are impossible to ignore. This time outrage was inevitable. And out of outrage comes redemption.

Or let us hope so. There is in these events a touch of tragedy in the true Aristotelian sense; the mighty fallen from high estate, the horror of inner flaws exposed, the fear that those faults may lie within us all, audience as well as actors. But tragedy also has its catharsis, and it is quite possible that out of all of this there may come a cleansing of the body politic. That will require, though, more than merely bringing the malfeasants to account, even if one of them turns out to be president. We cannot simply jail the ones or impeach the other and suppose we have thereby remedied all. No doubt it will be a long time before our future servants are so careless in their offices, but if we are truly to restore our public morality, we must look to ourselves.

The American Scholar, Spring 1974

FREE AT LAST

It's clear to everyone now that Jimmy Carter owes a great political debt to his native region. If he had not carried all the states of the former Confederacy (save only Virginia) he would not now be president-elect.

What ought to be noticed also is the great political debt the Southern states owe to Jimmy Carter. In becoming the first Democratic presidential candidate to carry the solid South since Franklin Roosevelt in 1944 and the first Southerner since 1848, Mr. Carter has freed the South from the past which has haunted its politics for a century. So doing, he may also have altered the political future of the nation.

First off, there's the striking fact that blacks in the South voted for him in overwhelming numbers. In the Georgia of Lester Maddox, the Alabama of George Wallace, the South Carolina of Strom Thurmond, the blacks poured to the polls to vote for this rural Georgian whose generations reach back through the turbulence of recent civil rights battles to Reconstruction and the Civil War.

To explain this by saying that Mr. Carter as governor proclaimed that the time for racial discrimination in the South was past explains it only in part. Mr. Carter's own record in this regard is not unblemished. He himself has said that like most Southerners of his generation he grew up accepting racial segregation as the normal order of things. In his earlier political forays, both as legislator and candidate for governor, he paid at least obeisance to custom, avoiding anything to alienate the supporters of Maddox or Wallace.

So it would have been possible for black voters to take Mr. Carter's proclamations with some skepticism. It would not have been the first time they had heard Southern politicians pay lip service to black aspirations while acting to frustrate them.

That this time black voters did not think so says much about Mr. Carter himself. He persuaded them that he had been born again not only in his views about God but in his views of his fellow man. Put simply, they believed him.

But this black outpouring for a Southern Democrat also says something about the South in general. These black voters were also saying that they believe the South itself has changed, that there would be no going back, no need any longer to fear gallus-thumping segregationists. They could trust Jimmy Carter because, at long last, they could trust the South.

Of course it was not only the black votes that carried the solid South for Carter. There are not enough of them for that. Mr. Carter had also to win a high proportion of white votes.

That he was able to do so was due in part to sectional loyalty. Just as many Catholics in 1960 voted for John Kennedy simply to put an end to the idea that a Catholic could not be elected president, without necessarily agreeing with his politics, so also many white Southerners voted for Carter while uneasy about his views on many issues. They wanted to end the century-old prejudice against a Southerner as president.

But that understandable motive also tells us something about the changing attitudes of the South. Less than a decade ago segregationist George Wallace carried five Southern states and very nearly won in several others. In that time a man of Mr. Carter's civil rights views could not have swept the South, native son or no.

What all this means, or so it seems to me, is that the South—black and white—has broken the grip of its past. So too in a different way has the whole nation, since it has now accepted a Southerner as president.

It's been a long time coming. The South has always romanticized the Civil War, brave boys in gray dying for a lost cause, but there was nothing romantic about the Reconstruction period imposed by the radical Republicans. Defeated, much of the countryside devastated, everybody reduced to poverty, the South was occupied by federal troops for twelve years. It was a bitter time, military governors ruling civil government, most whites disfranchised, illiterate blacks in legislatures and conventions to draw new constitutions, banks destroyed, havoc among farmers and the middle class.

The reaction to this, when reaction became possible, was inevitable and so was the fact that in part it should take the form of "white supremacy." It was also inevitable that against this sort of discrimination the rest of the nation should react in disgust. The South became a pariah, and feeling itself so also felt itself persecuted. (A hundred years after the Civil War the nation was still divided politically, north and south.)

In retrospect the great civil rights struggles of the fifties and sixties proved the salvation of the South. In anguish and turmoil the South made its peace with its racial division, and indeed can claim that in this respect it has done better than many of its northern neighbors. Today no political candidate, Democratic or Republican, can make political capital in the South by trying to pit white against black.

Of this change Jimmy Carter is the symbol. By winning the South with both white and black votes, by winning the presidency of the whole nation, he has put an end to the old political schism.

Thus this election, I suspect, may herald some major changes in American politics. For one thing, each party can hereafter pick its presidential candidates where it finds them, one-third of the nation being no longer out of bounds.

Another and paradoxical result of the Carter sweep of the South is that it could weaken the South as a solid Democratic bastion. Ever since the Republican Reconstruction, white Southerners have been born Democrats in the same way they are born Episcopalians or Baptists, not always keeping the faith in the one as in the other but always keeping the identification. Now that the South has done its own reconstructing, the tie that bound is loosened.

President Carter may carry the South again in 1980, but if so it will depend on what kind of president he is, not on the fact that he's a Southerner. That point once made, it afterwards becomes irrelevant.

About all that, we shall see. What is clear already is that the election of Jimmy Carter has emancipated the South from the political bonds of the past. Today Southerners, white and black, can join in the cry: Free at last.

November 24, 1976

THE POINT OF IT ALL

Not too many people any longer read the Constitution of the United States; it's possible to go through high school and college without ever having looked at it. Of those who have read it, even fewer pay attention to its preamble.

More's the pity. For while the Constitution makes an operating manual for our system of government, the preamble sets forth the point of it all. One tells us how, the other why.

For example, the articles of the Constitution, as amended from time to time, tell us such things as in what manner we elect a president and a Congress, and how taxes are to be levied. The preamble proclaims the purpose for which our government was organized in the first place.

And that makes it not irrelevant, I think, at a time when we are in the throes of choosing a president and a Congress to whom we will entrust our governing. It reminds us, or at least should remind us, what any election is all about.

The reason for having this Constitution, so said those who drew it, "is to form a more perfect union, establish justice, insure domestic tranquility, provide for the common defense, promote the general welfare, and secure the blessings of liberty to ourselves and our posterity."

Those words come heavy laden. In the beginning we didn't succeed in forming a more perfect union; that took a bitter war. We are still groping for the best way to establish justice, though we have more of it than any nation on earth. We still debate among ourselves what constitutes the general welfare and how to promote it. We still disagree on how to provide for the common defense, on how to secure the blessings of liberty.

But this debating, this groping, is what this election is all about. To lose sight of that in the turbulence of the political campaign is to put all in peril.

Foremost among the perils, surely, would be a failure to provide for the common defense. We may differ on how best to do that, on what kinds of weapons we should procure, on how many men-at-arms we need to secure the ramparts and how they are to be chosen. These are not simple questions because we no longer live in a simpler time when the great oceans stood as moats guarding us against enemies.

Yet if there are no simple answers it is to these questions that those who would lead us should give the highest priority, and it behooves us to listen carefully. To devote too much to arms, no doubt about it, would put a heavy burden upon the people. To devote too little would be fatal.

For there is one thing certain. If an enemy should defeat us, or even short of that wreak such destruction upon us as the atomic age makes possible, then all else would be beyond reach. We could no longer insure domestic tranquility, promote the general welfare or keep secure the blessings of liberty. We might not be able to preserve the union at all, save at the grace of our enemy.

Thus, or so it seems to me, those of us who have to decide who should serve us as president ought to make it our own priority to try as best we can to judge which one can lead us more safely in a parlous world. And then pray that God grant him wisdom.

That doesn't mean this is the only issue upon which we should judge the candidates. Even if we are granted peace, there are other matters upon which the general welfare turns, and they are proper matters for the public discussion.

Indeed, for some two hundred years we've debated what the phrase "the general welfare" implies. For some it means a government that stands aloof, or at least governs least, creating a climate in which each citizen is left free to provide for his own welfare. For others it means a government that supports a welfare state in which the government regulates the prices we pay, the wages we receive, and that supplies the food, clothing and shelter for all, regardless of individual endeavor or circumstance.

That debate won't end with one election. But it ought to be clear that if the government mismanages its basic economic policies, then the general welfare suffers no matter how you define it.

The Constitution, for example, gives the government the power to impose and collect taxes, to coin money and regulate the value thereof. This is an immense power because it affects the welfare of every citizen.

If the government taxes unwisely, it not only burdens everyone but can make it difficult, even impossible, for farms, factories and shops to supply the people's needs. If it does not wisely regulate the value of the money, it can not only destroy the people's savings but also the medium upon which all commerce depends—including, not least, the wages of all that labor.

As a matter of fact, the government's economic policies if ill-advised can undermine our ability to arm ourselves in our defense.

With all this we have lately had some experience. In the last four years alone we have seen our money depreciate at annual rates ranging from 7 percent to as high as 20 percent. At 10 percent inflation two-thirds of its value is destroyed every decade. In a lifetime there will be nothing left for those who trust it.

The cost of this can already be felt everywhere, in our foreign commerce (the dollar is no longer the standard of the world), in the increasing dollars that must be devoted to defense, in the prices people must pay for food or housing, in the value of those savings people may have put aside.

All those seeking our vote promise to halt this erosion of our money. None that I know of praises boldly the virtue of inflation. But it behooves us here too to listen carefully, for we must decide which one will have the most wisdom and courage to do what the health of the nation requires.

I do not mean to dismiss still other issues that concern people. Government over-regulation, for example, is as much talked of as it was when Jimmy Carter made it a central issue in 1976.

It refers, of course, to the fact that the auto industry or steel industry or oil industry is wrapped about with regulations to the point of near strangulation. It could as well refer to the fact that you are not at liberty to send your children to a public school of your choice; you send them where the government tells you, be it near or far. If you own a shop you aren't at liberty to hire whom you will at terms agreed upon; you must take care not to violate some government rule of employment. It's possible to wonder what happened to those "blessings of liberty" that were to be secured.

It's perfectly proper also for people to ask a candidate's views on the Equal Rights Amendment, on government-paid abortions, on prayer in the schools or anything else that troubles them. It's not improper for their votes to be affected by any issue on which they feel strongly.

I only submit there are overriding issues. If our leadership fails to provide for our common defense, if it cannot master the ills of our economy, then in the long run there will be no blessings of liberty at all and it will matter little whether or not we pass an Equal Rights Amendment.

In the long run. Those who wrote that brief preamble to the Constitution devised it not to serve just themselves but their posterity. We are their fortunate posterity. If we in our preoccupation with our immediate self-interest are too distracted to spare a thought for our posterity, we will have forgotten the point of it all.

October 1, 1980

VOICES FROM THE PULPIT

I'll begin with a very straightforward proposition:
That you have the right—God-given, if you think it so, or given by
our political Constitution, if you prefer—to decide what you believe
to be wrong, evil or immoral.

That you have the right to judge those who lead us, and to speak
that judgment, according to whether you think them right, good or
moral.

Further, that this right extends to those who would express their
view in public places, in print or on television. That it belongs to those
who believe in God as to those who don't. That it belongs to secular
philosophers, to rabbis, to itinerant preachers, to evangelical ministers, to cardinals of the Roman Catholic Church.

So saying I have, of course, made a suicidal leap into a hornets' nest.
For that simple proposition, to which once few might have taken exception, is presently the center of a political controversy which heats
emotions to a fever pitch.

The focus of it is those voices from the pulpit, Catholic and Protestant, which decry as immoral such practices as abortion, and which
call upon their followers to vote against those who advocate these
practices as public policy. What adds to the controversy is that there
are really two questions involved in the controversy, and it seems impossible to separate them.

The first question before the community is whether we agree with
those voices; after all, it's our collective view that decides public policy.
The second question is whether such voices should be raised at all, or
whether they violate the much talked-of principle of separation between church and state.

Both questions have lately had much attention in the media. The
pulpit preachers, especially those called fundamentalist or evangelical,

have been the subject of many newspaper stories, of "cover stories" in the news magazines, of extended programs on television.

The thrust of the media attention is clear enough. Anthony Lewis of *The New York Times* finds these voices "scary" and thinks they violate the intent of the Constitution by injecting religion into politics. On television Bill Moyers says our democracy cannot accept the view that makes "sectarian doctrine the test of political opinion." Richard Reeves, syndicated columnist, thinks the fundamentalist preachers "a clear and present danger" and that "under the American system they have no right to judge others."

I confess that I'm made queasy by the more extravagant rhetoric of the evangelical preachers. Many have the sound of demagogues. Some strike me as about as sincere as Elmer Gantry.

But I cannot share the idea that preachers have no right, moral or otherwise, to raise their voices or that "religion has no place in politics." It has been a part of American politics from the beginning. Pulpit voices played a role in making our revolution. They sounded loud and clear in their moral indignation at slavery and at those in politics who countenanced it. Their influence helped pass the Thirteenth Amendment, which abolished it.

To be sure, their influence hasn't always been salutary; they were largely responsible for saddling us with Prohibition. But there is nothing new, or inherently wrong, in their speaking out. Anything about which people feel deeply is the essence of politics.

If the Catholic Church believes that abortion is morally evil, then it is the right—nay, the duty—of its cardinals to say so and to urge their flock to oppose those who would make it acceptable public policy. It is then the right of the rest of us to accept or reject this view.

For reasons I can't fathom it's thought acceptable for those favoring abortion to demonstrate in the streets but unacceptable for others to raise their voices against it. People may organize and speak out under such names as Common Cause, but if they do so as Baptists, Methodists or Catholics they are, so many say, undermining the American way.

Nonsense. Our Constitution does prohibit the government from establishing any religion as a state religion. No one can be disqualified for president because of his religion or want of it, as one can for age (not less than thirty-five) or for foreign birth. Nothing prevents people, though, from taking into account a candidate's view on religious or moral questions when they cast their ballots.

Indeed, if there's anything surprising in the resurgence of voices crying against perceived immorality, it is that it has been so long coming. For more than a generation our society has been dominated by the view that "anything goes," that all morality is relative and no one should judge another's belief or conduct.

A reaction was inevitable. One always comes when societies see older values crumbling. It has been that way since old Cicero, in the dying days of the Roman republic, rose to cry out, "O tempora, O mores!" Savonarola, Martin Luther, every age has brought forth those to denounce the wickedness of their time.

Cicero was murdered, Luther excommunicated, Savonarola executed. And in the eyes of the fervent the wickedness of the world remained. So it will now, if that's what you think it is, despite all those pulpit voices. I even suspect that the political power of those voices is much exaggerated by those fearful of what they say. There are other matters that move people in presidential elections.

As for myself, I confess I'm always dubious about the self-righteous—including those who self-righteously proclaim that, alone among our citizens, those who stand in pulpits should keep silent.

October 8, 1980

THE QUESTION OF SUCCESSION

For a few hours that fateful Monday evening there was much concerned talk about the succession to the presidency. The wounded president was undergoing emergency surgery, the outcome of which was then uncertain. The vice-president was in a plane returning to Washington from Texas. What if something happened to both of them, a failing heart for one of them, an accident to the other?

By the next morning we all heaved a sigh of relief. The vice-president landed safely and was at the White House. The president was recovering rapidly. The question of succession faded from everyone's mind.

But that "what if" question is still troublesome. There would be no constitutional crisis, it's true, because the law clearly provides that on the death or disability of both the president and vice-president, the Speaker of the House automatically succeeds to the office. The transfer of authority would take place without interruption.

Nevertheless, in this case it would have been a worrisome prospect. That worry transcends the personal qualities of the present Speaker, Representative O'Neill of Massachusetts. Politically speaking, "Tip" O'Neill is 180 degrees away from Ronald Reagan. So the country would face the prospect of an abrupt change of presidential policy—foreign and domestic—from that which the electorate endorsed last November and which President Reagan has followed.

This is a problem which has haunted the country before, and which repeated efforts to grapple with haven't succeeded in resolving. It remains to plague us after two hundred years.

It first arose under the original Constitution. The Founding Fathers provided for a vice-president to succeed on a president's death or disability. Beyond that they left everything fuzzy, such as how to decide on "disability" and what to do if there were no vice-president. Worse, they provided that the presidential candidate with the most electoral votes should be president, the runner-up vice-president.

This very quickly produced a problem like the one today. For the two men were frequently long political rivals with diametrically opposed programs. This was the situation when Adams was president, Jefferson vice-president; when Jefferson was president (elected by the House) and Aaron Burr vice-president.

The Twelfth Amendment removed that problem by permitting presidents and vice-presidents to run as a "team," presumably sharing the same basic political philosophy. The problem of succession beyond that was delegated to the Congress.

Congress has done a lot of tinkering since then. In 1792 it provided that the president *pro tempore* of the Senate would be next in line followed by the House Speaker. In 1886 it put the secretary of state in line after the vice-president. In 1947, deciding some elected official would be better, it reversed the 1792 order and made the Speaker next in line.

Then came the Twenty-fifth Amendment which provided a way to fill a vice-presidential vacancy. Gerald Ford became president under its terms, being first confirmed by both houses as vice-president and then succeeding when President Nixon resigned. Since Ford was nominated by Nixon there was no unsettling change in national policy.

But that amendment didn't alter the further line of succession. In 1965, 1977 and 1979 Congress confirmed the Speaker as the next successor, followed by the president pro-tem of the Senate and then a designated line of cabinet officers headed by the secretary of state. That's the governing law today.

None of these solutions is really satisfactory. The Speaker and the Senate's president pro-tem are elected officials and have the status of being chosen as such by their political peers in their respective houses. But we have recently had repeated situations where one or another, or both, have been of a different party from the president and, in effect, leaders of the opposition.

That is certainly the case today with Speaker O'Neill. He is not only a Democrat but a leader of the more liberal wing of the party. He takes a dim view of almost every Reagan policy, foreign or domestic.

Any person succeeding to the presidency is bound to have some views differing from his predecessor. Truman was no Roosevelt; Johnson no Kennedy. Vice-President Bush would undoubtedly shift some emphases from those adopted by President Reagan.

But these are small matters beside what could be expected from a President O'Neill suddenly thrust into that office. Budget and tax policy would most surely be reversed. So would defense policy. So, most likely, would be many foreign policy objectives. It's hard to imagine two political leaders more philosophically different.

It's easy to imagine, though, the political turmoil into which the country would be plunged. And this in the face of the people's very clear endorsement of Mr. Reagan's political philosophy. Without judging Mr. O'Neill's politics, the drastic change is not comforting to contemplate.

How to resolve this I don't know. Having an appointive cabinet officer as automatic successor has its separate problem of electoral legitimacy. But perhaps an idea might be borrowed from the Twenty-fifth Amendment. That would be to have the elected president, upon assuming office, nominate one among his top officials as successor-designate after the vice-president with that nomination subject to confirmation by both houses of Congress as now provided for filling a vice-presidential vacancy.

But one thing is clear. The succession problem plagues us still and the present arrangement is fraught with danger. Congress should speedily get back to the drawing board.

April 8, 1981

BOMBASTUS INTERRUPTUS

My old friend, Theophrastus Bombastus, was in fine fettle. He laid about him with a hearty will, his rapier of words nicking on the swing Ronald Reagan, Tip O'Neill, Dave Stockman, Dan Rostenkowski—and me.

I hadn't seen Theo in quite a while. He shows up to keep me company only in the wee hours when I'm wakeful from too much pasta or too many bourbons. This time it must have been the pasta because I haven't had a hangover in years.

But he had me alert in a flash. "Never thought you'd be a turncoat," he grumbled. Not exactly the kind of opening to quiet rumblings in the tummy.

"Been reading your paper for years," he went on. "Best arguments I ever heard for balancing the government's budget. Admired the way you flayed Harry, Jack, Lyndon, Richard, Gerald, Jimmy and even Ike when he strayed from the narrow. Now what do I read? Cheerful mumblings about a deficit of $58 billion. Or is it $60 billion?"

I tried to explain I wasn't cheerful. I don't speak for the paper.

"Stuff and nonsense!" he exclaimed. "You reared the young fellow who does, didn't you? Didn't you learn him anything?"

That raised a hackle. In self-defense I pointed out most of the budget is being cut—cut to ribbons, so some say—and there wouldn't be any deficit if Reagan didn't have to repair the national defense.

"Ah, yes," he retorted. "Battleships, yet! They were anachronisms even in your war. You think we're going to fight another Jutland with the Russkies?"

As a destroyerman with Halsey task forces I thought it best to shift my ground. So I brought up carriers.

"Humph!" he huffed. "In the next war, atom bombs and all that, they could be the new dinosaurs. One bomb, one torpedo and puff! Anyway, why should one mastodon at $4 billion be better than several

smaller carriers? One can only be at one place at a time. That Stockman ought to be as tough on admirals as he is on secretaries of welfare,
or whatever they call them now.

"Besides," he went on, "I remember you lambasting the liberals for
thinking problems can be solved just by throwing money at them.
What makes you think throwing money at the Pentagon will buy the
best defense?"

That's Theo for you. Full of rhetorical questions, few answers. He
says he was in the Senate with Borah of Idaho, although I was there
then (as a reporter, that is) and don't remember him. I'm suspicious
too of his claim to be a lineal descendant of the Theophrastus who discovered zinc, even if I don't like to question a man's ancestry.

But like Borah he's irrepressible. When I tried to explain that, according to supply-side economics, three years of tax cuts would bring
in enough extra revenue to balance the budget anyway, his eyebrows
twitched.

"Read your piece on the Laffer Curve," he said. "Only thing it
proved was how hope triumphs over expectations. Not that I'm against
tax cuts. High time. I'm lucky I don't pay any. Where I am they don't
even collect Social Security. Just as well because when Reagan gets
through I wouldn't collect anything anyway."

I thought that a low blow. I assumed from his tone he sided with Tip
O'Neill in thinking Reagan was leading the nation to perdition. I mis-
took my man.

"Tip's tipping the wrong way," he said. "Reminds me of Canute. He
can't stop the tide. Like Rostenkowski, that Ways and Means Committee chairman. Drift with it. Laffer Curve or no Laffer Curve, people
want lower taxes no matter what they cost. They won't be happy with
anyone who begrudges them."

So at last, I thought, we'd found something we could agree on. That
the mood of the country's changed, Reagan is in tune with it and the
Democrats will have to live in the wilderness for a change.

"Od's bodkins!" he said. That's the way Theo talks sometimes.
"Haven't you learned anything about politics, boy? People want lower
taxes, right enough, and they're going to get them. They also want
those choice morsels that come from the Treasury. Rostenkowski
ought to read up on Kutusov, who won the war against Napoleon by
losing every battle."

Besides, he continued, "What if your supply-side economics doesn't work? What if people, having their tax cuts, find they've got just as much, or more, inflation? And withal fewer dainties from the public purse! What will that make the political situation in '84 or '88?"

He let that question hang in the cold night air. Then as a sort of afterthought he added, "If that happens, son, if disappointment lets the spenders back in, you ain't seen nothing yet!" Not the kind of vulgarism I expected from Theo but I took his point.

It was a prospect to make Jesse Helms shudder. But at least Theo would have to admit, I told him, that Reagan's doing all right so far. He's won all the opening games.

"So did Fernando Valenzuela, forsooth, that new pitcher for the L.A. Dodgers." Theo keeps up with everything. "Eight and ought for starters, if I remember rightly. But then the batters started hitting him. You think the Democrats are always going to strike out?"

The Republicans did for an awfully long time, I reminded him. Like Howard Cosell says, it's a matter of momentum.

But before I could press the point, Bombastus wandered off into the mist like Banquo's ghost. I awoke so depressed I swore off pasta.

June 10, 1981

O TEMPORA! O RES PUBLICAE!

"A most wretched custom," grumbled old Cicero, "is our election-eering and scrambling for office."

Ah, Marcus Tullius, thou shouldst be living at this hour!

Cicero was a great grumbler. He had the misfortune to live in the sadder days of the Roman Republic, and it was he, you'll remember, who uttered the famous exclamation "O tempora! O mores!" in telling the Senate what he thought of his times and the public morality, especially that of Lucius Sergius Catilina.

Of course, this sort of preachment made him political enemies, notably Julius Caesar and his successors, who charged the self-appointed moralist with not being above a bit of intrigue himself. In the end they did away with him.

All the same, you can't help wondering what that ancient complainer would have to say about present morals or the scrambling for office we witness nightly on our television screens.

Certainly the scramblers for the Democratic Party nomination this year haven't offered us a very edifying spectacle, however entertaining it may be. Of the original eight contestants only three remain, and the survivors seem more bent on mangling each other than their Republican opponent. They might remind Cicero of those gladiators in the Coliseum whacking away at one another for the crowd's amusement.

By the time the party assembles for the finals in San Francisco, there may be only one left standing. The leader at the moment is Walter Mondale, but the odds change with every successive encounter in the amphitheater where the rivals snarl at each other.

Whoever he is, he will be pretty well bloodied by then, not by Ronald Reagan but by his supposed political confreres. With such "friends," he may wonder if he has the strength left to confront the main opponent.

Hard-fought nomination battles, of course, are nothing new in

American politics. In recent times you think of Jack Kennedy marshaling all his forces to defeat Hubert Humphrey. Or of Jimmy Carter taking on the whole Democratic establishment and conquering it. But neither Kennedy nor Humphrey hurled at one another. Mr. Carter, the outsider, treated Henry Jackson, the insider, with the respect due a worthy rival.

This year it's been mostly snarling and snapping when Mr. Mondale and Gary Hart have sat face to face before the television cameras. Who is "naive" and who isn't? Who has the "purest" record in supporting Israel? Who's got the beef (whatever that means)? At times the wrangling makes you think of small boys squabbling in the playground rather than grown men debating serious public issues.

Their supporters have been even more acrimonious. For a time the big issue was whether Mr. Hart was a year older or younger. Whether Mr. Mondale as vice-president did or did not differ in council with President Carter on selling F-15s to Saudi Arabia. And so on with other matters hardly illuminating on the problems now facing the country.

In fairness to all, much of this snarling, bordering on discourtesy, grows out of the new ways of conducting the nominating process. The multiplicity of primaries involving constant travel, the practice of repeated personal confrontations on television, leaves little room for carefully thought out and uninterrupted talk that could really tell us what the candidate thinks on the major issues of the day. That older kind of campaigning for a nomination may be forevermore impossible.

This leads to a nagging question: With our present political ways, could Franklin Roosevelt or Dwight Eisenhower have won his party's nomination, that first necessary step to the presidency?

In 1932 Roosevelt hardly stirred out of Albany, leaving pre-convention politicking to Louis Howe and Jim Farley. For one thing, he had a physical handicap. As a governor, he also hadn't the time for cross-country campaigning. And I think he would have considered it undignified anyway. He did make one radio talk (in which he first used the "forgotten man" phrase) and an impressive commencement speech at Oglethorpe University in Georgia. But that was about it. It was his record as governor that won him primaries in a half-score states and helped him defeat Al Smith and John Nance Garner.

Once Dwight Eisenhower let his name be put forward in 1952 he did make several campaign speeches, but barnstorming it was not. It was his personality, his reputation and the efforts of Thomas E. Dewey and other supporters that turned back Robert A. Taft at the Chicago convention. Eisenhower, too, had a strong sense of dignity that prevented him from "scrambling" for office.

Neither of them, I might add, made personal assaults on his rivals. Thus Garner could later join the ticket with Roosevelt. Taft could become a strong voice supporting Eisenhower. And neither FDR nor Ike, I fear, would today make it through the grueling contest a nomination race has become. I doubt if either would lower himself to such a scramble.

I also wonder whether under the present system we will see their like again. Sitting governors are ruled out; they have too many duties to attend to. Roosevelt was the last one; Mr. Carter and Mr. Reagan made it only afterward. As a practical matter, we thus deprive ourselves of fifty people who may have demonstrated their capacity for executive leadership.

The new way to the nomination is said to be more "democratic." Perhaps. But does it bring the best candidates to the fore, which after all should be the hope of a democracy? That's why I'm tempted to grumble, "O the times! O our politics!"

May 18, 1984

VI

Eye on the Press

THE AMERICAN PRESS AND THE
REVOLUTIONARY TRADITION

I

Among the many revolutionary ideas to emerge from the American Revolution, none proved more revolutionary than the idea of freedom of the press. None has proved more durable, for it has withstood two centuries of assault. None has brewed more controversy, for it remains today even in this country as revolutionary an idea as it was in the eighteenth century and in its American form it exists now only in this country. And of the many changes which time has worked on the political ideas of the Founding Fathers, none would more surprise them—and perhaps disturb them—than what has evolved in the succeeding two centuries from their views of what constitutes freedom of the press. All the evidence suggests that when they embraced this philosophical idea, and embodied it in the First Amendment to our Constitution, they knew not what they wrought.

Certainly when they spoke of freedom of the press they did not envision a press of very nearly unrestrained license, which is for all practical purposes the legal privilege of the twentieth-century American press. That idea was foreign to the liberal philosophers, mostly those of the seventeenth and eighteenth centuries, from whom they drew their concepts about the nature of man and society on which they founded the American political system. Nor was there anything in their own experience, even in the midst of rebellion against a distant government, that led them to suppose a civil liberty, whatever its nature, could be severed from civic responsibility and therefore from all restraint. They thought this especially true when one liberty—or, if you prefer, one unalienable right—clashed with another. In few things were they absolutists. So in their view this freedom of the press, as every other freedom, existed only within certain parameters of responsibility, not always precisely definable but existing nonetheless.

Even in our own time the idea of freedom of the press without restraint, which is what that freedom often appears to have become, is disturbing to many people. It is not merely that this freedom is irritating to our governors, although there are many examples of that. It is also disturbing at times to philosophers, to men of the law, to the citizenry generally and not least to some of those within the press itself. Not only is the performance of the press criticized, but the very extent of its freedom is questioned, both from within and from without. So it is that the right to speak and to spread abroad whatever one wishes remains to this day a revolutionary idea; that is to say, one which has not yet lost its controversial nature through unquestioning acceptance.

Yet we have come to accept so much of this idea of freedom of the press that we are scarcely aware of how far we have come from its beginnings. The parameters within which we today debate possible, or desirable, restraints on the freedom to publish, or the terms in which we discuss the need for both a free and responsible press, are quite different from those used by Mr. Jefferson, Mr. Madison or Mr. Franklin. They would have some difficulty, I suspect, comprehending the recent controversy over the Pentagon Papers; they would be puzzled by the near-disappearance of private libel from the canons of the law, or the total disappearance of seditious libel, not to mention the untrammeled performance of the press in the Watergate affair. Certainly they would be aghast at today's license, under the shelter of the First Amendment, for published pornography.

Nonetheless, that we have come so far is in part a logical extension of those very ideas about man and society and the nature of political freedom that permeated the thinking of those who embarked on the American experiment. Just as other of their ideas set in motion political events they did not fully anticipate, so it was here. Their declaration that all men are created free and equal inevitably led not only to the abolition of slavery but to universal suffrage and to an ever-widening concept of civil rights. So with the declaration that freedom of speech and of the press shall not be abridged. That declaration once made, it became ever more difficult to find a point of abridgment.

There is also, however, another reason why in the area of political reporting and publishing the American press has pushed the borders of permissible freedom beyond those in any other country including countries which share our heritage of general political liberty, such as Great Britain itself. That reason lies in geography, that in the time before and during our rebellion the colonies were both remote from the mother country and separated even from each other. Geography made restraints less practical, the opportunities for freedom of expression more available.

Ideas fertilized the American Revolution; it would hardly have come without them. Geography made its success possible; it was the great gulf of ocean that, in the end, made it impossible to put down. These same two things, ideas and geography, also provided the soil for the revolutionary tradition of the American press, a tradition suspicious of all government and fiercely opposed to all restraint. In the two centuries since, it has proved a lasting tradition.

The ideas here involved, as so many others, might be traced back to the Greeks when Plato and Aristotle were debating the nature of man and of government. We are heirs of them both, teacher and pupil, but in politics more Aristotelian than Platonist. It was Plato, after all, who would have had the state lay down rigid rules for poets and philosophers and who would have had their works submitted to magistrates to decide whether they were fit for the people. As we shall see, there are Platonists among us yet. Aristotle, though he defended the slavery of his times and was fearful of pure democracy, did broach the thought that the citizens exercising their collective judgment had the right not only to choose their leaders but to call them to account. The echoes of this are heard in that Declaration of 1776; they reverberate today whenever there is heard a clamor in the press to impeach the president.

But it was the Reformation, with its revolt against the authority of the Church, that more immediately opened the Pandora's box and let escape the idea that each man had a right to make "free inquiry" with his own mind. The inquiry began about God; it was not long before it extended to the state.

Not long, but slowly all the same. In England, which is the principal source of our political heritage, the sixteenth century had ended with absolutism triumphant. By the end of the seventeenth century, having suffered the absolutism of Cromwell, England was a ferment of liberal ideas. The Declaration of Rights of 1689, forced upon William and Mary as the price of their crowns, foreshadows in many particulars not only our own Declaration of Independence but later provisions in our Constitution; it proclaimed among other things that at least in Parliament there must be freedom of debate.

This was the century, too, of John Locke, with his thesis of popular sovereignty under which government was merely the trustee of power delegated by the people and which the people could withdraw. And the century of John Milton, who in his *Areopagitica* argued that men can distinguish between right and wrong ideas if these are allowed to meet in open encounter. Locke sowed the seed of rebellion, Milton the seed of the First Amendment of our Bill of Rights.

Still, at the beginning of the eighteenth century they were seeds only. Milton, like Locke, spoke a minority view. Moreover Milton himself, whose motivation was irritation at Puritan censorship of his own theology, would not extend the full freedom of expression to Roman Catholics or to insidious pamphleteers and journalists. And no matter how majestic his argument, it had small effect even upon the intellectual men of his time and none at all upon the political authorities. In England, as elsewhere, the printing press remained subservient to the needs of the state. When the first small cracks did appear in the system of press control—and here, of course, we are speaking primarily of books and pamphlets, not newspapers as we know them—those cracks were caused less by the pressure of ideas than by the practical difficulties of enforcement.

Until well into the seventeenth century the printing press was controlled in England by a system of patents, that is, licenses. The Crown gave patents to a group of printers organized into the Stationers' Company. This company had the power to admit and expel members from the printing trade and to discipline the members for such transgressions as might be charged against them by the authorities. For some two hundred years this system worked well in controlling the printing press, the Stationers' Company being assiduous in protecting its monopoly. It began to break down only as technology made printing presses cheap and therefore readily available. By the beginning of the eighteenth century the proliferation of presses had made it impossible for an official censor to read and approve every piece of printed matter before it was published. Practicality, then, demanded both a different system and a different rationale, legal and philosophical, to justify it.

The English answer to this problem was both ingenious and far-reaching in its effects. Necessity forced the abandonment of prior restraint on publication. In its place was substituted the idea that the printer, while he could not be restrained in advance, could be held accountable afterwards for what he caused to be published. Gradually what could not be prevented came to be hailed as an unalienable right; what could be adjudicated came to be accepted as a proper restraint upon that right. In time this new concept of freedom of the press, its extent and its limitations, was debated and shaped by men as varied as Dr. Samuel Johnson and Sir William Blackstone.

Blackstone, most especially. For this English jurist not only capsuled the new philosophy and the new law on the press in his famous *Commentaries* but he was also the great teacher for the law-minded revolutionists in the colonies. Today few lawyers read his *Commentaries*, even as a classic, but in the latter part of the eighteenth century and through much of the nineteenth his influence on American jurisprudence was immense, far greater here indeed than in his own country. Before the advent of law schools every budding lawyer began his reading with Blackstone as his guide and oracle. His *obiter dicta* on the common law were pervasive among those who launched and nurtured our experiment in political liberty.

In his *Commentaries*, first delivered as lectures in 1758 and formally published in 1765, a decade before Bunker Hill, Blackstone defined the freedom of the press this way:

> The liberty of the press is indeed essential to the nature of a free state; but this consists in laying no *previous* restraint upon publications, and not in freedom from censure for criminal matter when published. Every freeman has an undoubted right to lay what sentiments he pleases before the public: to forbid this is to destroy the freedom of the press; but if he publishes what is improper, mischievous or illegal, he must take the consequences of his own temerity.[1]

There, in two sentences, is the whole of the law and the philosophy of the press as it appeared to Englishmen of the eighteenth century, including our own revolutionists.

It is, as you can see, an effort to reconcile the irreconcilable. For plainly if there is to be political liberty the citizens cannot be constrained in what they think and what they speak by the power of government, whether it be a government of a king or of ministers. To subject the press to such restrictions, in Blackstone's words, "is to subject all freedom of sentiment to the prejudices of one man, and make him the arbitrary and infallible judge of all controverted points in learning, religion and government." But also plainly, or so it seemed to the men of those times, no man would be safe and no government secure if all

---

[1] William Blackstone, *Commentaries on the Law of England*, Book 4 (London, 1969), chap. 11, pp. 151ff.

manner of libels could be uttered with impunity. Thus to punish dangerous and offensive writings, said Blackstone, "is necessary for the preservation of peace and good order, of government and religion, the only solid foundation of civil liberty."

It was, perhaps, an unsatisfactory thrust at the Gordian knot to say on the one hand that a man is free to publish what he will without let or hindrance but, on the other hand, that he is not free from accountability for what he publishes, leaving undefined what later may be judged punishable as improper, mischievous or illegal. Yet if that answer seems unsatisfactory to logical minds, it is one we have not bettered two centuries later. In that famous Pentagon Papers case, of which more later, the justices of our own Supreme Court were unable to discard the Blackstonian concept.

However that may be, such was the philosophical view and the legal doctrine about the press and its freedom commonly accepted in those memorable years leading up to 1776. Now, if we are to understand the American press tradition, it is necessary to look at the special circumstances in these English colonies which gave those ideas an indigenous cast.

2

In 1734 the royal governor of the colony of New York was one William Cosby, by the evidence of his contemporaries an avaricious, haughty and ill-tempered man who was among the worst of these representatives of the distant Crown. The publisher of the New York *Weekly Journal*, a four-page poorly printed sheet, was John Peter Zenger, an itinerant printer. Before the year was out they were to clash, with consequences neither of them foresaw.[2]

The origin of it, briefly, was a dispute between the governor and the council of the colony over the governor's salary. As part of that dispute Cosby discharged the colony's chief justice, Lewis Morris, and appointed in his place one James Delancey, a royalist supporter. Zenger's print shop issued a pamphlet giving the deposed chief justice's side of the case, and there began a long and acrimonious fight between the royal governor and the *Weekly Journal*. Ultimately, having failed to get

[2]Frank Luther Mott, *American Journalism*, Third Edition (New York: Macmillan Company, 1962), pp. 31ff., has a good account of the Zenger case, which I have followed. For documents in the case, including Hamilton's defense, see Leonard W. Levy, ed., *Freedom of the Press From Zenger to Jefferson: Early American Libertarian Theories* (New York: Bobbs-Merrill Co., 1966).

an indictment of Zenger from a local grand jury, Governor Cosby had Zenger jailed on his own authority. The charge was seditious libel. Zenger, who had not written the offending articles but who had published them, was refused reasonable bail by the new chief justice and languished in jail for nine months. The next year, 1735, he came to trial.

It was a disappointing trial if the hope was that the issue of freedom of the press from seditious libel would be squarely joined. Zenger's counsel was Andrew Hamilton—not to be confused with Alexander Hamilton—and he saw his task, as lawyers are wont to, to free his client rather than to win some great judicial principle. Thus Hamilton did not attack the concept of seditious libel. Instead he argued that it was designed to protect the king, not provincial governors, and that if the people could not remonstrate truthfully against despotic governors the people would lose their liberty and the king would be ill served. Then in an impassioned appeal directly to the jurors he asked them, in effect, to ignore the court's rulings on the law and acquit Zenger notwithstanding.

This is what the jury did, quite possibly for no other reason than that Cosby was an unpopular governor and this was a way to strike back at him. Anyway, the Zenger case did nothing to alter the common law of seditious libel nor to advance any new principles with regard to freedom of the press. Nonetheless, the Zenger trial is justly renowned in the history of the colonial press. Cosby vanished in obscurity; Zenger took his place in the pantheon of journalistic heroes. In a very dramatic fashion a small newspaper had challenged royal authority, been brought to trial in a royal court and acquitted by a jury of colonial citizens. That was enough.

There were other cases before and after Zenger, with varying results. As early as 1692 one William Bradford, a Philadelphia printer, had been tried for seditious libel, Thomas Maule for the same charge in Boston in 1696, neither of whom was ultimately imprisoned. But Andrew Bradford, William's son, was later imprisoned for publishing a letter critical of the English government. Benjamin Franklin's brother was jailed for being critical of the Massachusetts colonial government, and also in Massachusetts John Checkley was convicted for distributing a book critical of Calvinist doctrines. Until the eve of the Revolution, there was little consistency, either from time to time or from colony to colony, in the boldness of printers or in the reaction of the

authorities to criticism. For the most part, however, boldness was not
characteristic of these early printers. Their shops were commercial enterprises; they sought out official business and were inclined to do little
to disturb it. They also shared the general attitude of the time, which
consisted of much grumbling at particular authority but without any
disposition to challenge the principle of authority from the Crown.

This is not the place for recounting the history of the colonial press.
It should be noted, though, that the present view of colonial America
as a society that everywhere cherished freedom of ideas and expression
is a romantic one. There was indeed an enormous diversity of political
and religious ideas among the various colonies, due to their origins
and geography, and this diversity was ultimately to have an enormous
effect. But each colony, sometimes different colonies within a colony,
had its own orthodoxy and guarded it zealously, being quite willing to
suppress the dissidence of the non-orthodox, whether political or religious. In John P. Roche's phrase, "Colonial America was an open society dotted with closed enclaves."

If there was a turning point for the press, a point at which it generally turned rebellious toward the Crown and began to acquire its revolutionary character, it was the same as for the colonists generally,
namely, the Stamp Act of 1765. That tax struck very hard at printers.
Since it amounted to a penny for each four pages and two shillings for
each advertisement, it came to a tax of nearly 50 percent of revenue for
many papers. It thus united the printers as no other issue could. The
Pennsylvania *Gazette* draped its last pre-tax issue with the black column rules of mourning. The New York *Gazette* openly defied the law
by continuing to publish with unstamped paper. A few papers sus-
pended, but many others shifted to irregular publication dates to claim
status as handbills not as newspapers. Similar taxes were levied in England and were enforceable. In the colonies, far removed from the
home country and with the presses scattered over a huge geographic
area, the taxes were largely unenforceable.

A year later this Stamp Act was repealed, thanks in good measure to
the persuasiveness in London of that Kissinger of the day, Benjamin
Franklin. But by then the situation had been permanently altered. Until then the dissatisfaction of most of the printers with the remote government of the Crown had been no more than that generally shared by
other colonists; now they had a personal grievance and a warning to
what extent they personally could be injured by that remote govern-

ment. Arguments about the power of government against the press ceased to be abstractions. Equally important—and I am inclined to think more so—the printers learned that in fact this distant government could not enforce its laws against them. Thus the Boston *Gazette*, which in 1765 had printed the bitterest attacks against the Stamp Act, did not relent after its repeal in attacks on Crown government. Indeed, it became even bolder as spokesman for the "radicals," or, if you prefer a different term, for the "patriots."

How much the practical situation had altered is shown by the reaction of the Crown authorities to these new attacks. Governor Bernard of Massachusetts called the *Gazette* "an infamous weekly paper which has swarmed with Libels of the most atrocious kind," made several feeble attempts to get a libel indictment against its publishers, but in the end found it more politic to suffer the paper. He would risk no more Zenger cases. The situation in the other colonies in varying degrees, was much the same.[3]

Meanwhile, all those other forces which led to 1776 continued to do their work; I will leave to others to decide the proportion in which they were economic, political or philosophical. Slowly but relentlessly the colonists moved from being loyal complainants against particular Crown actions to open rebellion against the Crown itself. Whatever the causes, the movement required a major change in public opinion and in that change the printers of the colony played a major role. Through newspapers, through broadsides, through pamphlets, the printing presses of the colonies proved as dangerous as muskets. The newspapers issued by these presses were outlets for the exchange of information among the colonies (one picking up its "news" from the mailed copies of another), for letters to the editor and for anonymous articles signed with such pen names as Cato or Publius. There was little "objectivity" in the news reported. For example the Salem *Gazette* in its issue of April 25, 1775 began its account of the battles of Lexington and Concord this way:

> Last Wednesday, the 19th of April, the Troops of his *Brittanick* Majesty commenced Hostilities upon the People of this Province, attended with Circumstances of Cruelty not less brutal than what our venerable Ancestors received from the vilest Savages of the Wilderness.

This was the tone of the news reported throughout the Revolution,

---

[3] Mott, *American Journalism*, p. 75.

though often the news was sparse and late due to the difficulties of communication. When there was none many of the printers carried rumors, second- and third-hand reports and on some occasions seem to have made up their information.

But we must not suppose that in this period there had been any advancement in the *philosophy* of freedom of the press. The patriot, or rebel, newspapers had indeed thrown off the yoke of Crown governors, and having got the bit in their teeth made the most of it. The loyalist papers, of whom a few survived even after the war's outbreak, did not fare so well. The patriots were no more anxious to extend freedom of the press to them than the Crown governors had been to extend it to the seditious patriot press. Great pressure, including violence, was exerted to silence the Boston *Evening Post*, the New York *Packet*, and the Maryland *Journal*, all loyalist papers. In an outbreak of mob violence the New York *Gazetteer*, a Tory paper, was totally destroyed. In every faction, freedom of the press meant freedom for *us*, not for *them*.

What did result from the Revolution, if not new philosophies about freedom of the press, were habits and an attitude. The attitude, natural under the circumstances, was one of antagonism to government, or at least distant government; after all, that was the root of the Revolution itself. The habits were of fiercely venting that antagonism without check, at least from any distant government. In a very pragmatic way these two things were to have important consequences. For one, they bestirred a renewed interest among publishers, writers and intellectuals generally in philosophical thinking about the nature of a free press, if for no other reason than to find a respectable rationale for what these writers and printers were in fact doing. The other consequence was that in time the revolutionary habits became transformed into a tradition.

Neither the habits of free-speaking nor the critical attitude toward distant government were, to be sure, limited to printers. Both had been acquired by the former colonists generally. In fact when the Constitutional Convention convened in 1787 the delegates had two problems. One was to devise an acceptable form of national government. The other was to persuade the citizens of the new states to accept *any* national government stronger than the loose Confederation. The extent of this second problem shows up clearly in *The Federalist* papers of Madison, Hamilton and Jay. Again and again while defending the structure of the proposed government they had also to answer critics of the very concept of a national government. Eight of the papers are devoted to explaining the inadequacies of the original Confederation; one (Number 23) is devoted wholly to justifying the need for central government and another (Number 84) to explaining away the need for further checks on the power of the national government. Nonetheless, in the end they had to add such checks, known as the Bill of Rights, in order to get their new government accepted.

One of these checks, embodied in the First Amendment, was that "*Congress* shall make no law . . . abridging the freedom of speech, or of the press" (emphasis added). But this was not then the sweeping doctrine it has since come to appear. The key word then was "Congress"—that is, the *national* government was to be prohibited from abridging the press. What was done under state government was to be left to the states; they were not prohibited from regulating the press. Indeed, the Pennsylvania Constitution of 1790 and the Delaware Constitution of 1792 expressly imposed liability for abuses of free speech; even in Virginia a 1792 statute provided sanctions against "abusive" uses of free speech. Thomas Jefferson explained, "While we deny that Congress have the right to control the freedom of the press, we have ever asserted the right of the states, and their exclusive right to do so."[4]

Jefferson, having now made his entrance in our story, is worth a moment's pause. He has, and with some reason, become the patron saint of the press, having proclaimed that if he had to choose between government and no newspapers or newspapers and no government he would do without government. But Jefferson also reflected other views of the press, not untypical of his times. His 1783 draft for the Virginia Constitution provided that the press should be subject to no restraints *other than* "legal prosecution for false facts printed and published." Again, in a letter to Madison he remarked, "A declaration that the federal government will never restrain the presses from printing anything they please, will not take away the liability of printers for false facts printed."[5] That view, as you can see, is essentially Blackstonian; the press should be free of prior restraint but could be liable afterwards for injury by falsehoods. On seditious libel he was ambiguous, or at least

[4]Letter to Abigail Adams, September 4, 1804.
[5]Letter to James Madison, July 31, 1788.

changeable. In 1803, angered by its "licentiousness and its lying" he thought the press ought to be restrained by the states if not by the federal government; "I have long thought," he said, "that a few prosecutions of the most prominent offenders would have a wholesome effect in restoring the integrity of the presses."[6] Yet as president he pardoned those convicted under the Sedition Act of 1798. Finally, of course, like all presidents before or since, he had a low opinion of the performance of the press and angrily assailed the calumnies of the press against himself and against the government. Jefferson, like scripture, can be quoted to one's own purposes.

The next great leap forward for freedom of the press, both in philosophy and in practice, came from that 1798 Sedition Act. This law made it a crime to publish any "false, scandalous and malicious writing" bringing into disrepute the government, the Congress or the president, and it immediately plunged the country into bitter controversy. The press was outraged; victims among newspapers included the New York *Argus*, the Boston *Independent Chronicle*, the Richmond *Examiner*. One of the more famous trials was of Thomas Cooper, who in the Reading *Weekly Advertiser* had called President John Adams an incompetent, and who was imprisoned for six months. Of perhaps passing interest is the fact that at his trial Cooper tried to get Adams as a witness but the court refused to subpoena the president.

The Sedition Act forced Americans to rethink their views on the nature of press freedom. In the Virginia Resolutions against the act, James Madison brought forth a new concept. Noting the common law principle that freedom of the press was limited to imposing no prior restraints on publication, Madison said that could not be the American idea of press freedom since a law inflicting penalties afterward would have a similar effect to a law imposing prior restraint. "It would seem a mockery," he wrote," to say that no law should be passed preventing publication . . . but that laws might be passed punishing them in case they should be made."[7] And for the first time a loud voice—that of George Hay, prosecutor of Aaron Burr and later a federal judge—was raised to proclaim the idea that freedom of the press was absolute in terms of criticizing the government, whether the criticism be true, false, malicious or otherwise. "Freedom of the press," he pro-

[6] Letter to Thomas McKean, February 19, 1803.
[7] Levy, *Freedom of the Press From Zenger to Jefferson*, reprints the text of Madison's argument for freedom of the press (document 28, p. 197).

claimed, "means total exemption of the press from any kind of legis-lative control." He would admit only private actions against the press for private injury, as for any other tort.[8]

These sweeping ideas of Madison and Hay were in advance of their own time. Indeed, it is not fully accepted even yet, Justices Black and Douglas to the contrary, that the press should be free of all account-ability to government—that is, to society as a whole—for what it pub-lishes, for in that extreme form freedom of the press raises all manner of political and philosophical questions that are still disturbing. None-theless, the outcome of the outcry was that the Sedition Act was re-pealed. The press emerged freer than ever, its habits of independence and its attitude of suspicion toward government strengthened. The stage was set for the development of the modern American press.

3

As we approach the last quarter of the twentieth century the Ameri-can press occupies a unique position. By the word press I refer, of course, not just to the newspapers of mass circulation but to the whole of the press in all its multiplicity and diversity. To the thousands of weekly papers and journals; to the little offset presses and portable du-plicators of nameless number scattered in every town and hamlet turn-ing out posters, pamphlets, handbills, and broadsides; to magazines overground and underground speaking the ideas of the respectable and the disreputable and aimed at whatever audience—churchgoers, atheists, lesbians, militant blacks or Ku Klux Klan whites, Puritan and prurient, reactionary or rebellious. Each of these is a part of the press, and the whole of it is all of them.

This American press, each part choosing what it will, can publish what it will. It can seize upon secrets stolen from government archives and broadcast them to the world. It can strip the privacy of councils and grand juries. It can pillory those accused of crimes before they are tried. It can heap calumnies not only upon elected governors but upon all whom chance has made an object of public attention. It can publish the lascivious and the sadistic. It can advance any opinion on any sub-ject, including the opinion that all our government is corrupt and that the whole of the social order proclaimed in 1776 should be swept away and another put in its place.

[8] Ibid. (document 27, p. 186).

This is unique, for such full freedom to publish exists nowhere else in the world. In many countries nothing can be published save with the imprimatur of some politburo. In others, the press has many of those freedoms. But in what other country is the press free to do all of these things with impunity? Even in that England which is the wellspring of our liberties there remain, after two hundred years, official secrets acts, strict libel laws, rigid rules on the reporting of judicial proceedings, and other restraints which put some limits upon the freedom of the press. In newer countries the authorities have taken early heed against too much license. Only in America are the boundaries of freedom so broad.

If, even in America, we have not yet extended the same freedom to the new electronic media it is due in part to the fact that for technological reasons there does not exist the multiplicity of outlets and so the same diversity is lacking. But it is also because these media are so newly upon us that there is no history to guide either public policy or media practice. We are just beginning to grapple with the political issues and philosophical conflicts that have long embroiled the printed press.

We have had some glimpse of those press conflicts and seen how they were resolved in our early days, at least partially, by argument and experience. In the century after the Sedition Act new spokesmen here and abroad came forward to expand thoughtfully and eloquently on the nature of civil liberty, notably John Stuart Mill. They provided a philosophical underpinning for a broader concept of freedom of the press.

At the same time the practical situation of the press continued to play its role. The proliferation of printing presses, the geographical expanse of the country and the separation of regions one from another, made for a diversity of political views—or at least a diversity of orthodoxies—and imposed very practical difficulties on the government in controlling the press even when it tried. With the western expansion across the continent this factor was intensified. The newspaper editor on the moving frontier was in practice answerable to no one for what he printed, except upon occasion to an irate reader with a horsewhip. He became accustomed to independence and fiercely defended it until gradually this independence became ever more deeply imbedded in the tradition of the craft.

Not, of course, that the government did not try to curtail it from time to time. In the Civil War President Lincoln, in defiance of the First Amendment, arrested the proprietors of *The New York World* and *The Journal of Commerce* for what seemed to him seditious libel. In peacetime President Theodore Roosevelt tried and failed to convict the *World* and *The Indianapolis News* for "a string of infamous libels," even sending a special message to Congress on the subject. These and other instances, some open, some more subtle, intensified the feeling among writers and printers that only eternal vigilance would preserve their laboriously won independence. Quite understandably, they continued to see government as an antagonist.

And not government alone. By the arrival of the twentieth century the complexities of an industrial society had created other centers of power seeming to the people as distant and even more mysterious and uncontrollable than government. In the shorthand of the day these were the "trusts," or Big Business, but in a larger sense they were all the institutions of society which have power but without clear-cut accountability. Thus there was ushered in the era of muckraking, at first aimed only at those "trusts" but gradually against other parts of the nongovernmental Establishment. The daily press—notably the papers of Hearst, Scripps and Pulitzer—took up the cudgels but the heaviest blows were struck by magazines such as *McClure's* and *Collier's*, and in books, both fiction and nonfiction. So the press began to acquire not merely an anti-government but an anti-institutional cast which remains with us yet.

Meanwhile, one by one the legal barriers against any restraints on the press toppled. The Fourteenth Amendment, as interpreted by the Supreme Court, extended the prohibition against press abridgment under the First Amendment to the states as well as to the national government. With the court's decision in *New York Times* v. *Sullivan* private libel was, for all practical purposes, stricken from the law books; the press is not liable even for publishing falsehoods unless it can be proved that the intent was "malicious." In the Pentagon Papers case (*New York Times* v. *United States*) the press was allowed to publish stolen government documents without either restraint or liability.

We must not think, however, that efforts to put some limits on the freedom of the press were not often supported by public sentiment; to many people the press seems often to abuse its freedom to the injury of both individuals and society as a whole. Nor should we think that philosophy and reason are all on the side of untrammeled freedom.

Thoughtful men have found moral, ethical and practical arguments for not letting liberty turn into license.

Let us go back for a moment and imagine how the argument for putting some restraints on the press might have been put by an articulate philosopher in the Crown colonies. It might have run something like this:

> Freedom of the press is essential to political liberty. Where men cannot freely convey their thoughts to one another no freedom is secure. But freedom of the press to appeal to reason may always be construed as freedom of the press to appeal to public passion and ignorance, vulgarity and cynicism. So it is always dangerous. The moral right of free public expression is not unconditional. When a man who claims the right is a liar, a prostitute whose political judgments can be bought, a dishonest inflamer of hatred and suspicion, his claim is groundless. To protect the press is not always to protect the community. Libel, obscenity, incitement to riot, sedition, these have a common principle; their utterance invades vital social interests. So the extension of legal sanctions to these categories of abuse is justified.

In fact, the above quotation is not imaginary. Every phrase of it is taken verbatim from the report of the Commission on Freedom of the Press, done in the twentieth century by a group of scholars and teachers, one of whom was an eminent philosopher and another the chancellor of the University of Chicago. No foes of liberty, they; no blind reactionaries, no partisan politicians. All of them thoughtful men, deeply disturbed by the fear that the abuse of liberty can destroy liberty.[9]

The report of the Commission on Freedom of the Press, more popularly known as the Hutchins commission, was issued in 1947. It was greeted by outraged outcries from the press, to whom it was heresy. And its import, without any question, was to challenge the absolutism of the idea of freedom of the press, threatening to take us back beyond Mill, beyond George Hay, beyond Madison and Jefferson and John Peter Zenger.

True, the Hutchins commission did not really grasp the nettle. That is, it did not say what ought to be done to restrain abuses of freedom of the press, or even who should be the judge of what they are, beyond the general thought that not every restraint on the press is wrong and

[9] Commission on Freedom of the Press, *A Free and Responsible Press* (Chicago: University of Chicago Press, 1947). Among the commission members were William E. Hocking, professor of philosophy at Harvard, and Robert M. Hutchins, then chancellor of the University of Chicago.

some strong urgings that the press itself exercise self-restraint. But the commission did remind us that the nettle is there.

It always has been. The fundamental assumption of all who cherish freedom of the press and who have nourished it over the centuries is that it is the cornerstone of liberty. The safeguard of the citizens against tyranny is their freedom to remonstrate against despotic governors. A society of self-governing people is viable only if the people are informed. Men have no way of discovering the best ideas about man and God or man and society unless all ideas are free to confront each other, the good and the bad, in the cauldron of the intellectual marketplace. Without the right of free inquiry all other freedoms vanish. Such are the premises of free speech, from Milton to our own day.

Yet another assumption is that no man is free if he can be terrorized by his neighbor, whether by swords or by words; this is the justification of laws against violence and against libel and slander. Nor can a citizen be truly informed if falsehoods come masquerading as truth; false advertising for ideas is as injurious as those for foods or for drugs. Moreover the liberty of the citizen also depends upon the stability of society, which is why governments exist, and society has a right to protect itself against the predatory. Such are the premises of those who say no right is absolute, including freedom of the press, when it clashes with other rights.

Therein lies the nettle and it grows ever more prickly. If the right of a fair trial is fundamental to liberty, what happens to it if the press is free to prejudice a fair trial by what it publishes? If it is wrong for other institutions of society to have power without responsibility, is it right for the press—surely one of the more powerful institutions of society—to have no accountability for what it does?

These questions, raised a quarter of a century ago by the Hutchins commission, are now disturbing others. In that Pentagon Papers case the court reaffirmed the Blackstonian doctrine and refused to uphold prior restraint, but several of the judges were uneasy even with that as an absolute doctrine when it seemed to give sanction to the stealing of government documents. Justice White, for one, plainly said that while he would not restrain prior publication he might well sustain a decision holding the newspapers accountable for their actions as receivers of stolen property.

Within the press as well there is also a groping for some way to reconcile this freedom of the press with the other needs of liberty. A

quarter century after the Hutchins commission there is much talk of
press councils and other means of achieving both a free and responsible press. And two centuries after 1776 the reconciliation seems as
difficult as ever.

Perhaps more so. For certainly the Founding Fathers would be as-
tounded by how much we have enlarged the parameters of the debate.
After all, when they met to draft the Constitution they did so in secret,
barring the press entirely and pledging themselves to confidentiality of
their discussions. They did so not because they feared open debate on
their handiwork but because they saw values to liberty in the privacy
of council. Certainly the purloining of state papers would have stirred
even President Jefferson to outrage. None of them thought freedom of
the press was a license to do anything whatever.

Yet the changes that time has wrought on the idea of freedom of the
press were, I think, inevitable. Freedom of the press, once proclaimed,
admits of no logical limit. If the national legislature may not abridge it,
by what logic should state legislatures? If all ideas should be freely expressed, how can information on which ideas are based be suppressed?
If government must be open, how can the governors keep secrets from
the governed? And if the governors will not give information freely, is
there not a right to wrest it from them? Each progression leads inexorably to the next.

In this country there has also been the pressure of historical experience, thrusting the boundaries ever outward. The very nature of our
Revolution created a bias, first against distant government and then by
extension against all government save that which governs least. Although the twentieth century has forced an acceptance of enlarged
government, it has been a reluctant acceptance and it still divides the
people. We remain unruly under the long arm of government, as when
mothers parade to protest school busing or truck drivers block highways to protest fuel allocations. We remain equally suspicious of, and
hostile to, other institutional sources of power.

This bias has been shared by those who report and comment on the
news, and their habit of displaying it has been reinforced by the privilege of independence so fiercely fought for. "Print the news and raise
hell"—that has been the traditional battle cry of the press. Except in
rare moments it matters not who holds the power, what president the
reins of government, the press will soon be sniffing at his spoor and
thundering at his actions.

That such freedom can be abused is undeniable. Good men can be slandered, justice thwarted, base passions aroused, people misinformed, government subverted, all the institutions of society undermined. It should surprise no one that there arise from time to time voices asking how we shall protect ourselves. As our society grows more complex these voices will, I am sure, grow more clamorous.

But this is true of all liberty. There is none that cannot be abused. And if the people cannot be trusted to find their way amid the abuses then there is no hope for the American experiment. For that experiment rests less upon logic than upon a faith that the danger of unbounded liberty is not so great as that of putting liberty in bondage. It is a faith so far justified. In our two hundred years we have been better served by our freedoms, including most especially our freedom of speech and of the press, than we would have been served without them. That is the answer, perhaps the only answer, to those who would no longer trust those freedoms.

All the same, the story is not ended. Freedom of religion. Freedom of person under the protection of habeas corpus. Trial by jury. Freedom of the press. "These principles," said Jefferson in his first Inaugural, "form the bright constellation which has gone before us, and guided our steps through an age of revolution and reformation."

Freedom of religion, habeas corpus, trial by jury. All these have become so much a part of us we hardly remember that they were once things men fought over. Of that constellation only freedom of the press remains in the heat of controversy—as revolutionary an idea now as it was in the beginning.

Lecture delivered at Stanford University
under the sponsorship of the American Enterprise Institute,
March 6, 1974

ON THE FREEDOM AND RESPONSIBILITY
OF THE PRESS

When I first came to Washington as a fledgling journalist forty-two years ago, the Washington press corps, in total, numbered only a few hundred and you could know almost all of them by sight. There was no radio and television press gallery, not even a gallery to accommodate the periodical press. Today I am stunned by the number of pages it takes in the *Congressional Directory* to list the accredited press in all its forms; I refuse to use that word "media."

That was not all that was different. I well remember my first presidential press conference. For the record, the date was Friday, May 15, 1936, and Franklin D. Roosevelt was holding his 295th press conference since he had become president.

I presented my shiny new press credentials to the guard at the Pennsylvania Avenue gate, walked up the winding driveway and entered the West Wing of the White House. To the left of the room was a modest office for Steve Early, the president's press secretary. Beyond and out of sight were the offices for Marvin McIntyre, the president's only other regular aide, and for Missy Le Hand, his private secretary. There were two others, designated as executive clerks. And that was all—the entire White House staff. The press conference itself was held in the Oval Office. When the door opened, we gathered around the president's desk, no more than twenty of us. There were some desultory questions; I remember being overcome at being a few feet away from the president, at being one of the little band entitled to this privilege.

Press conferences of cabinet officials were equally informal. The Agriculture Department was my first beat and usually only four or five of us would meet with Henry Wallace in his office. There were no microphones, no snaking cables for lights and television cameras. It was no different with Henry Morgenthau or Harold Ickes or Cordell Hull.

In those days all the major government departments were within easy walking distance—Agriculture, Treasury, State, the White House, even War and Navy—and, since *The Wall Street Journal* office was then equally informally organized, I would often wander to other press conferences, not because journalistic duty demanded it but because it was fun and helped give a feel for the whole of government.

The working rules for press conferences were, by and large, those applied by the president. In general we could paraphrase what he said but could use no direct quotes without express permission. He could also give us information "for background only" which we could make use of but not attribute to him. And he kept the privilege of going "off the record" entirely when he chose.

I do not need to tell you how different it is today. That old State Department building has become the Executive Office Building, and it houses more staff aides to the president than, in those olden days, there were members of the press corps.

Presidential press conferences are now TV events. The last one I attended was in the time of Gerald Ford, and I swore I would never attend another. Unless you want to get your face on television, there's not much point to it.

Press conferences of cabinet officers and other high government officials are also now staged with almost equal panoply.

Though I am reluctant to admit it, there are some gains in the way the new technology has altered the manner of doing things. The ordinary citizen today does get a chance to see the president in action and doubtless to form impressions not just by what the president says but by his style. His grace under pressure, or his lack of it, is not wholly irrelevant to his performance as our national leader.

The same is true, of course, of others in the public arena—a secretary of state speaking on some matter of foreign policy, an economic adviser testifying before a congressional committee. Even a ten-second snippet on the evening news tells us something about the person, and that too is not irrelevant to his public performance.

But I am not persuaded that the technological changes are all for the better. President Roosevelt could, and often did, just think out loud without fear that every word was put indelibly on the record. He could share with the reporters around his desk some information that would help them to do their jobs better, help them understand what was involved in some public question. He could, and sometimes did, misstate himself at first expression, as everyone may do in casual conversation, and then on second thought rephrase his remarks.

The modern president has no such latitude. He must live in constant fear of the slip-of-the-tongue. A misstated name from a lapse of memory can be an embarrassment. Awkward phraseology on some matter of public import is beyond recall or correction; it is flashed around the world irretrievably.

One consequence of this, it seems to me, is that presidents today try to say no more at a press conference than what might be put as well in a carefully drafted statement. The loss here is both to the president and to the press.

The president has lost an opportunity to be frank and open. The press has lost an opportunity to share his thought processes which, without being the stuff of tomorrow's headlines, nonetheless could help reporters on their own to do a better job of informing their readers and listeners.

I might add, by the way, that the president has also lost the opportunity to deal bluntly with the stupid question, not unknown at a presidential press conference. Anyway, I cannot imagine President Carter telling a reporter on television that he had asked a silly question and to go stand in the dunce corner, something President Roosevelt didn't hesitate to do.

So much for the changes wrought by technology, with their subtle differences in the relationship between the press and government as it was and as it is. The surface differences encapsule more profound changes—in our government, in our craft, and not least in the role this journalistic craft plays in the society in which we live.

I have heard it said that the old relationship between the Washington press corps and the government was too "cozy." The implication is that we were "taken in" by the informality of, let us say, Mr. Roosevelt's press conferences or the more casual relationship between the few regulars around a cabinet officer; that we were too flattered at being admitted as at least semi-insiders, too easily accepting the off-the-record conversation; that all this somehow intimidated us from doing our job.

I don't believe it. The competitive instinct among reporters then was no less than now. On my first beat, Agriculture, Felix Belair of *The New York Times* knocked naivete out of me in a hurry and he never

seemed to be intimidated by Henry Wallace. I never noticed Eddie Fol-
liard of *The Post*, Turner Catledge of *The Times* or Harrison Salisbury
of the UP passing up a good story out of deference to authority.

Investigative reporting isn't new, either. It was the press that exposed
the Teapot Dome scandal. In my time—for one example—Tom Stokes
of Scripps-Howard won his Pulitzer for exposing graft and corruption
in the WPA. The defeat of FDR's court-packing scheme was due to the
spotlight the press kept on it.

But there was one thing about the press then, I think, which was
different from today. We did not think of ourselves and the government
as enemies.

We were cynical about much in government, yes. We were skeptical
about many government programs, yes. We thought ourselves the
watchdogs of government, yes. We delighted in exposés of bungling
and corruption, yes. But enemies of government? No.

In any event I don't recall hearing much in those days about the "adversary relationship" between press and government. Today I hear the
phrase everywhere.

It reflects an attitude that shows in many ways. At these new-style
press conferences, including those of the president, the questions often
seem less designed to elicit information than to entrap. Even the daily
press briefings by Jody Powell have become a sort of duel, an encounter
that would have astonished Steve Early and the old White House press
regulars.

There appears to be a widespread view that here on one side are we,
the press, and over there on the other side are government officials,
none of whom can be trusted.

I suppose it's a result of Watergate. We blame everything now on
Watergate—much as the Chinese blame everything on the Gang of
Four. But it is, I must confess, an attitude that leaves me uneasy.

Under our Constitution the three official Estates of the realm are the
executive, the legislature and the judiciary. Each has a different role
and sometimes they disagree, one with another, about what is proper
public policy. But no one supposes that because a president may differ
with Congress on a particular matter that they are "enemies" by
nature or that the Supreme Court is an adversary of both. Unless each
gives the others a full measure of respect, our society will dissolve into
anarchy.

The press is not an institution of government. But it is most definitely an institution of our society, made so by the First Amendment to our Constitution. It is not too much to say, I think, that one intent of the First Amendment was to make the press, collectively, a part of the system of checks and balances that helps preserve a free society.

That is, in Macaulay's felicitous phrase, we in the press constitute a Fourth Estate of the realm. But that very phrase, "Fourth Estate," implies that we are part of the self-governing process of our society, not something set apart from it.

As such we are permitted—nay, invited—to inform the people what the other Estates are doing and upon occasion to criticize what they are doing. In that last respect, of course, our right is not different from that of other citizens, all of whom are free to speak their minds. We differ from other citizens only in the fact that watching government perform is our full-time occupation.

But that role, or so it seems to me, is not the same thing as casting ourselves as adversaries, enemies even, of government as government. There's a distinction, and an important one, between differing with *a* president in some editorial or commentary and being an adversary of *the* presidency.

To think ourselves adversaries of government as government makes me uneasy for several reasons. For one, if the press collectively thinks of itself as an adversary of government, why would not the government begin to think of itself as an adversary to the press?

We have, in fact, already seen some signs of that. Some of us have been spied upon—our mail opened, our telephones tapped—as if we were agents of some hostile power. Some of us have been hauled into court and thrown into jail.

The reminder here is that in polity, as in physics, every action creates a reaction. We have in turn reacted to this harassment, as well we should. We ought to cry alarm whenever the government, whether the executive or the judiciary, seems bent on intimidating us by harassment. But we ought also, so I think, take care that we in turn do not overreact.

We should, with all the energy that is in us, defend the rights of all citizens against executive spying. When citizens cannot write to one another freely or speak to one another without fear, then all liberty is endangered.

We should demand for all citizens due process against unwarranted searches and seizures of their private papers. We should hold both the executive and the judiciary strictly accountable that the right of the people to be secure in their persons, their houses, papers and effects be not violated.

We should insist that no warrants or subpoenas be issued against any citizen except upon probable cause; warrants should be duly supported before the courts and particular in describing why and what is to be seized.

We should be zealous in our protection of all citizens in their right to a public trial by an impartial jury. That means we should take care that nothing we do prejudices the minds of those who will be called to give judgment on a person accused. That also means, surely, that we should uphold the right of an accused to obtain witnesses in his favor— by compulsory process, if need be, as the Constitution provides.

We should remember that the First Amendment protects the freedom of speech of all citizens, not just our own voices. That is where we should stand our ground, defending the rights of all. Beyond that we should be wary. We should be especially wary of claiming for ourselves alone any exemption from the obligations of all citizens, including the obligation to bear witness in our courts once due process has been observed.

The risk, if we do, is that someday the people may come to think us arrogant. For there is nothing in any part of the Bill of Rights, including the First Amendment, that makes us a privileged class apart.

And it cannot be said too often: Freedom of the press is not some immutable right handed down to Moses on Mt. Sinai. It is a political right granted by the people in a political document, and what the people grant they can, if they ever choose, take away.

But what a precious right it is that they have granted us.

So long as the First Amendment stands, the American press, each part choosing what it will, can publish what it will. When we think it necessary to the public weal we can seize upon documents taken from government archives and broadcast them to the world. We can strip privacy from the councils of state and from grand juries. We are free to heap criticism not only upon our elected governors but upon all whom chance has made an object of public attention. We can, if we wish, publish even the lascivious and the sadistic. And we can advance any opinion on any subject.

This is unique among the nations of the world. In what other country is the press so free? Even in England, which is the wellspring of our liberties, there remain, after two hundred years, limits upon the free-dom of the press.

Only in America are the boundaries of that freedom so broad. That is why I cherish it and pray the people will never think we abuse it. For there is no liberty that cannot be abused and none that cannot be lost.

Policy Review, Summer 1979

A SMALL CONFESSION

Back in the summer of 1962—and a long time ago it seems now—twelve American editors were offered a unique opportunity to visit the Soviet Union as guests of the Union of Soviet Journalists. Although they were, as travelers always are in that strange land, shepherded by their Communist hosts they nonetheless saw more than most visitors.

The group included, besides me, representatives of most of the major American newspapers—Lee Hills, head of the Knight papers and then president of the American Society of Newspaper Editors; Paul Miller, head of the Gannett papers and president of the Associated Press; Robert Estabrook, chief European correspondent of *The Washington Post*, to mention only a few. There were also editors from geographically scattered smaller newspapers.

When we returned after a journey of some 8,000 miles from Leningrad to Central Asia, we spent an afternoon with Ambassador Thompson sharing our impressions. Later a few of us were invited to visit President Kennedy, and all who would were asked to visit the State Department to talk with officials there.

I do not know what the others did but I spent more than an hour one morning with State Department officials especially interested in Soviet affairs; the group may have included, for all I know, someone from the CIA. I also answered questions, at its request, from the Joint Economic Committee of Congress about economic conditions, as I saw them, in the Soviet Union.

All this personal reminiscence would be nothing more than a minor footnote to history except for the fact that there has lately been much public controversy about the propriety of journalists and others who may acquire foreign information "cooperating" with the CIA and similar government agencies.

Not long ago there was quite an uproar when it became known that a number of American foreign correspondents share such tidbits of information as they may come by with the American mission in that country. It was argued, at least in some quarters, that this made them "spies," not journalists.

More recently there has been a flap at Brooklyn College because a political science professor there, whose special interest is research in terrorism, agreed to report to the CIA any interesting information he came across on a research trip to Europe. There are those at Brooklyn College who think he ought to be fired forthwith.

This raises an interesting philosophical question. If an American citizen traveling abroad acquires some information that might be useful to his government in understanding conditions in a foreign country, what should he do? Should he share the information with those in his government to whom it may be useful? Or should he refuse?

It's not a question that arises for journalists or political scientists alone. A knowledgeable businessman traveling abroad may gather information about industrial production methods that would be highly useful in understanding economic development in that country. So might a banker about impending currency developments or an airline pilot about the state of aeronautical technology.

Sometimes even an ordinary tourist who has a local friend, or perchance strikes up an informal acquaintance, may glean from conversation some clues as to the mood of the country helpful in assessing possible future developments. Rarely is such information meaningful by itself. Put together with a mosaic of other information it might be very useful in understanding social, economic and political developments in the country.

Certainly there were no "secrets" uncovered in that Soviet visit of long ago; we saw nothing and heard nothing but what our hosts allowed. But we did spend two and a half hours with then Premier Khrushchev, many hours with the editors of *Pravda*, *Izvestia* and local editors from Georgia to Uzbekistan. We saw farms and factories, talked with peasants, university professors, young students, actors, musicians and poets.

Whether any of that was helpful to those whose task it was to better understand the Soviet Union, I cannot say. I doubt whether those journalists who later made similar visits to Red China, including Robert Bartley of *The Wall Street Journal*, can say that this or that piece of information they came upon was a revelation to those seeking to understand that inscrutable country.

But that is not the question, really. The question, rather, is whether the journalist—or the businessman or college professor or casual tourist—having had the experience is acting improperly if he shares his information, impressions and judgments with interested officials of his own country.

I confess that fifteen years ago the question never occurred to me. Neither I nor anyone in the group had stolen secret Russian papers, bribed any informants, taken any forbidden pictures or otherwise done anything unknown to our Soviet hosts. Most of what we had seen or heard we had written about in our newspapers anyway.

Yet I saw no reason why I should not talk about what I had seen and heard if, perchance, there was some observation which put together with other information might be helpful to those who had to deal with the Soviet Union. It never crossed my mind that the foreign affairs officials of my country were somehow "enemies" to be avoided.

Today, at least in some quarters, that attitude is considered immoral and it may even get a poor college professor fired. That's because in many intellectual circles there is a war on against the CIA and all intelligence gathering agencies. Much of this the CIA has brought on itself with its rather strange covert activities. But by some alchemy that criticism has been converted into the idea that it is wicked for a citizen to do anything to help those in his government better understand what is going on in the countries with which it must deal.

Perhaps so. But while I cannot speak for my colleagues, I confess that I do not cease being a citizen of my country because I am a journalist and I do not think that, as a citizen, it is immoral for me to share with my government such information as I may gather about the world around us.

March 9, 1977

THE COMMENTATOR

U nless you've been visiting on Mars these past ten days you must know that Eric Sevareid has retired. And if you were a visitor from Mars you might well wonder what the fuss was all about.

For Mr. Sevareid is not a general who led armies to victory, a political leader who reshaped the country or even a captain of industry who built a great enterprise that increased our material well-being. He is simply a man whose chief claim to the public attention has been about six minutes a week on the CBS "Evening News."

Yet CBS gave him as many farewell performances as Sarah Bernhardt, rival networks cut into their own news time to pay him homage (NBC, *mirabile dictu*, even ran his final commentary on its program) and newspaper columns were full of enough encomiums to stock an obituary.

The personal qualities of Mr. Sevareid, splendid though they be, are not enough to explain all this fuss. You have to also understand the role of the commentator, which is an old one, and the forum in which he performed it, which is something brand-new. The phenomenon known as Eric Sevareid, you might say, is the result of a concatenation of circumstance.

The role of the commentator—the non-participating observer of the passing parade—is probably as old as the first gathering of nomads, where the witch doctor and the minstrel regaled the fireside with their observations on tribal affairs, past or present. They learned early, I suspect, the uses of show business to make themselves heard.

Time has promoted the peripatetic commentators of ancient Athens to the status of philosophers, but their purpose was less to speak to the ages than to the policies of Pericles or whoever was running things at the moment. This called for a certain amount of arrogance and they were not always well received; after all, who had elected them?

Their forum was the marketplace, and their instrument was the spoken word. With the coming of print the number of commentators multiplied and their voices reached further, though possibly with a diminution in quality. Anyway, by our mid-century the journalistic commentator flourished like the green bay tree. If public affairs were run no better it wasn't for want of critical commentary.

Some of this came from persons of considerable attainment and intellectual capacity. No one would have proposed Walter Lippmann, Anne O'Hare McCormick or Arthur Krock for president, but when they wrote they usually said something worth remarking.

Today, in the print medium, there is a plethora of self-appointed commentators of varying philosophic persuasions. We can choose among James Reston, David Broder, George Will, Tom Wicker, Meg Greenfield or Mary McGrory, to mention a few. All are respected. But the retirement of none of them would be a public event, because none of them are public figures to be instantly recognized like politicians and show business performers.

With television it is otherwise. This medium, for all its marvels, has not yet found a way to accommodate the diversity of commentators available in print. Others besides Eric Sevareid have played that role intermittently; Howard K. Smith and David Brinkley on the networks, a scattering of others on local stations. But Mr. Sevareid is the only one with unbroken longevity on a particular network.

That is what has made his position unique. With television we are back to the spoken word, not in the marketplace this time but in people's homes. Mr. Sevareid is thus a familiar acquaintance in a way not possible for any newspaper writer. That uniqueness makes it a position of opportunity, but that same uniqueness also poses possible peril to the public weal.

Mr. Sevareid has recognized this from the beginning and his personal qualities have at once contributed to his stature and minimized any perils from his position. He is not a man given to arrogance about his own opinions. He is soft-spoken with those he has and he puts them forward in a soft-spoken manner, not as certainties but as something one might want to think about. Sometimes he is so soft-spoken and tentative you cannot be sure when he has finished what opinion he meant to advance.

This can make for dullness; the person who is certain he has all the answers can speak with more fire. But it is a quality, I think, well suited to his unique role. A firebrand would have long since worn out his welcome in our home.

Mr. Sevareid has understood better than many the difference between the advocate of political causes and the journalist who by happenstance has been thrown into the role of commentator on public affairs. The journalistic commentator can lay no claim to expertise on all the topics of discussion; he is arrogant if he thinks himself wiser than those who read or hear him. The only real justification for his unelected position is that his job gives him full time to follow and to think about public affairs. His vocation is the avocation of the butcher and the candlestick maker.

If that gives him some credentials to have a thought one day about the Middle East and, on another, about a president's energy program, they are thoughts to be spoken with some humility and heard with some reservation. The service to the public comes not from one commentator but from the many, putting all manner of observations before the public for their weighing.

The attention now being paid to Mr. Sevareid's retirement is a reminder that television has not yet solved that problem.

Indeed, the real encomium for Eric Sevareid, I think, is that he understood the uniqueness of his role, felt its responsibility and played it with an innate sense of fairness. The best response to his departure would be not simply to replace him with another but for this great new medium to find a way to offer a broader diversity of opinion from its commentators.

December 12, 1977

AN ANACHRONISTIC MAN

In 1936, when I joined *The Wall Street Journal*, its newsroom seemed an appropriate setting for *The Front Page*, although the newspaper it provided its 35,000 subscribers hardly fit the raucous Chicago journalism Hecht and MacArthur described.

The open room was a cavern packed with desks cheek-by-jowl. Most were littered with journalistic detritus providing ammunition for wadded paper fights when the reporters got bored. Here and there were visible some whiskey bottles hard by the old-fashioned upright telephones.

There's nostalgia for me too in the remembered technology. In room center there was still a working Morse telegraph wire, its receiver jammed with a bent tobacco can (Prince Albert, no doubt) to magnify its clickety-click for the operator. The Dow Jones News Service wire was served by a spinning type-wheel—all caps, no punctuation—that printed the news at a languid pace. The New York Stock Exchange ticker was one now found only in museums, sprouting a glass dome.

Then there was Thomas F. Woodlock. At seventy he had been writing for the *Journal* since the days of Charles Dow. A scholarly Irishman, he by now wrote a regular column of commentary under the same rubric, "Thinking Things Over," as this one, displayed on page one instead of hidden inside.

But Woodlock had never come to terms with the typewriter. He wrote everything in longhand, which meant somebody had to transcribe it for the Linotype operators in the basement. Although that was a nuisance, he was both privileged and stubborn. To any who dared grumble, he retorted, "I'm hired as a writer not a typist, and nobody expects Paderewski to tune his own piano."

Today Tom Woodlock wouldn't recognize the place. The reporters now have glassed-off privacy so the newsroom looks like a bank. No Morse wires, no clanking Linotypes below. No paper fights, no whiskey bottles—at least that you notice. The newspaper isn't even printed in the home office.

Instead, it reaches its more than two million subscribers by being printed each night in seventeen places, coast to coast. All this by sending signals to satellites in the sky. What's delivered isn't eighteen to twenty pages but up to fifty-six. The few oldsters left can only marvel.

And things are still a-changing. As Suzanne Garment recently reported the staff is switching to the newest computer system for writing copy that will soon displace the typewriters of the Hecht-MacArthur days.

They are marvelous contraptions. You sit before a video screen which displays what you write. When you're finished you push a button and all the copy goes automatically into a central computer which spews it out as "paper type" all ready for page make-up and then the presses. That is, unless there's a glitch and it all vanishes to never-never land.

Here is the wave of the future. In journalism schools today they devote as much time teaching students how to put words into these Video Display Terminals (VDTs) as they do to what words to put in them. More, maybe. *Time* magazine was in tune with the times when it replaced the Man-of-the-Year with a fleshless machine.

Mrs. Garment confesses that when a temperament like hers comes up against the computer "there are going to be a few weeks of hard going." But she notes that other colleagues young enough to have already joined the modern world adapt to it well. "There is little doubt that in the end I will succumb."

My personal interest in this is that the Honorable Editor has made some mutterings that I too should have one in my office at home where these weekly effusions are written. That way I could be typographer for my own copy which would pass into the central computer untouched by other human hands, and possibly other human minds as well.

But there are a few little problems unmentioned by Suzanne. For one, you can't pick up a VDT with keyboard, move to the breakfast table for a cup of coffee, glower at what you've written, scratch a word here or add one there in that futile effort to say what you want to say.

You can, it's true, go back to your keyboard where the magical machine will let you do this. But the thinking process isn't the same when you wander about, brooding, and when your bottom is anchored to a chair staring at a video display. I suffer from *cacoethes scribendi*, a mania nourished by long years at that typewriter Tom Woodlock deplored but one that's satisfied only when I can actually scribble, scribble on an old-fashioned piece of paper.

There's another little problem. For this machine to do its job the words must be typed into it letter-perfect. Otherwise, garbles in, garbles out. After fifty years of haphazard typing by hunt, peck and hope, correcting and re-correcting my typos would add hours of arduous labor and lead to a nervous breakdown. I'd have no one but myself to blame for those errors that slip by the most skilled typographers.

So I beg patience of the Honorable Editor. Patience, I have no doubt, will be rewarded one day by a machine that will think things over for itself. Push a button and he'll get a computer-packaged column on the situation in the Middle East or the Reagan budget, brilliantly original and letter-perfect.

Of course, when that day comes, why will the *Journal* need an editor at all?

Meanwhile, put me down as an anachronistic man, like Old Man Woodlock. He at least would agree that an electronic piano, note-perfect though it be, is not an improvement on Paderewski.

January 19, 1983

THE INSUFFERABLE

"Columnists," so remarked George Will in a *Newsweek* column, "are incorrigible, not to say insufferable."

Indeed so. And so for that matter are not only signed columnists but other journalistic "givers of advice" to mayors, governors, congressmen, cabinet officers, prime ministers and presidents. This includes editorial writers who hide their incorrigible certitude beneath a cloak of anonymity.

In this case, I have no doubt, George was trying to disarm his readers with the ploy of self-deprecation, because he immediately launched into gratuitous advice "for the next Republican president" on a range of matters from energy to defense to labor and the welfare program. No real humility there.

Such self-acknowledgment of a personality image (or should I say personality disorder?) may have disarmed Mr. Will's readers, so skillful is he with words. The confession is undoubtedly good for the soul. I can assure him, though, that such winsome words won't smooth away the prickly question that lurks in every reader's mind.

One of my own readers recently put it in stinging fashion. "What gives you the nerve," he asked, "to sound off on anything and everything that happens in Washington or the world?"

In one form or another the question has been put to journalists by every president from George Washington to Jimmy Carter and it crops up wherever soi-disant commentators encounter their fellow man. For those who labor in this vineyard there is no balm in Gilead.

Moreover the question is properly put. Journalistic commentary is a peculiar occupation. The writer perforce deals with many topics and issues on which he is not, and cannot be, an expert. One day it's taxes, the next the economy or some Constitutional issue, and on another day a question of foreign policy involving perhaps some distant and unfamiliar part of the world.

This helps explain why the general level of journalistic commentary is so mediocre. Most journalists come to it because they have been good reporters and it's assumed that since they are knowledgeable about, say, government or foreign affairs they may have an opinion worth listening to. Sometimes it's true, sometimes not. Many a good reporter has been ruined by asking him to think.

Nonetheless the poor fellow paid to comment must have something to say about all these things, sensible he hopes, and furthermore must compress his thoughts into a narrow space. That's an art, like juggling tenpins. The marvel is that every once in a while the craft produces a George Will or a Richard Strout, worth listening to whether you agree with them or not.

Still, the rest of us, too, have some credentials, though they are more modest than we may admit.

It's not a matter of intelligence. The lawyer, the doctor, the businessman, the shopkeeper or the carpenter may be smarter. They may, and often do, have a commonsense perspective sharper than those who profess to offer perspective in the public prints.

But most people most of the time are busy with their day's occupations, with all the demands these put on their time and attention. It's only with their left-over time that they contemplate the SALT treaty, muse on the problems of Palestine, mull over the arguments between the Keynesians and the monetarists, or consider the details of the president's budget.

On the other hand, following public affairs is the full-time occupation of the journalistic commentator, be he anonymous editorial writer or famous columnist. The news of the day is his workaday world. He can spend his time reading the full text of the president's speech, poring over that proposed tax bill or international treaty, and some of them actually do so.

That is not, by itself, the making of a sage. The journalist, almost by definition, is a professional amateur, knowing a little bit about a lot of things and not very much about anything. His only claim on the reader's attention is that he is paid, albeit a paltry sum, to do what the doctor and the businessman might do if they had the time.

Very modest credentials indeed. But that's all he has.

There's a great difference, be it noted, between being informed and being thoughtful. On the latter, the reader must make his own judgment. Opinions, after all, are a dime a dozen; most of us have them on every subject. Movie actresses expound freely on nuclear physics and the physicist on foreign policy. Whether their opinions are worth listening to is another matter. It's a rare person, journalist or otherwise, who knows why he thinks what he thinks well enough to tell you why.

The trouble with commentators is that reticence does not fit well with their peculiar occupation. As my vexed correspondent suggests, it does take a bit of nerve to "sound off" on anything and everything that happens in Washington and the world. But want of nerve won't earn one's daily pittance when confronted with a blank sheet of paper in the typewriter.

The occupational hazard is the danger of losing it once one begins to fear one might be wrong.

So be not disarmed, dear reader, by George's confessional.

If those who practice the craft appear incorrigible it's because we must. If we admit to being insufferable, it's to make a virtue of the inevitable.

But there's no reason for you to suffer. You can pick and choose according to your own prejudices. And, though the thought be treasonable, there's nothing to prevent you from turning the page.

September 5, 1979

VII

Money, Money, Money

DEFICITS AND DEFENSE

If reading this you think me out of tune with the times, you won't be the first. For years liberals labeled me an anachronism for my views on everything from government economic policy to the threat of the Soviet Union to world peace.

Now, ironically, I find myself out of tune with some of what's called the new conservatism.

Specifically, I think that deficits matter—government deficits, that is—in their effects on the nation's economy. And after years of bewailing the disrepair of our defense ramparts, I find myself uneasy with the idea that we best repair them with a crash program of just throwing money at the Pentagon.

The attitude of the new conservatism, if I read the signs aright, is that government deficits don't matter. Or in the words of Representative Jack Kemp, one of the more thoughtful and articulate spokesmen for the new attitude, Republicans as conservatives "no longer worship at the shrine of a balanced budget."

Similar views, less colorfully expressed, have been heard from others on the pages of *The Wall Street Journal* and elsewhere. Their burden, at least until very lately, is that the Reagan administration need not overly concern itself with the president's promise of a balanced budget by 1984. Shades of Walter Heller and John Kenneth Galbraith!

The rationale for the new conservatism is that government deficits don't of themselves create the inflation which so much plagues us. Moreover we shouldn't worship at the balanced budget shrine because the nation faces another problem, the sad estate of our armed forces compared with those of the Soviet Union.

There is truth in both of these arguments. Inflation, as these pages have long insisted, arises from the excessive creation of money and credit from whatever sources. It would be quite possible to have inflation, even a rampant one, while the government's budget was precisely balanced between revenue and expenditures. That would happen if monetary policy remained expansionist.

By the same token it would be possible for the government to run a budget deficit with little or no inflationary effects if the deficit was not "monetized"; that is if the government borrowed real savings to finance it rather than having it "paid for" with money and credit pumped out by the Federal Reserve system. If that were the case a "small" deficit would make no difference.

There remain a few difficulties nonetheless. The greater the government's demand for "real" savings the greater the squeeze on the savings supply, raising the cost (interest rate) for all borrowers, from home purchasers to industry. Even without inflation the economy would have mammoth problems.

Perhaps I'm too cynical, but experience suggests also it is highly unlikely that a deficit of any size would in fact be met by borrowing only "real" savings. The pressures on the monetary authorities against standing fast would be enormous even with the support of a president as tough as Mr. Reagan. Already we've heard mumblings from the secretary of the treasury about the the present restraint by the Federal Reserve Board, not to mention complaints from business and industry about the prevailing high interest rates.

So I persist in my anachronistic view that deficits do matter. Handled one way they cause one kind of problem, inflation. Handled differently they create all manner of other problems.

The Reagan administration came to office with three main objectives, all worthy and all overdue. To reduce the growing size and cost of government. To lower the people's taxes. To rebuild our neglected armed forces.

The first two were carefully thought out and a splendid beginning made on each. The third hasn't been. The approach was simply to increase the defense budget without weighing its overall effects on the cost of government and, equally importantly, without pause to consider carefully how the money should be spent.

To pinch-penny with our defense is foolhardy. To merely hand the Pentagon money and leave it to decide how to spend it is reckless. No branch of government can waste money easier, or in such large amounts, as the military. We need hard thought on what kind of planes, ships, missiles, guns or troops will be best adapted to the next war, not the last one. If that means difficult decisions by the president, that's what we have one for.

Another thing. One of the reasons we could gird ourselves for World War II with a minimum of strain was that we entered it with no inflationary pressures. The country could absorb huge wartime expenses. The next war, big or little, will bring new inflationary pressures—make no mistake about that—as we should have learned from the half-war of Vietnam. The less strain on our resources at the beginning, the easier we will bear the burden.

So it's with relief I see some cracks in the attitude that of all the activities of government, defense alone should be immune to discipline. Money may be the sinews of war but its use should never be left to generals alone.

I'm relieved too at what seems a recognition that deficits matter after all. Anyway, there are hints the administration will seek to shrink them and won't shrink from a rigorous look at all spending, not just part of it.

For the two are related. Military safety depends not only on the ramparts we watch but on the economic strength behind them. Conservatives also need to relearn old lessons now and then.

September 9, 1981

THE GOLDEN GLITTER

Put me down as a bit of a gold bug. I'm among those who believe that any people are better served when the value of what they use for money isn't subject to the whims of their governors, be they kings of yore or the chosen officials of today. And of all the commodities used for money, none has proved more useful and dependable than gold.

Put me down also, however, as more than somewhat skeptical about all this talk of returning the country to the gold standard, whatever economic ills it might relieve.

The problem with the gold standard is not what so many of its opponents allege, that is, that it "won't work." Quite the opposite. It works very well indeed, forcing a monetary discipline upon kings, dictators, parliaments and people.

And that's the real problem. When money is anchored to gold, the gold governs the governors. It limits their political power because they can't manufacture all the money they'd like to spend. It also chafes those who want money from the government, be it for education, roads, welfare, arms, subsidies or whatever. In time the restraint to these aspirations becomes intolerable and, upon one excuse or another, the gold standard is abandoned.

At least that's the way it's been since sometime in the seventh century B.C. Many commodities, of course, can and have served as media of exchange—iron, cattle, stone disks—but the Lydians in Asia Minor seem to have been the first to coin money with a gold content and give it a "mark" as warranty it was what it said it was. Such coins proved felicitous for the conduct of commerce and their use spread. The gold standard was born.

But there was a problem right from the beginning. The limited supply of gold limited the coins available. So kings, always eager for more money, would clip the edges of the coins and use the shavings to make more coins. This worked until people realized there were more short-weighted coins circulating, thus reducing the exchange value of each. Inflation had come, if not yet the word.

Modern times, modern techniques. Those clever Chinese who invented printing also invented paper money, a thing at which Marco Polo marveled on his visit to Cathay. Each piece of paper stood surrogate for gold supposedly in the emperor's treasury. Paper money was another improvement for commerce (easier to carry than a pocketful of coins) but also for the emperor's treasury. He quickly discovered that paper was easier to print than gold to coin.

That's the way it's been ever since. Periodically, as the printing press has made inflation rampant, prophets have preached a return to a gold standard as to some Garden of Eden. At times they have succeeded, but never for long.

The British held to it for most of the nineteenth century, making the pound sterling the world's most trustworthy currency and giving Britain a prosperity the world envied. In our country, after the greenback inflation of the Civil War, we returned to the gold standard in 1879, launching an era of industrial expansion. Except for some bending in World War I we remained on it until 1933, when President Roosevelt abandoned it and even made it illegal for ordinary citizens to own gold except in jewelry.

Recent history is more familiar. The Bretton Woods conference created a "gold exchange standard" as between nations, hoping to anchor the relative value between currencies. This lasted until President Nixon ended the payment of gold for dollars even between countries.

That link between gold and dollars severed, people were again permitted to own gold. Whereupon to the astonishment of our governors (and most economists) this "useless" metal which once sold for $32 an ounce now sells for more than $400, a rough measure of what's happened to the value of our paper dollars anchored to nothing.

Thus history makes a solid argument for a return to a gold standard. Wherever and whenever it's been held to, the people have prospered. They're induced to save money, trusting it to retain its value. Commerce is encouraged because a price bargained today will be good tomorrow. Industry more readily expands because it can calculate today the cost of a plant to be finished five years hence. The laborer knows today's wage will suffice for tomorrow's food.

It's argued by the objectors (economists as well as politicians) that we've no need of the gold-standard discipline if our monetary authorities will discipline themselves. This is doubtless true, and for the moment anyway our governors seem to be trying to do just that. But on the morrow our governors may change—or even change their minds.

However, history also reminds us how fragile this gold standard is. Even within its restrictions, it can be tampered with. Just as kings could clip their coins, modern governors can stretch the amount of currency issued against their gold holdings and it will be a time before the people know it. And there also comes a day—inexorably, it would seem—when the shackles of the gold standard become too frustrating to those restrained by it.

The excuse can be war; no nation ever fought a major one without debasing its currency. Or it can be only the desire of politicians (or the pressure on them) to do "good things" which is frustrated by a restricted money supply. Then the cry goes up that we ought not to be "enslaved" by a foolish and outmoded adherence to the "myth" of gold.

Out of such musings comes my skepticism that we will in fact return to the gold standard, however much glittering talk is heard about it. Or, should it happen, that the adoption will last. It chafes too much for either governors or the governed to long endure it.

October 28, 1981

THE POOR AND THE RICH

What this country needs is an official definition of who's rich. The federal government out of its compassion defines who's poor. In fact, it has a number of definitions of who's above or below an official poverty line, depending on whether you are talking about food stamps, Medicaid or Social Security.

For example, to be eligible for Medicaid—that's the poor person's version of Medicare, which covers hospital bills without payment of any premiums—a single person's income must be below $2,100. For a family of four, the equivalent poverty line is anything below an income of $3,396.*

If you're applying for food stamps, a single person can't have an income of more than $4,320. With a family of four, you're considered poor enough to be eligible if your income is less than $10,922. Unless, that is, one member of the family is over sixty years old and drawing Social Security, in which case the rules are different.

As for Social Security itself (assuming you've been paying Social Security taxes during your working life), you're eligible to have it pay off at sixty-five if you don't earn more than $5,500. Moreover, if in any month you earn more than $270 your benefits are cut equivalently for that month and you'd jolly well better tell the government about it. When you get to be seventy-two, happily, you can earn as much as you can without losing any benefits, which is generous of the government.

The inverse of all this doesn't apply. That is, if you've a family of four and earn $11,000 no one considers you "rich"—neither the government nor your neighbors—even though you don't any longer get food stamps.

All this is a bit confusing but at least the government is making some

*Since 1980 all these figures have been adjusted and seventy is the age at which one can draw Social Security regardless of income.

effort to define the poor so we can know, officially, who is and who isn't. But where's the official line that separates the "rich"? Nobody knows. That leaves a great many higher income people in a sort of limbo.

This may not strike you offhand as a vital deficiency in public policy. The assumption is that the rich can take care of themselves. Indeed, most people share Scott Fitzgerald's view that the "rich are different from the rest of us" and can be viewed with unconcern.

Trouble arises, however, with another aspect of public policy, taxes. Some politician is always arising to propose that we should "soak the rich," tax-wise. Just the other day David Stockman, the budget director, created a bit of a flap with a suggestion that the recent Reagan tax bill mainly benefited the rich, a remark that had the White House groaning and Democrats chortling.

What are we to think of that, and how are we going to devise ways to soak the rich, if we don't know who they are?

We could get hoist with our own petards if we simply put anyone with a larger income than our own into that category. A year or two from now, with diligent application or merely the effects of inflation, we might find ourselves at that income level and get soaked. No, we need a more precise and official guideline.

Should we draw the line, say, at a $50,000-a-year level, well above any poverty line and more than most people earn? If so, we've made "rich" people out of a goodly number of public servants paid by the taxes of the rest of us. A senator or representative gets $60,662.50 a year. A cabinet officer draws $69,600.

If we hike that line to $75,000 a year we've still got Speaker Tip O'Neill in that rich category where, presumably, he should be soaked. He's paid $79,125 and gets a free limousine in the bargain. Supreme Court justices, by the way, are paid $81,288, the chief justice $84,675.

Then there are football players, baseball players, country singers and TV personalities whose incomes run into seven figures, topping the president of General Motors and many of those "rich" big businessmen.

One problem with using any income level as a dividing line, of course, is that with the exception of Supreme Court justices (appointed for life) most earned pay is ephemeral. Reggie Jackson won't have his for long, and even Tip O'Neill could lose his a few years hence. A high income isn't to be sneezed at but it doesn't necessarily make a person wealthy, although that's the premise of those advocating soak-the-rich taxes.

There's a difference, finance-wise, between a basketball player or business executive earning a big paycheck and someone who has a high income without the bother of working.

That opens up a whole new can of worms. J. P. Morgan is supposed to have once remarked that a man with a million dollars was almost as well off as if he were rich. Sadly that's not as true as it was in Morgan's day. If you had a million dollars worth of IBM stock today you wouldn't need food stamps, to be sure, but you still wouldn't do as well income-wise as Speaker O'Neill, much less Dan Rather. And even Mr. Rather, I rather suspect, would today have to consider the price before he ordered a yacht like Morgan's.

So we could, I suppose, shift from income taxes to some form of capital levy in order to soak the rich, something that's advocated from time to time by politicians and college professors who don't have to worry about it. But we're still left with the problem of whether being rich means $1 million or $10 million of stocks and bonds. Let's face it, the dollar ain't what it used to be.

That means whichever criterion we use it will have to be adjustable for inflation. Every year the government will have to refigure the upper dividing line as it now does poverty lines.

That will be tricky. But how are we going to judge the political oratory about the rich if we don't have an official definition of who is and who isn't?

November 25, 1981

THEOPHRASTUS—AGAIN

I hadn't seen my old friend Theophrastus Bombastus for over a year, and there he was, in the wee hours of the morning as usual, a shadowy figure at the end of the bed. I was in no mood for him because I was on a holiday and probably indulged too much the evening before.

He started right in. "What do you think of your man Reagan now?" he asked, obviously pleased with himself.

"He's not 'my man,'" I replied. "But he's the only president we've got."

"A profound statement of the obvious," he retorted. "All the same, he isn't the same president you had a year ago. Then he was cutting the budget and your taxes, still talking of balancing the budget. Now he's raising taxes and both the budget and the deficit are bigger."

I explained Mr. Reagan still wants to balance the budget. That's why he's raising taxes. In fact, he's urging a constitutional amendment to force a balanced budget.

"Since your man Reagan can't do the job himself," Theo riposted, "he wants somebody else to make him—or to blame it on if he doesn't. A man running away from himself needs skirts to hide behind."

I winced again at that "your man Reagan" but didn't try to wiggle away. Instead I pointed out there were still Republicans more kingly than the king, or at least as the king used to be. Some remain preachers of the original Reaganomics.

"Ah, yes," he came back. "You might say that Reaganomics has become un-Kemped. That young ex-football congressman is raising Keynes to argue you don't increase taxes in the midst of a recession."

It's just such bombastic puns, I suppose, that won Theophrastus his sobriquet. I refused to be cowed. This year's tax increases, I quoted the president, are mainly to close loopholes for the corporations and the rich.

"Such as raising taxes on cigarettes, on airline tickets to visit the grandchildren in Texas or call them on the telephone?" The question was rhetorical. "When government wants more money it eyes the simple pleasures of life, which are few, that are left to the poor, of whom there are many."

Theo then went on to tick off statistics on rising unemployment, growing bankruptcies, frustrated home seekers, shaky banks confronted with defaulting borrowers, including whole countries such as Poland, Argentina and Mexico.

So I ticked off the declining inflation, the dropping interest rates and the big boom on the stock exchange floor. Not everything is gloomy, I protested.

"Give the credit to that Kaufman fellow everybody listens to," said Theo. "The market took off when he predicted lower interest rates because business is so bad nobody wants to borrow. That's cheerful news?"

Having no ready answer I thought it best to change the subject.

At least give Mr. Reagan credit, I said, for trying to keep little wars from becoming big ones by standing up to the Argentines, the Russians, the PLO and the Israelis.

Theo grinned. "It was Maggie Thatcher, not Reagan, who stood up to Argentina. Reagan and Haig were trying to mediate that argument, which means giving a little something to both sides. If it hadn't been for Maggie the Argentines would still be in the Falklands.

"As for the Russians, Reagan is feeding them grain while trying to stop their having a gas pipeline. That's only sowed discord among our allies. I'll bet in the end the Kremlin will get both grain and the pipeline, to happy chortling in the Politburo."

Not being willing to bet on that, I brought up the Middle East. There Mr. Reagan succeeded, I said, in persuading the PLO to leave Lebanon and in restraining the Israelis in order to save West Beirut.

"Fiddlesticks!" Theo uses old-fashioned words like that, disdaining more expressive modern epithets.

"What was left to save in West Beirut? You seen those pictures on the television? What Reagan saved was the PLO. You think scattering them around Syria, Jordan and elsewhere will turn them into peace-loving folk? Begin's big mistake was that he didn't know his Shakespeare as well as the Talmud."

I looked puzzled.

"If you'd learned anything from all that schooling," he lectured me, "you'd remember Macbeth's shrewd remark. If something's to be done, it were well it be done quickly. Once the Israelis got to Beirut they should've marched right in. There'd have been cries of outrage all over the world, including from Reagan, who likes the word. But that would have spared us those long agonizing weeks. There'd have been less damage to Beirut, fewer civilian casualties. And there'd be no more PLO at all."

I was shocked by this ruthless cynicism until I realized that Theophrastus was a child of the third century B.C. He just doesn't fit into our age of enlightenment.

I sighed. "Theo, you're depressing. You see only gloom everywhere. More depression here at home. Inflation abroad as well as here. Disarray among the Western allies. Wars and rumors of wars in far-off places. No wisdom among statesmen, including our president, to lead us out of despair. To hear you tell it, the whole world is in a helluva fix."

"It is, my boy, it is," he said as he began to fade from view. Then just as there was nothing left of him except a grin like the Cheshire cat, he added quietly, "But it always has been."

I struggled out of bed, took two aspirins and vowed to be more temperate with food and drink on my next holiday.

September 8, 1982

CHAINS OF THE CONSTITUTION

One of the deepest articles of our national faith is that the chains of the Constitution securely bind our governors.

And so they do for the most part. Congress does not challenge the right of the president to veto its laws nor the president the right of Congress to override him, the procedure set down in the Constitution. Neither Congress nor the president defies the Supreme Court when it interprets the meaning of that document.

It's from this faith in the Constitution that there spring efforts to enlarge it whenever there are desires among the people unsatisfied by the ways of the president, the legislature, or the courts. We have already amended the Constitution twenty-six times, once amending an amendment. And there is scarcely a year in which there are not proposals to amend it further.

This year one such proposal, as yet unfulfilled, will again draw national attention. This is the so-called Balanced Budget Amendment to force the government to do what neither the president nor the Congress has succeeded in doing, end the spending prodigality of our governors.

It has a worthy objective. But, I fear, it puts too much faith in those constitutional chains. For those chains do not always bind as tightly as we suppose; our governors can be clever in getting over, around or under them.

For example, Section 7 of Article I of the Constitution plainly states that "all bills for raising revenue shall originate in the House of Representatives." Yet only last summer what has been called, not quite accurately, our largest tax increase originated in the Senate.

For political reasons the House figuratively shrugged its shoulders at this usurpation of its clear prerogative.

And no one thinks that the Supreme Court will invalidate all those tax increases just because they were passed unconstitutionally.

Section 8 of that same article not only gives Congress the sole right to coin money but directs it to "regulate the value thereof." When, since the creation of the Federal Reserve System, has Congress made any effort to regulate the value of our money?

Or when has any state insisted that only "gold and silver" be legal tender in payment of debts, despite the fact that this is firmly ordered in Section 10 of that first article? Just try refusing to accept Federal Reserve paper money from someone who owes you a debt.

Then there is our famed Bill of Rights prohibiting restrictions on freedom of speech or the right of the people peaceably to assemble. That same Bill of Rights also demands a "speedy" trial of all accused of crimes, something unknown in our judicial system as it in fact functions.

Finally, there is the Tenth Amendment: "The powers not delegated to the United States by the Constitution, nor prohibited by it to the States, are reserved to the States respectively, or to the people."

That amendment has been a dead letter since the day it was adopted in 1791. Had it not been stillborn, people would not be now complaining about too much intrusion of the federal government in every aspect of our lives, commercial and personal.

I mention all this not to disparage the Constitution, which for any failings in its observance nonetheless remains the most durable political document of history. Nor to object on principle to future changes in it. A living, changing society must from time to time take a fresh look at the fundamental charter that governs it.

But these examples serve as a caution that all is not immutably fixed simply because of a clause in the Constitution. They remind us that politicians can be very ingenious in finding ways around the ties that supposedly bind.

This has some bearing on the proposed Balanced Budget Amendment. Supposedly it requires Congress prior to each fiscal year to adopt a statement of receipts and expenditures and see that the latter do not exceed the former by the end of the fiscal year. Indeed, the president as well as Congress is enjoined against an excess of expenditures.

But the appearance of rigidity is deceiving. Perhaps expenditures can be calculated a year in advance, although they've never been so accurately. Receipts can only be guessed at wildly, for they are imponderables of the economy. What if they don't match? Do we recall the Congress? Impeach the president?

So the proposed amendment itself has to offer exceptions and procedures for escape. This would, in fact, be a longer amendment than any of the twenty-six adopted and more complicated in language. It requires more than an act of faith—it takes considerable naivete—to believe that it would become an iron chain to bind the government to a balanced budget.

Even Milton Friedman, its most ardent supporter, no longer promises that it would assure us a balanced budget. The best he can argue is that support for it, and its possible approval by Congress and the states, would show a popular will for a balanced budget. And the politicians do follow the election returns.

This much, I concede, can be said for the drive to popularize it. There is no gainsaying that the government's budget is out of hand, with spending increasing every year, with deficits rising and the national debt mounting. We've had only one balanced budget in a generation, and that by accident. None is in prospect from either this president or this Congress, and small hope from their successors.

But the fault lies not altogether with either the president or the Congress. The people pay lip service to a balanced budget but when they see the billions that must be cut from expenditures or the taxes that must be paid to achieve it they are as reckless as any of our politicians.

Let us all pray for fiscal sanity. But a little skepticism, please, about a mere declaration for it. Even our Constitution is a document men have chosen to honor or ignore as the spirit moved them.

January 12, 1983

MR. MICAWBER IN WASHINGTON

Everybody agreed, including his patient wife, that Wilkins Micawber was a most improvident fellow. He kept spending money he didn't have until he wound up in debtor's prison.

Mr. Micawber himself said the trouble was he didn't follow his own advice. It was he, you'll remember, who told David Copperfield: "Annual income twenty pounds, annual expenditure nineteen pounds—result happiness. Annual income twenty pounds, annual expenditure twenty pounds nought six—result misery."

Unexceptionable advice, to be sure, but like most copybook maxims easier to honor than to follow. Micawber preferred the pleasures of spending, waiting confidently for "something to turn up" to rescue him.

Dickens reports that Micawber fled to Australia. I have a feeling that by now he's gone to Washington, at least in spirit, to be with other congenial spirits. There he'll find a whole town of merry spendthrifts. It's not that they don't honor Micawber's maxim. It's just that, like he, they find it easier to spend what they haven't got.

There's nothing new in that, of course. The first president I remember to preach the Micawber message on government spending was Franklin Roosevelt. He held Herbert Hoover to be a profligate and vowed to return frugality to government.

That lasted less than a year, and before he was through Roosevelt had outspent all his predecessors and increased the government debt by multipliers hard for his successors to match, including President Reagan.

No president since then, or presidential aspirant either, has preached profligacy; all have promised economy. A few, like Eisenhower, even managed to balance income and expenditure for a brief year, by accident if not design. But year after year, in good years or in bad, the government's debt has moved relentlessly upward.

Jimmy Carter went so far as not only to promise a balanced budget but to put a date on when he would achieve it. He didn't make it and left behind still bigger debts.

Ronald Reagan wasn't to be outdone. "We must move boldly and quickly to control the runaway growth of federal spending." He promised this would lead to future budget surpluses. That was about a month before his election. This month he proposed the biggest peacetime spending ever, with the biggest deficit.

It's unfair to blame all this on presidents, though. Year after year Congress has appropriated more spending money than presidents have asked for. It will doubtless do so again this year.

Nor are the rest of us blameless. Mrs. Micawber, that genteel lady, would faint over the prospect of financial ruin and then cheerfully eat with relish expensive breaded lamb chops downed with a tankard of ale, all bought from pawned silverware. We too may feel faint at the government's horrendous fiscal figures, but we happily gobble up whatever morsels come our way from that government spending and cry in pain at any diminution of our own particular "entitlements."

The nub of the matter is that no more than Wilkins Micawber do we really believe that misery will overtake us from our wastrel ways. After all, how long has that been going on—fifty years? And where are those woes that killjoys warned of?

Here we are with deficits measured in hundreds of billions (some of us remember when one first touched a billion) and debt measured in trillions. Yet here we are also, just as Mr. Reagan says, enjoying prosperous times.

The inflation rate is down, so is unemployment. So, too, are interest rates from a couple of years ago. Likewise the cost of living. Meanwhile most wages are up, as are business profits.

Moreover, even the gloomier forecasters expect the momentum of recovery to continue into 1984. There are expected to be further drops in unemployment, further rises in corporate profits and real personal incomes.

Opinions differ on what happens after that. Democrats see only woe and misery ahead. While President Reagan concedes both deficit and debt are too high, he thinks the economy can absorb them without disaster. Non-political economists seem to worry less about current deficit and debt than at the prospect that both will continue to increase. The stock market, for whatever that's worth, certainly acts nervous.

All I can say, not being an economist, is that I've never heard of an individual, a bank or business, or a government that kept on continually spending more than it took in that didn't ultimately get into trouble. I've no doubt that the United States with all its resources will take longer than, say, Brazil. I doubt very much that we are immune from the Micawber principle.

So I'm happy to hear all this talk in Washington about provident copybook maxims. What makes me nervous is that this leads mostly to talk about boosting my taxes. Doing that would only give Washington more money to spend. Nobody—Democrats or Republicans, president or Congress—is actually doing anything to get expenditures down to fit the actual income.

Just hoping, I guess, that something will turn up to spare us any miseries.

February 22, 1984

VIII

Trials on Trial

FAIR TRIAL—FOR WHOM?

There are two tales told by Robert Morgenthau, district attorney for New York County, that are worth pondering.

One of them, as recounted by Mr. Morgenthau in a recent issue of *Barron's* magazine, is of an informant who told the Bureau of Narcotics that a heroin "drop" would take place one day at the corner of 116th Street and Pleasant Avenue. A man carrying a *New York Times* with heroin concealed in it would cross the street and pass the newspaper and its contents to another man.

Two bureau agents watched the corner and saw the first man, who met the description, pass the newspaper to a second man. The agents arrested both and found the heroin.

When the case came to trial this evidence was disallowed and the case against both men—the man who passed the heroin and he who received it—was dismissed by the judge.

The reason given by the judge, and upheld by an appeals court, was that the informant who told the police about it was not, in Mr. Morgenthau's words, "a person of known reliability."

The second story, also told in that *Barron's* interview, was of a call to the New York Police Department from a local bar reporting that there was a man at the bar, wearing a red shirt, who was brandishing a gun. The police responded, found the man in the red shirt who was wielding a gun as reported. He was arrested but again the evidence against him was disallowed on the same grounds, that whoever called from the bar was not a person of "known reliability" to the police.

In neither case was the validity of the evidence as such disputed. The courts' ruling was that the manner of obtaining it—that is, from a "tip" from a person of unknown reliability—violated the defendants' rights to a fair trial under the Fourth Amendment, which prohibits "unreasonable" searches and seizures.

Imbedded in these two tales are some knotty questions about justice in our society. There is, first of all, the question of when it is reasonable and when it is not for the police to search and seize evidence. Beyond that is the larger question of what constitutes a "fair" trial.

We certainly do not want the police to go about promiscuously searching people with no reason for doing so; that is why we have that Fourth Amendment as part of the Bill of Rights. But it is proper to ask, I think, whether the police are to be barred from even investigating information that comes to them simply because the person giving it is not one previously proven reliable. That puts a heavy burden upon the police in investigating crime; they cannot be everywhere at once and they cannot know in advance everyone in a bar who may witness a crime and call them.

This question, difficult as it is, is wrapped inside another. What is a "fair" trial? "Fair" to whom?

We instinctively think of the fairness of a criminal trial in terms of the defendant and the defendant only. If the defendant is acquitted, we hardly ever challenge the "fairness" of the trial. Acquittal is seen as almost prima facie evidence that justice has been done.

There are historical explanations for this attitude. But in guarding against the danger of abuse of the police power, we have somehow lost sight of the fact that there are two parties in every criminal trial and justice is not done unless it is "fair" to both parties.

One is the defendant. The other party is society, you and I. Mr. Morgenthau, or any other prosecutor, represents our interest; he is our counsel before judge and jury. Our interest is, first of all, that the criminal laws be obeyed. If they are not, then that transgressors be brought to book.

This view, too, has a historical basis. Once there was a time when crimes against persons—murder, rape, mayhem—were not thought the king's business. They were considered torts to be rectified by civil action, or, perhaps more likely, by personal retribution. It was in the slow growth of the English common law that there arose the concept of the "king's peace," that an injury to any person was an injury to the realm to be prosecuted by the king's ministers.

Today in many jurisdictions criminal trials are still called "The People versus So-and-so" in recognition of the fact that we the people are party to the trial. It follows, though we sometimes forget it, that fairness in the courtroom means that the evidence and arguments of both parties be fully presented. If it becomes otherwise, the order and stability of society break down.

We must insist, as we always have, that no one accused be judged guilty until a jury of ordinary citizens is so convinced and that the burden of proof rest upon those who accuse. The problem, still unresolved both in law and in our sense of equity, is what evidence of guilt may fully be laid before the jury.

Our courts have been diligent, as they should be, in protecting the rights of an accused so that no person will be judged guilty on rumor, hearsay or evidence of questionable origin or dubious credibility. Our police, our prosecutors are almost unique in the world in the limits put upon them to safeguard against the injustice of star chamber proceedings.

Yet it is not amiss to wonder, as Mr. Morgenthau does, whether the courts have not gone so far in this direction as to injure society. That is at least a proper question to put when our city streets cannot be walked safely by you and me.

We cannot pretend, and certainly I do not, that it is a question easily answered. It's one we must continually wrestle with. But we will come closer to resolving it if we remember that in every criminal trial there are always two parties to be fairly heard and to whom justice should be done.

August 8, 1979

THE EMPTY-MINDED JURY

"Can a suspected criminal such as John Hinckley receive a fair trial after being convicted in the headlines?"

The question is from an ad in *TV Guide* for a television program examining what it calls a "provocative question." It's rather badly put because every story I've seen in newspapers or on TV has referred to Hinckley only as the "accused" or "alleged" attacker of President Reagan.

Nonetheless, the same question involving pre-trial publicity has been raised in various forms ever since Jack Ruby shot Lee Harvey Oswald in a Dallas jail. In that case, for the first time, a murder took place not only in a crowd of witnesses but in the full glare of the television cameras, there being hardly a citizen of the country who did not see those pictures.

The same thing happened in the attempted assassination of President Reagan and now, most recently, in the attempt on the pope's life. In those circumstances, if we are to ask whether those accused can receive a "fair trial" we are going to have to re-examine the concept of a fair trial. Doing so, we'll have to look again at some prevalent ideas about what makes a trial fair or unfair.

One is the concept of the "empty-minded jury." That is, the idea that the jurors in a criminal case should have no prior knowledge of the crime, of the accused or of the witnesses to be heard. In current trial procedure a prospective juror can be disqualified if the lawyers think he may have knowledge about almost anything connected with the case.

Another question buried in popular ideas about a fair trial: Fair trial for whom? Most of the time we only raise the question in terms of a defendant. We've almost forgotten that in every trial there are two parties, not just one, and that to be fair a trial must be fair to both.

For a long time in history the redress of an injury against a person, including murder, lay in a civil suit for damages by the injured party or his family: It was considered a tort in legal terms. Then kings began to realize they had a stake in the peace of the realm and so they became parties to what we call criminal cases. From "the king versus John Jones" we came in time to substitute "the people versus John Jones."

In short, then, in every criminal case the people, all of us collectively, are a party at the trial. We have wisely done everything we could to ensure fairness to an accused for we are aware that kings, or whoever governs the realm, are capable of injustice. But in so doing, we've sometimes forgotten we all suffer from any murder because each touches on the safety of every man. To be fair, a trial needs be as fair to "the people" who accuse as it does to whomever the people accuse.

The current idea of a trial as a presentation of evidence before a jury totally ignorant of the case is of relatively recent origin. The forerunners of the modern jury were the "jurata" of Norman times, men called to help decide a case because they were familiar with the matters at issue. Its weakness was that a king's ministers would rarely choose jurata unfriendly to his side of the case. The substitute, slowly evolved, was the jury of freemen chosen by lot.

In the English common law they were always freemen of the same county. They were locally chosen precisely because local jurors would have some knowledge of local affairs, of the character and reliability of any witnesses and even of the character and history of the accused.

This idea carried over when we drafted our Bill of Rights. The Sixth Amendment—the one which calls for a speedy as well as a public trial, for the right of an accused to witnesses in his favor—also includes an almost forgotten phrase. It provides that the jury shall be drawn from "the state or district wherein the crime shall have been committed."

The intent was to avoid having an accused person's fate put in the hands of strangers in some distant court knowing nothing of the circumstances, nothing of the accused, nothing of the witnesses. There was no feeling, either among the developers of English common law or among drafters of the Sixth Amendment, that an impartial trial could not be had before jurors already acquainted with the case. Quite the contrary.

But somewhere in the evolution of modern trial procedure the substance of what constitutes a fair trial got lost in the observation of form. Impartial came to mean ignorant. A fair trial came to be seen only as one fair to one party, the defendant. The rules of evidence, the

procedure in the courtroom, the multiplication of technicalities to protect a defendant have become so complex that the rights of society
have been nearly forgotten. You never hear an outcry about injustice
after an acquittal.

This change more than anything else accounts for the rumblings of
discontent among the people about the handling of criminal cases in
our courts. There's a widespread feeling that it's becoming increasingly
difficult to bring common criminals to account. As any poll of public
sentiment will show, people are asking, What of the victims of assault,
rape or murder? What of the rights of peaceful citizens to protect
themselves against malefactors?

Yet now we have it solemnly asked whether there can be a fair trial
for the assailant of President Reagan because the whole world has
heard about it, discussed it and thought about it—and millions have
seen the attack photographed by television cameras.

If all that makes justice impossible through "pre-trial publicity,"
then we might as well declare an open season on presidents and popes.
A would-be assassin who acts publicly enough makes certain that no
venue anywhere can assemble an empty-minded jury.

May 27, 1981

MADNESS AND MURDER

The facts have never been in dispute. Some hundred spectators saw John Hinckley shoot President Reagan, a Secret Service agent, a police officer and presidential aide James Brady. Moreover, the action was captured by TV cameras and the whole country has seen the tapes played over and over. So the witnesses are legion.

The president, fortunately, was not killed and the two security officers have recovered from their wounds. But James Brady, though alive, suffered brain injuries from which he will suffer for the rest of his life. The intent, if not the result, was murder.

It was a year before Hinckley could be brought to trial, a comment itself on the law's delay. When he was, the defense plea was that he was insane, emotionally disturbed or temporarily deranged, depending on one's choice of phraseology.

That too, it seems to me, is beyond dispute. His wild letters to an obscure movie actress and his decision to shoot the president as a way of attracting attention, all this is not the mental or emotional state of a "normal" person.

The question, then, was not whether he did the deed, firing wildly at the president and those around him, or even whether he was sane enough to understand what he was doing, that is, to know right from wrong. For the few moments in which he fired wildly into the crowd he surely did not.

The real question is whether madness absolves a person from responsibility for his acts and therefore makes him not guilty in the eyes of the law. That was the question before the jury. It is also a question for all in our society, for more and more often we are seeing the plea of insanity put forward in defense of violence, including murder.

Juries are asked not only to decide whether the accused did or did not commit the crime but also to choose among disputing psychologists whether at the moment of the shooting or knifing or whatever, the perpetrator was mentally deranged and therefore "not responsible."

I am not a psychologist but I venture the thought that there is never murder without madness. John Wilkes Booth was mentally deranged when he shot Abraham Lincoln. Lee Harvey Oswald when he shot John Kennedy. Sirhan Sirhan when he shot Robert Kennedy.

The terrorists of today who go about killing people at random with bombs and machine-gun bursts are madmen all, killing for the sake of killing whatever "cause" may be locked in their psychotic minds. Psychotic is the only word for the Manson family killers or those who, passing an old man on a bench, cut him up to see the blood flow. If insanity is a defense, they are all innocent.

This is also true, though in a different way, of those who commit spur-of-the-moment violence, or what the law refers to as "unpremeditated murder." The man standing at a bar who in the heat of an argument stabs the person next to him, quite possibly a friend, may ordinarily be the most placid of companions. Afterward he may be truly contrite.

So also with the woman who suddenly, to the surprise of all, shoots her husband. Or the teenager who takes gun to both mother and father. Most of these are never thought of by anybody ahead of time as being insane. Neighbors brought to testify will bear witness that he or she was known to them as a quiet, pleasant person.

Yet these people too can rightly be called at least temporarily deranged, whether by a flash of anger, a fit of jealousy or the bursting of resentment at some parental action.

This is true as well of those cases in which a jury may justly return a verdict of "justifiable homicide," as in self-defense. None of us, no matter how emotionally stable we think ourselves, are immune to the emotions of anger, jealousy or resentment. Nor from the emotion of fear engendered by facing a would-be attacker or one threatening those we love.

In short, every act of killing involves an abnormal mental state, however briefly. Given sufficient provocation any of us might succumb. What restrains most of us are the behavioral inhibitions instilled since childhood or, for some of us, the fear of punishment. Tell me I can kill mine enemy without fear of retribution and there but for the grace of God go I.

It follows that mental derangement, or insanity, should not by itself absolve a person from violent acts, including murder. The law should not accept that alone as a plea of innocence.

It doesn't follow, though, that every murderer should be hanged or even imprisoned. Every civilized society tries to make the punishment fit the transgressor as well as the crime. He who steals a loaf of bread from hunger is judged differently from him who robs a bank from greed, the calculating or wanton killer from him whose transgression is a once-in-a-lifetime derangement. For one person imprisonment is justice, for another humaneness calls for different treatment.

Thus the jury in the Hinckley case faces agonizing questions. An obviously disturbed young man—insane, if you will—goes on a rampage shooting wildly at the president and into a crowd of bystanders, ruining the life of one of them. Should he, being deranged, be excused from responsibility for the consequences of his violence?

Should the jury answer that question "yes," finding him not guilty on the grounds of temporary insanity, then I, for one, will think it a miscarriage of justice. For if insanity, emotional disturbance—call it what you will—absolves a man from attempted murder, then no man's life is safe and all society is at peril.

June 9, 1982

TRIALS ON TRIAL

Pose the question to your neighbor: What is the purpose of a criminal trial?

If your neighbors are like mine the reply will be to the effect that a trial is supposed to get at the truth of the matter. That is, for twelve ordinary citizens as best they can to decide whether the defendant did or did not do the deed for which he is charged. That is the common view of laymen.

The law, however, sees the matter somewhat differently. It too presumes that the purpose is to arrive at a verdict of guilty or not guilty, but in the eyes of the law this is not sufficient. The manner of arriving at the verdict is as important as the verdict itself. The law's purpose is also to see that the trial is conducted with due process. Among other things that often means not all of the available evidence may be presented to the jury, no matter how relevant.

For example, the police may not burst into your house and search it on mere suspicion. They must first go to a magistrate, convince him that they have reasonable grounds for a search and obtain a warrant to enter. If they act without a warrant, any evidence of wrongdoing they may find is not admissible at a trial.

Moreover, strict observance of due process requires that if the police have a warrant to search for stolen silver, find none but find instead a supply of cocaine, that cannot be used as evidence on a drug charge. Our Constitution provides that every warrant must specify not only the place to be searched but the person or thing to be seized.

There are other examples. The use of confessions made to the police, for instance, is wrapped in many restrictions on their disclosure to the jury. Altogether these are known as exclusionary rules.

These we inherited from the common law of England. They grew there, slowly, as protection against arbitrary power which left no man's home safe and wrung false confessions from the rack and the screw.

They are, in short, fundamentals of our liberty. Yet in recent times there has come a questioning of many exclusionary rules which have been multiplied with time. Violent crime has become a growth industry and it has become harder and harder to convict and imprison malefactors. The view spreads that one reason lies in the rules which keep relevant evidence from trial juries and so criminals are freed on "technicalities."

This feeling is not without cause. Over the years there has been a steady accretion of exclusionary rules; the laws of evidence have become so complicated not all lawyers or judges are sure of them. To these have been added other technicalities which, in the name of protecting the accused, have seemed to let known criminals go free.

An example of the latter is the so-called "Miranda rule." This requires an arresting policeman to read formally to his prisoner a long list of his "rights" almost before he can ask the prisoner's name. If the policemen forget to do this, any statements of a defendant can be barred at his trial. Another is the broadening of the insanity plea as a defense against guilty verdicts. This is what won acquittal for John Hinckley though there was no doubt at all he shot President Reagan and maimed James Brady for life.

What has happened to the law, I think, is a forgetfulness that there are two parties in every criminal trial. One is the accused, a real person easily visible. The other is "the state," a seemingly impersonal and institutional entity. An injustice to the individual is readily understood. Injustice to "the state" is not so readily recognized. To many, including lawyers, a "fair trial" has come to mean only fair to the accused; fairness to the other party is forgotten.

Yet that entity "the state" is not only all of us but each of us. The person called the prosecutor is in fact a public defender. His task is to try to make our homes and streets safer by removing from society those whom twelve ordinary citizens decide have been guilty of injury to one or more members of society.

For those twelve citizens to decide is crucial to justice. They cannot decide intelligently or fairly unless they have before them all the relevant evidence. If some is excluded the verdict cannot be true or just.

This brings us back to an old dilemma. How do we let all the evidence be heard and at the same time prevent police and other authorities from obtaining it in ways that violate such cherished liberties of citizens as those against arbitrary searches and seizures, against false confessions wrung by force or guile?

I know no simple answer. But one way might be for the law to reconsider the remedy for improper actions of authority in acquiring evidence. At present the policeman who without warrant breaks down your door is rarely brought to account. Nor are those who engage in third-degree interrogation methods. To use that remedy instead of excluding the evidence obtained, if it is in fact relevant, would serve better to check arbitrary authority while permitting a jury to have and to weigh all the evidence.

What I do know is that the public sees an alarming increase in violent crime and is increasingly alarmed at what it thinks, mistakenly or otherwise, is such a tangle of "technicalities" in our courtrooms that crime perpetrators walk out of court unpunished. If this mood grows there is a real possiblity that an aroused public will demand changes which could endanger those fundamental safeguards of liberty won at such cost over so many years.

Certainly this is a problem to which lawyers, legislators and especially our courts must address themselves. For in the present public mood the conduct of criminal trials is itself on trial.

October 27, 1982

LAWS AND NASTY HABITS

When I was a college undergraduate, more years ago than I care to mention, the making and selling of whiskey was illegal. So far as I could discover that did nothing to discourage its drinking.

At any rate, there were two friendly bootleggers within easy reach of the campus, and for those unable to drive to them they would make dormitory deliveries, usually in gallon jugs. These would be handily displayed at every social gathering and almost everybody I knew partook from time to time. There were even those who partook sufficiently to become blotto.

What was perfectly legal in those ancient days was the growing, selling or smoking of what was then known by its more formal name, marijuana, or sometimes referred to as "loco weed." The traffic in and use of pot didn't become a federal crime until 1937.

Meanwhile, of course, whiskey and similar alcoholic beverages were stricken from the forbidden list by constitutional amendment. Today these are readily available from public stores hard-by my old college campus. I'm told that there is still quite a bit of imbibing among present-day college undergraduates but that drinking is now rivaled in popularity by inhaling *cannabis sativa*. To call it marijuana, or even pot, marks you as a member of the drinking generation. All sorts of "in" words have cropped up, including tea, grass, weed and Mary Jane, with new ones being invented daily by the cognoscenti.

I must leave it to the sociologists to explain fully why, in my time, drinking was a main collegiate pastime while pot smoking was almost unknown; I recall not a single "tea party" in my days in that undergraduate milieu. But I suspect some of the difference had to do with the relative charms of the permitted and the forbidden fruit.

Be that as it may, I note that the noble experiment of Prohibition did nothing to stay the drinking habit. Society was as plagued by alcoholism as it was before.

Repeal didn't end alcoholism either; it remains today a serious problem. It did, though, put the bootlegging syndicates out of business. Organized crime had to turn to other endeavors, prostitution or gambling, which were no way as remunerative. We had some years of a reduction in the breeding grounds for the lawless. There was no longer any place for rumrunners, speak-easies or sub rosa entrepreneurs of distilling or beer-making.

The crime climate changed again after the addition of pot to the narcotic proscribed list. In fact, it is now far worse. At least during Prohibition it was possible for the ordinary citizen to walk city streets with little fear of being mugged.

Not any more. The popularity of pot grew and with its wider use many people succumbed by stages to even stronger drugs, such as cocaine and heroin. Unlike alcohol these are addictive to all users, the addiction grows by what it feeds on and the need to feed it has opened a whole new wave of crime, reaching down to the city streets.

No one knows how much money is made by the purveyors of dope in its various forms but it is enormous. The newspapers are daily full of stories of the battle between our customs officials or the Coast Guard and the importers; no matter how frequent or how large the "hauls" they do no more than put a small crimp in the business. The huge sums to be made make the risks worthwhile.

That is only part of the problem. Any addiction—whiskey or dope—is a woe for the individual and his family. It becomes an agony for society when the addict, denied, must turn to criminals to sustain the habit.

The growth of crime in the streets of late is not due merely to the presence of addicts. Most of them would be harmless to others except that feeding their habit can be exorbitantly costly. They mug the passing stranger to get money to feed the addiction.

Meanwhile, a whole new occupation has been created. That of the "pusher." It pays the dope purveyor, and well, to create new addicts, especially young ones. So he will push his wares by at first selling them cheaply. Then, once his new customer is hooked, he can keep raising the price confident that whatever he asks the victim will be driven to get it. Sometimes the victim will get it by reducing himself or his family to penury, sometimes by embezzlement, sometimes by knocking someone on the head to steal a purse.

That makes for the kind of social problem that's an agony for anyone who thinks about it. The idea of making the various forms of addictive drugs, especially cocaine or heroin, freely available, is abhorrent to most people. Legally available, they would be so cheap as to be an easy temptation to the susceptible, including the young. That is why, beginning early in this century, we adopted a series of laws against narcotics, including marijuana, the weakest of all.

Yet it's the kind of problem that needs agonizing thought. We are confronted today not only by a widespread "dope" problem with an uncounted number of casual pot smokers and an equally uncounted number of addicts to the worse narcotics. We also have with it a crime problem unknown ever before, far worse in its extent and social cost than anything we knew even in the days of Capone and his kind in the unlamented days of Prohibition.

I profess to no answers. I doubt if removing the restrictions on marijuana will now reduce its use; the habit has become too widely socially acceptable. And removing all the narcotic laws won't end the habit of narcotic use; it was widespread before we had any such laws.

All I'm sure of is that nasty habits, even the worst of them, have never yet been ended by statutes and that sometimes such laws breed worse evils. And that therefore it behooves us to think much on the present condition.

June 8, 1984

IX

School Days

THE PENDULUM IN EDUCATION

C onsider two propositions. The first is that for at least two generations the educational system in this country has been falling to a
low estate (if it has not actually failed) because it was built on a false
philosophical base. The second—and one I find more cheerful—is that
within the past few years there has been a widespread effort to re-
examine that philosophical base. Many of the faults in the system have
been recognized. The pendulum of educational fashion may not yet
have swung far, but it is indeed beginning at long last to swing.

So that the reader may understand my own prejudices, let me explain their origin. I am the product of a most peculiar education, one
that will strike you at once as an anachronism. It was begun by a father
who never felt comfortable in the twentieth century. He would have
been more at home in the age of Pericles or in classical Rome. I was
thus chanting the principal parts of Latin verbs before I could read. A
six-year-old can delight in chanting *tango, tangere, tetigi, tactum* with
no idea of what they mean.

My earliest formal schooling was in a classroom run by an Episcopal minister. He still made use of those McGuffey Readers, once ubiq-
uitous in American schoolrooms. McGuffey treated children as adults,
though not yet fully formed. He believed they could understand even
difficult things if given in short doses, so when he included a dollop of
Samuel Johnson in a reader, the young student got his Samuel Johnson pure.

Thereafter, I graduated from the public high school in Raleigh,
North Carolina. It may seem strange, but in 1929 the Raleigh high
school included in its curriculum four years of Latin and an introductory course in Greek (the latter having two students in the class, including me).

From there I went to the Webb School in Tennessee, an anachronism
even in 1931. Not only did it require four years of Latin and two of

Greek before you could graduate, it also followed the dictum of its founder in every subject—"one must *know*, not *almost know*"— whether it was the dates of history or the manipulation of equations in calculus or the uses of the subjunctive in English composition. I next attended the University of North Carolina at Chapel Hill, where I majored in the classics and English literature. Indeed, I went into journalism because a nodding acquaintance with Euripides hardly qualified me for anything more useful.

With that as background, let me leap forward to the time when my two daughters were in the public schools of a Westchester County village, one we had chosen because of the good reputation of its schools. One day my elder daughter came home with word that she was going to read *David Copperfield* in her English class. I was delighted because I remembered it fondly. That evening I picked up her book to renew the pleasure, but as I read, something seemed awry. That led me to rummage among old books and find my schoolboy copy. Then I discovered Dickens's language had been "simplified." When I took this up with the principal, he was puzzled by my outrage. Much of Dickens's language, he noted, was archaic and therefore difficult for the pupils. He also explained that many of his high school students didn't go on to college, and this way they at least got the Dickens story. My reply was that they could get the story from a movie and that an acquaintance with the original Dickens was more important for those *not* going to college than for those who were. The latter might make up the deficiency later. The principal was not impressed with my argument that to let the pupils believe they had read Dickens, when in fact they hadn't, was a form of cheating.

A couple of years later, this same school employed as a temporary English teacher a young man with a master's degree from DePauw, who was working on his doctorate at Columbia. He knew his subject, was enthusiastic about it and transmitted that enthusiasm to our younger daughter. With other parents, we petitioned the school to keep him as long as he was available. It was explained that this was not possible because he had had no education courses and so wasn't qualified under New York State rules.

You won't be surprised at this point to learn that my wife and I took our daughters out of the public schools and sent them to a neighboring private school—this at a time when we could ill afford it—where they received a good secondary education, despite the fact that many of its teachers weren't "qualified" to teach in public schools. Their excellent French teacher, for example, was a native French lady who had no American schooling at all. If you wonder at the persistence of private schools in a country that provides public education at public expense, perhaps this helps explain it. Anyway, it was the beginning of my long war with the "educationists," which is not yet ended.

Let me now leap further forward in time. In 1972, after I retired as editor of *The Wall Street Journal*, I was invited to teach both journalism and political science at Chapel Hill—neither of which, incidentally, I had ever formally studied. I found the university much changed from my own undergraduate years. For instance, I discovered it was possible for a student to get a bachelor of arts degree either without studying mathematics or without learning a foreign language—any foreign language, never mind that Latin or Greek bit. That is, a student could take *either* mathematics *or* a foreign language, the one being accepted as a substitute for the other.

The political science course I was to teach was "Modern American Politics." In explaining it to the departmental faculty meeting, I said students could not understand politics of the 1970s well without some understanding of the New Deal period of the 1930s. The faculty approved the course, but afterward one of its distinguished members came up to me and remarked that they had abandoned "the historical approach to political science." I held my tongue in deference to my betters.

But the real shocker came in journalism. At Chapel Hill a student may not enter the journalism school until at least his junior year. Yet I found that so many of the would-be students were so poorly prepared in spelling and the fundamentals of English grammar that the school had been forced to institute a required test in these subjects. It counted for no credit, a student could take it several times, but he or she had to pass it before graduation. On the average, 50 percent of the entering juniors failed the test—a simple one designed for high school graduates—on the first try. I soon learned that the students could not be blamed for this woeful situation. Many of them were bright, articulate, and no more reluctant to study than their parents had been. The problem was that they had passed through four years of high school and two of college without ever being taught their own language.

Some universities, my own included, tried to meet this problem with remedial courses in basic English for entering freshmen. Here they encountered a new problem. Too few members of the English faculty were sufficiently grounded in English grammar to teach it—or even thought teaching it important. Many felt such assignments demeaning to their academic dignity; they preferred to lecture on "Trends in the Modern American Novel." Hence, these remedial courses were left to young instructors who were products of the educational system that had created the deficiencies in the first place. With the disappearance from grammar school of the Blue Back Speller and the practice of parsing sentences, competence at spelling and the constructing of English sentences diminished. Soon only a few elderly schoolteachers— or the rare eccentric—were left to teach these skills, and the new educational philosophy discouraged them from doing so. A vicious circle had set in.

I was also invited to lead a seminar for graduate students and advanced undergraduates called "The Press and Society." Its purpose was to explore for would-be journalists, historically and philosopically, the role of the press in American society: What are a journalist's ethical obligations, if any, to the other institutions of society, including government? This is a topic much debated these days by the public and within the press itself.

I had the conceit to begin with the problem of Socrates, who disapproved of some of the laws of Athens and yet, being condemned by them, chose not to flee but to submit to his own death under those laws. On my first day, I began by asking for a volunteer to recount the story of Socrates. Dead silence. After some futile efforts in this endeavor, I asked how many had *heard* of Socrates. At this point ten of sixteen hands went up. That was something, I suppose, but I couldn't help thinking that perhaps two thousand years later Socrates was, after all, at last dead. Now ignorance does not necessarily derive from want of intelligence. If the students I encountered who had never learned the story of Socrates had other amazing gaps in their general knowledge of history and were woefully deficient in knowledge of their native language, none of this could be blamed on them. The fault lay in the education that had been offered them all the way through college.

Let me here quickly enter a disclaimer lest I be misunderstood. I do not mean to imply that the university at Chapel Hill did not offer a sound education to those students with both an aptitude and a desire to learn. In 1971, as in 1931, a student had only to ask and it would be given. The university had excellent departments in the classics, in history, in mathematics and in other areas. The problem lay elsewhere.

It began with an administration that was unwilling to take a stand on what constituted a well-rounded education. It was fearful, I suppose, of "regimenting" the students, of crushing their "individuality," of being "authoritarian." By 1971 all these words had become pejorative terms. Instead, a student was offered a sort of smorgasbord from which he might choose as he pleased. The result was that many students simply took a little bit of this, a little bit of that, and ended up with a smattering of ignorance. If they didn't like mathematics, let them take Spanish—or Swahili.

This attitude carried over into some of the departmental faculties. For example—and here I cite from the catalogue—a student could major in history with a survey course in "The World since 1945" or one in the history of Islamic civilization. Thereafter he could pick among courses such as "Women in Europe," "The Urban World in the Twentieth Century," "Race Relations in America" or "Revolutionary Changes in Contemporary China."

Each of these could be valuable in itself. My point is that it was at least theoretically possible for a history major to emerge with little grasp of the sweep of history. How could he or she understand the changing role of women in Europe, or race relations in America, without a thorough understanding of the progress of history in Europe or America in its many other aspects? And how is an undergraduate to understand the revolutionary changes in contemporary China without some prior knowledge of traditional China? A course in earlier Chinese history was indeed there for the taking but catalogued as one for advanced undergraduates or graduate students. I thought—and I think—that's putting the cart before the horse.

When I broached questions of this sort with my colleagues, I was told that a student should have had, for example, American history in high school and therefore would have no need to pursue it further unless that was the student's major interest. Like examples could be drawn from other departments—in the study of English literature for instance. As for those deficiencies in spelling and English grammar that I encountered among junior-level students in journalism, a contributing factor was certainly that many professors in other fields, such as history, paid little attention to composition faults, even in essay exams. Their interest, so they told me, was in content, not writing style. It wasn't *their* business to teach English.

I realize it's dangerous to generalize from all this and that I do so at my peril. Nonetheless, when I put together in my mind those encounters with modern high school education and my reaction to what I found at the college or university level, I cannot avoid certain impressions. One is that the root of the problem in much modern education is the idea that young people shouldn't be *required* to learn anything. The prevailing doctrine has long been that if a young person put in the requisite number of years in high school, he was *entitled* to a diploma. To set standards of accomplishment, to require the student to wrestle with something strange and difficult (as with the language of Dickens or the precision of algebra and trigonometry) was unfair, not socially acceptable.

A consequence of this practice has been the devaluation of a high school diploma. It can't be trusted to mean anything—as every college admissions officer and every would-be employer has come to recognize. The student himself has suffered the greatest loss; he has been led to think he has an acceptable secondary education, when in fact he hasn't. He has been left ill-prepared to make his way in the real world. It is also a very real loss to society. This has done particular injury to those underprivileged in their home environment. The public schools have failed to make up for the handicaps of those not reared in families where reading is a habit and learning is a family tradition.

The fault at the college level is somewhat different but alike in kind. We are all familiar with grade inflation. Here again, to give an undeserved A or B—or even an undeserved passing C—cheats the student in a subtle but very real way. It is an extension of the widely accepted view that young people should not be *required* to learn anything, to meet any standards anyone might claim are "arbitrary." This fault extends all the way to graduate school. In the graduate school at Chapel Hill we do not use A, B and C. The grades—that is, those above failure—are "passing," "satisfactory" and "honors." I've had graduate students who received a satisfactory grade come to me in much unhappiness to ask what was wrong with their paper or exam. When I've replied that they wouldn't have received a satisfactory grade if they hadn't done work of merit, they remain puzzled. If there was nothing wrong with their work, they wanted to know, why not an honors grade? I've had difficulty explaining why, at least to me, the honors grade should be reserved for those who do, not merely satisfactory, but exceptional work. The distinction escapes some students.

To what can I attribute these matters of which I complain? I think they grow out of a philosophy of education that has lately had much currency. Some of that philosophy is an improvement over what existed before and ought to be adhered to. My complaints—and I think those of the public as well—grow out of the distortions and misapplication of a changing philosophy, although I'm not sure that the public recognizes the cause-and-effect relationship.

A little more than a hundred years ago education was considered an elitist enterprise. In the late eighteenth century, Thomas Jefferson was unable to persuade the state of Virginia to provide even as little as three years of elementary education at public expense. The first public high school did not open until 1821, in Boston. It provided three years of free instruction in such subjects as English, mathematics, geography, history, logic and civics; and the curriculum included as well both Latin and Greek. It thus reflected in matter and manner the private schools already in existence. Over the next hundred years education came to be looked upon as something society should provide for all its citizens—including education at the higher levels. The University of North Carolina became the first operating university supported by state funds. The national government entered the picture with the founding of the land-grant colleges. The contribution of all these events to the welfare of society cannot be overestimated.

By the beginning of this century, under the influence of John Dewey and others, ideas also began to change as to what ought to be taught in these public schools and how it ought to be taught. Dewey's seminal work was published in 1900. Unfortunately, or so I think, Dewey's followers did not always have his common sense. "Learning by rote" became a pejorative term, as if there were any other way to learn such things as the multiplication tables. Schools sprang up to teach the technique of teaching, which indeed stood in need of improvement. Gradually, though, the technique of teaching came to seem more important than what was taught. So it is that in time we have come to have English teachers who cannot write simple English and math teachers who are lost beyond simple algebra. We have arrived at the point where holding a master's degree in English, or even a doctorate, does not "qualify" a person to teach English to high school students.

The absurdity of all this has been compounded by the populism that has overtaken education in the past generation or so. Every student, regardless of aptitude or interest, is compelled to receive the same instruction. It has become politically impossible to separate young people according to their ability. All have to be taught at the same pace. The inevitable result is that many brighter students become bored and lose interest, while others become lost in the horse latitudes of education.

At the university level, quite apart from the problem of poor preparation at the time of admission, there's another philosophical problem. Perhaps I can get at it best by posing this question: What range of knowledge does it take to make an "educated person"? There was a time, once, when that question would have been unnecessary. There was a common consensus that an educated person should feel at home with language, especially his own language and its literature, with the principles of mathematics, with the basic concepts of physical sciences, with an awareness of the progress of history from ancient times to his own and with the questions that have perplexed philosophers since antiquity. A learned person might be more learned in one field than another. But to be called an educated person he should at least have some familiarity with all areas of learning.

Then, somewhere along the way, we lost the consensus of what constitutes an educated person. One reason for this has been the proliferation of knowledge in every realm. We have long passed the point where a Jefferson could take all human knowledge to be his province. It is almost impossible now to encompass all the knowledge in one field or to have more than a superficial acquaintance with fields outside one's area of specialization. In the face of that seemingly insuperable problem, those who directed higher education threw up their hands and gave up even the concept of the educated person.

One consequence of the abandonment of this concept was the fragmentation of graduate-level education. Our universities no longer have "a" graduate school; they have many. There are graduate schools of medicine, of law, of business administration, of journalism, of library science, of education, of engineering, of social work and so on—and each with its own dean.

Now, I have no quarrel with specialization. When it comes time to take out my gall bladder, I want a highly trained person who knows where it is, how to get at it and what to do after he's found it. I respect the truly expert in any field, from carpentry to computers. But I know doctors—very competent ones—who couldn't be called educated by anyone's definition; so too with lawyers, engineers or MBAs—not to mention journalists.

That one has a doctorate in history or classical languages may not warrant any familiarity with the physical sciences or an understanding of the mathematical way of thinking. A certificate as a doctor of philosophy may disguise a woeful ignorance of Newton or Einstein, for all that these men have influenced our view of the world more than any since Aristotle or Plato. Despite the title, he or she may know little not only of those ancient thinkers but also of Spinoza, Locke, Hume or others who have thought much on the human condition. Moreover, the reading of doctoral dissertations is not a cheering experience. Usually research has been diligently done in whatever corner of learning the candidate may be pursuing—the examining committees are demanding on that point. It is the organization of the material, the effort to communicate by sentences and paragraphs, that causes disappointment.

A friend of mine is director of a university press hungry for scholarly books to publish. He is flooded with manuscripts, but few impress him with their intellectual merits. And he tells me that even when he finds one, it all too often requires the labor of Hercules to get it into presentable form through editing and rewriting. He finds that depressing, and so do I. The explanation, I think, is that the graduate schools are inheriting from the educational system below. They get the pick of the crop and at times find someone exceptional, but graduate school is too late to make up for earlier educational deficiencies. Mediocrity is mediocrity wherever you find it.

Now, having said all this, let me go on to say that I sense a change of direction, a swing of the pendulum. In my own state, North Carolina, we are abandoning the idea that mere attendance at high school entitles one to a diploma. Bodily attendance for four years will get a young person a certificate attesting to that. A diploma of graduation will hereafter be reserved for those who meet established standards. Those standards may not be of the highest level in reading, writing and arithmetic—there is much argument about how high they should be set—but some standards are better than none. A high school diploma in North Carolina, at least, will cease to be a meaningless document. The state has also established within the public school system special schools for those who are exceptionally talented in the arts, in mathematics or in other fields. It is even in the process of establishing a publicly supported boarding school to better prepare students of ability for college. In one sense this is a return to elitism in education, but it will be an individually earned elitism, not one based on family fortune or racial or other background.

New Jersey and other states are also experimenting with what are called "magnet" schools. I note with amusement that one of these, for grades one through eight, is to be called a "classical school." Translated from educational jargon, that designation has nothing to do with classical languages. It simply means a school in which there is special emphasis on reading, writing and arithmetic—once the purpose of all elementary schools.

The same changing tide is creeping into higher education. It was Harvard that began the trend toward the smorgasbord curriculum at the university level, other colleges following like sheep. Now Harvard has reversed herself, and others are again following her to school. I can illustrate this point with the new curriculum that has been approved for undergraduates at my university in Chapel Hill. Henceforth, freshmen and sophomores must complete two courses in English composition; at least one mathematics course beyond the level of simple algebra; two courses in one foreign language; two courses in Western or comparative history, which must span at least two centuries; and two courses in the physical sciences, of which one must be a laboratory course. In addition the students must take at least one course in what is termed "philosophical perspective," a set of courses that addresses questions about forms of government, the purposes of social organization and the scope of human obligations. During their junior and senior years those seeking a bachelor of arts degree must complete one additional course in each of these categories, regardless of the major field they have selected.

When this new curriculum was finally approved by the faculty, I read it with some amazement and dug up the university catalogue of 1931, fifty years earlier. As I suspected, the present proved an echo of that distant past.

If the same kind of ferment has reached postgraduate education, it has escaped my notice. But if the revolution—or rather counter-revolution—that is talked of at the undergraduate level lives up to its manifesto, graduate education cannot escape being affected.

As things are at present, clearly not every graduate student, as a product of the educational system of recent years, appears to me an educated person. That is, while their knowledge may be deep in their chosen specialty, it is limited in scope. This is not altogether a fault of graduate schools per se, but they cannot escape its consequences, and, as far as I can see, they do little to lessen the deficiencies. This seems particularly true of the professional graduate schools—law, medicine and business administration—but the other traditional graduate schools do not escape it.

What is more, while examining committees for master's degrees and doctorates are diligent in examining candidates on the quality of their research, they do not pay much attention to the willingness or ability of candidates to relate their newly acquired knowledge to broader questions, even within the general field of their specialty. The result is, all too often, dust-covered theses or dissertations, which languish unread upon library shelves—and deservedly so.

But here, too, the pendulum, I think, is bound to swing as the philosophy of education swings. We should soon begin to see students entering graduate school better prepared in the fundamentals acquired at the primary and secondary levels of schooling and with a broader perspective opened up to them by "new" undergraduate curricula. The net result, I'm confident, will be an improvement in the quality of education for those earning graduate degrees.

So I am by no means a pessimist about the future of American education. When I look at the whole continuum, from the first grade all the way through the higher levels, I see a ferment in current-day educational philosophy. Out of it is coming—slowly, perhaps, but surely nonetheless—a revolution, or, more accurately, a counter-revolution against the educational philosophy of the past half-century or more.

Two things about this counter-revolution strike me especially. One is that its seeds were not sown in academia. This counter-revolution sprang from a dissatisfaction among the people generally—parents who saw that their children, who had been exposed to eight to ten years of basic education, still could not read or write or do simple sums. The parents began to realize something was wrong, even though they may not have known what, and they began to cry for change. The best that can be said for the educational establishment is that it is beginning to respond to this cry.

The second thing that strikes me is the slowness with which the counter-revolution has reached into the upper levels of the educational establishment. It was only last year that my university re-examined, and was willing to change, its basic educational philosophy as reflected in its undergraduate curriculum. Many other universities have not done so yet. As for graduate education, it has hardly begun to change at all.

Schools of law and medicine still discourage the applicant who has sought a broad education, preferring those who specialized early with premedical or prelaw courses. The result is the lawyer who cannot write clear, concise, intelligent English even in a letter. In medicine, the rarity of a physician who is also an educated, thoughtful person makes him a celebrity, like Lewis Thomas. And what of the more traditional graduate schools? Alas, here I fear we are still turning out far too many ignoramuses.

In English departments, or at least in some of them, a student does not study novels, plays or poetry; he "decodes" them or "deconstructs texts." He does not read great literature in order to learn from the author's perceptions of the human condition and certainly not to examine and evaluate the writer's style in the use of language—no, he seeks to discover how the author performs "linguistic acts." With such jargon bandied about, who should be surprised at the turgid language of the critically acclaimed novels of today?

As for history—well, let me give a personal example: I am an adviser to a graduate student whose specialty is Soviet history from Stalin through the rise and fall of Khrushchev. He reads Russian well, as far as I can tell. He has done excellent research on that period, and I've learned much from him that I did not know before. But when our conversation turns to Czarist Russia or to the parallel political and social developments in Western Europe during the eighteenth and nineteenth centuries, he seems puzzled that I think them pertinent to the understanding of why the Communist rise took place in Russia rather than—as Marx himself thought would happen—in more industrialized Europe. His knowledge of that part of history is even more superficial than my own.

Another example: I am the official adviser to a graduate journalism student working on a paper about the history of the First Amendment, particularly its free speech and free press clauses. He is well informed on its political and judicial history since 1776. I have had to prod him, however, to go back as far as the concordance signed in 1689 by William and Mary when they were offered the English throne only on condition that they sign a "Declaration of Rights," which for the first time gave to Englishmen those rights later embodied in our own First Amendment. That hadn't occurred to him.

What is wanting in both these examples, or so it seems to me, is an understanding of the relationship between one period of history and another, of how so often ideas interlock with one another. I'm reasonably confident the same complaints could be made about graduate education in the physical sciences. I feel sure that a graduate student in mathematics suffers if he knows no language but his own and is unaware how long it took the human mind to grapple with the problem of limits—as in defining the slope of a curved line—however skilled he may be today with calculus.

In any event, I think that the next area ripe for re-examination, for a counter-revolution, is that of graduate education. It is not enough to turn out doctors of medicine who know the uses of antibiotics but have given no thought to the purpose of life; or lawyers who know all about the latest tax statute but know nothing of the long reaches of the English common law to which they are the heirs; or doctors of education who are familiar with the latest audiovisual aids but who have given little thought to the basic purposes of education; or doctors of philosophy (which should still be an honored title) who have never read a philosopher and who, anyway, think philosophy a waste of time.

I do think a re-examination of the role and purpose of graduate education will come whether or not academia wills it. A revolution, or a counter-revolution, once underway cannot be stayed or confined. We have lately seen this in the political arena, and it will be so in education; for education, too, is a political matter, not in the partisan party sense of that word but in the Aristotelian sense of being something that concerns the interests of the body politic. And I know of few things more properly the concern of the American people than the kind and quality of education we offer new generations.

What is coming to be seen is that education should not be the same for everybody, for that inevitably means education reduced to the lowest common denominator. The public is beginning to recognize that the worthy goal of equality of opportunity for every young person does not mean equal entitlement to the rewards of accomplishment.

Education is a proud tower that everyone should be free to climb; but the climber should be able to halt at any stage without loss of dignity, without stigma, without shame. Standards, therefore, should not be lowered so as to put their achievement within the reach of all. Education, at any level, does not fulfill its function if it aims no higher than mediocrity. The education of a carpenter should aim to teach the highest skills of carpentry.

That is what the present ferment is all about. At the university level we are once again groping for an answer to that old question: What makes a truly educated person? It is because of that ferment that I keep a cheerful countenance. I cannot help, though, being struck by a certain irony. From the first grade through the last, the university postgraduate, we are seeking to make progress by going backward.

The American Scholar, Spring 1983

TURMOIL IN ACADEMIA

A university—is it not?—is a collegium of scholars devoted to handing on to the next generation the accumulation of learning, diligently seeking to increase that store of knowledge, making its corridors an oasis of civilized discourse in a turbulent world.

Well, not always.

You need only attend a meeting of any faculty senate—sometimes called an academic council—to be disillusioned. Since ours is an open society you are free to do so, though you'll be expected to keep silent in the presence of your intellectual betters. What you'll find, possibly to your surprise, is as much raucous disputation as you'd expect from a congregation of sophomores.

Sometimes these disputations burst from the walls of academia into the outside world, as they have recently done at Duke University where the issue is whether it's appropriate for the university to harbor a library of historical documents.

Or, more specifically, whether Duke should accept and make available to scholars the papers of Richard Nixon, a graduate of its law school and lately president of the United States.

The suggestion was advanced by the university president, Terry Sanford, a liberal Democrat who was formerly governor of North Carolina and a political opponent of President Nixon. Mr. Sanford, no academic scholar himself, thought it would be useful to gather together the scattered Nixon papers where they could be examined at leisure by historians, political scientists or others wishing to study in depth an extraordinary time in the nation's affairs.

Mr. Sanford had no sooner made his suggestion than, to put it mildly, all hell broke loose in Duke's Gothic halls.

The cause of the turmoil, as you've doubtless surmised, is that Richard Nixon was a controversial figure throughout his political career and is our only president to have resigned in mid-term under threat of impeachment. To many in and out of academia he was, and remains, a target of opprobrium not far short of a modern Caligula.

Setting aside for the moment the validity of that judgment, you might suppose the controversial nature of his career and especially his presidency would make his papers, private and public, of more, not less, interest to scholars. They could be the raw material for hundreds of doctoral dissertations, of shelves of biographies of the man and histories of the period.

You think, for example, of poor Suetonius struggling to write his lives of the Caesars and having to rely on secondhand information from rumor and gossip. What would he have given for a full collection of the papers of that Caligula, or of Tiberius or Nero? And what a gold mine the papers of Pompey or Marcus Brutus would have seemed to Plutarch.

Yet, astounding though it may appear, it was the history and political science departments that took the lead in crying outrage against having the Nixon papers housed in the hallowed halls of Duke. They would tolerate no "memorial" on their campus to the university's most famous—or infamous—alumnus. Never mind the role he played in the nation's history.

Consider, for example, James David Barber, a political scientist and former chairman of that department. Dr. Barber has earned considerable renown writing books on "The Presidential Character," most of them necessarily written from distant observation. One of these dealt with the character of President Nixon. Does he welcome the opportunity to have at hand a mass of material to confirm (or perhaps alter) his assessment of the Nixon character? Not at all.

"We can't let our students down," Dr. Barber says. "They deserve the truth—the bipartisan truth," presumably not to be found studying the Nixon papers. And then with his gift for the elegant phrase, he adds, "I say it's broccoli and to hell with it."

Perhaps I should note that not all the opposition (the faculty voted against accepting the papers 35 to 34) seems to come from principle. Some of it lies in a complaint that the faculty wasn't "adequately consulted" beforehand; professors, it seems, can be human, simply getting their noses out of joint.

I should also note that not all the faculty shares the outrage over the Nixon papers. Some is directed at their colleagues. A sociology professor called the objectors "Duke's Moral Majority" (a pejorative phrase) and claimed they were trying to censor Nixon's papers. A professor of medicine said of the objections, "Gosh amighty, that sounds anti-intellectual."

Altogether it's been a grand uproar for the spectators, and unhappily a revealing one about the dispassionate discourse supposed to be found in the groves of academe as scholars search among the debris of history for truth, whatever it may be. It lends credence to the canard that among university professors there are some who are educated beyond their capacity.

For my part, I merely hope that somewhere the Nixon papers will find a resting place and that from them we will learn more about the man and his times. After all, he was vice-president of the United States for eight years, was twice elected president, the second time by a landslide exceeding that of President Roosevelt in 1936. If his career ended in the disgrace of Watergate it also embraced one of the major turning points in American foreign policy, the long-overdue reversal of our relations with China.

Richard Nixon was indeed a major political actor, for good or ill, on our political stage over more than two decades. We cannot wipe them from the record. And whether scholarly study confirms or revises the verdict of his time we can only profit from the examination.

September 16, 1981

SCHOOL DAYS

When the National Commission on Excellence in Education last May 1 charged that there was a "rising tide of mediocrity" in our public schools and made a plea for higher standards, there were voices raised in criticism of the commission.

Some, like the superintendent of schools in North Carolina, retorted that the accusation just wasn't so. "The charge of lax standards and misguided priorities," said A. Craig Phillips, "is a cop-out on the part of the commission." His remark reflected the view of many within the educational establishment.

Then there were spokesmen for teachers' unions who said that if the public schools were mediocre, it was because the nation didn't devote enough of its resources to education. They called for a massive increase in education spending, particularly by the federal government.

But to me the most curious reaction was from those who said demanding higher standards from public school students in reading, writing and arithmetic would be "elitism" and unfair to disadvantaged pupils.

In this context, of course, the word "disadvantaged" meant primarily blacks from lower-income families but also children from immigrant groups not yet assimilated into our general culture. These latter include the Creole-speaking Haitians, of whom there are many in Miami, or those Hispanics all over our Southwest, among other places.

To raise the school standards in the English language would supposedly penalize those accustomed to "black English" or to whom English had to be taught as a second language.

In fact, not long before the commission's report the federal government had launched a drive to require the teaching of Hispanics, Indians and others in their native language, that spoken at home.

It always seemed to me that this had the argument backwards. The public schools are not places where disadvantages are created. They are, or ought to be, the places where disadvantages are corrected. It is not "racism" to elevate educational standards. Raising them is the best way to help eliminate any vestiges of racism or discrimination and to give equal opportunity to all as they reach adulthood.

Now I find that I am not alone in so thinking. Many civil-rights leaders have begun to change their tone.

Bayard Rustin, for one, the man who organized the 1963 march on Washington, which was dominated by the eloquence of Martin Luther King. Writing in *Newsweek*, Mr. Rustin says the continuing plight of many blacks today rests not upon the old "white racism" but upon other factors: the displacement of unskilled or semi-skilled blacks in the shift from heavy industry to high-technology industry "for which many blacks are unprepared."

He has many items on his agenda for correcting this, some of them very controversial, but education is high on his list. We need, he says, a national commitment to excellence in education, including vocational training, not just for blacks but the white poor as well.

An even stronger statement aimed at blacks comes from Mayor Roy West of Richmond, Virginia, who is also the black principal of a junior high school there.

Much of what he said in a speech to students at Virginia Union University is worth repeating and heeding:

"I suggest it is time for blacks to wake up. . . . It saddens my heart, for example, when I think of the belief fostered by many that there is a value in the use and mastery of so-called black English by black students. . . . We must realize that much of our unemployment and underemployment among blacks are the results of some black Americans not being able to communicate correctly with other parts of society. . . .

"To me it is one of the worst types of discrimination to tell students that because they are black it doesn't matter if they drop their plural endings or imply there is no need to learn the English language."

Mayor West then went on to challenge the Virginia Union students in several areas of learning. First of all in English, "to master the rules of subject and verb agreement."

Then: "Learn how to factor an equation . . . learn not only the significance of America's discovery but [to think] what would have hap-

pened to this world if America had not been discovered . . . experiment with the principles of science to understand better those forces
which undergird human life."

Here, truly, is a Daniel come to judgment, and I hope that those students listen to him rather than to those who tell them that because
they are black it is unfair to ask of them high standards in the classroom. There is room for argument as to how high those standards
should be in the classroom, none that it is "racism" to require them to
be the same for all, black or white.

There are, indeed, disadvantaged students. The advantaged is one
from a home where reading is a habit, where learning is encouraged
from childhood. The disadvantaged is the child who comes to school
with none of this home background.

There is some correlation between the economic and educational
level of the parents and the home background, but it's by no means the
whole of the matter. America is rich in stories of those who came from
poor parents, even uneducated ones, and yet who rose to promi-
nence—success, if you will—in many walks of life—law, medicine, science, business, politics or philosophy. This is true of the white poor as
well as the black poor.

The school is, as it always has been, the equalizer, the only place that
can lift a child over a disadvantage. If our public schools fail, if they
teach differently black and white, rich and poor, then there would be
in truth little hope for the future of the disadvantaged.

October 26, 1983

WORDS, WORDS, WORDS

In one of those Rex Stout tales of Nero Wolfe there is a delightful scene in which Archie Goodwin, the faithful amanuensis, discovers the corpulent detective diligently tearing out the pages of a huge book and consigning them to a roaring fire.

Book burning? inquires Archie. An irrelevant question, replies Nero. "I'm not a government or a committee of censors. Having paid for this book and found it subversive and intolerably offensive I am destroying it."

What Nero Wolfe found so subversive was the then newly published Third Edition of the Merriam-Webster unabridged dictionary. What he found intolerably offensive about it was that this one-time bastion of lexicographical purity seemed to him to have surrendered to Spockian permissiveness.

"Do you use 'infer' and 'imply' interchangeably?" growls Wolfe. "This book says you may. Pfui!"

The horticultural detective may have been unfair and subjecting himself to unnecessary discomfort—he hates open fires and the chair he was sitting in was too small for his girth. He was inferring more than the Merriam-Webster implies. A careful reading of the entries for "infer" and "imply" shows that the compilers were aware of and noted the distinction.

No matter. Nero Wolfe was reflecting a widespread reaction to the Third Edition among those who care about the purity of English, or American, usage. When it first appeared in 1961 it was greeted with howls of anguish from the self-appointed guardians of the language. The tone of nearly every review was denunciatory.

What caused the outrage was not that the Third Edition recorded colloquial usages, reflecting the language as it is often written or spoken, but that in so doing it dropped the label "colloquial," leaving the unwary reader to suppose such usage endorsed by authority. Indeed, the editors quite frankly said they would not "attempt to dictate what usage should be."

Consider "like" as a conjunction, as in "Winston tastes good like a cigaret should." The famed Second Edition (1934) said: " 'Like' introducing a complete clause, or an incomplete clause in which the predicate, and sometimes the subject, is to be supplied from the context, is freely used only in illiterate speech and is now regarded as incorrect."

In the Third Edition "like" is listed as a conjunction with no suggestion of impurity amid the seemingly authoritative citations from Art Linkletter and the St. Petersburg (Fla.) *Independent*.

Ah, well; it was enough to send the Puritans to the wailing wall. It was also enough to spawn the making of new dictionaries designed to fill the vacuum left by the Merriam-Webster.

One of the best of these is the *American Heritage Dictionary*, edited by William Morris and published in conjunction with Houghton-Mifflin. The *AHD* also records colloquialisms, slang and non-standard usages (including some the Merriam-Webster modestly eschewed) but it endeavors to offer guidance between good usage and bad. To do so, it called for advice from a Usage Panel drawn from those for whom language is a professional occupation, poets, novelists, journalists, lawyers and teachers.

Now Mr. Morris, with the help of his wife, Mary, has edited the *Harper Dictionary of Contemporary Usage*, which as the name implies is less concerned with definitions in the ordinary sense than with distinctions of usage both in terms of meaning and grammar. Once more he called to his aid a panel of "experts" from the late W. H. Auden to Herman Wouk.

I must confess a certain prejudice here, since by some process of selection I served as a member of that Usage Panel. All the same, it is a book to fill a need, even if it is flawed by being a bit sketchy and sometimes whimsical in both selection and judgment. Hopefully (mea culpa!), it will inspire the Morrises or others to a more detailed and comprehensive guide.

In the present work you will find "hopefully" (in the sense of "it is hoped") frowned upon by 76 percent of the panel, "like" as a conjunction rejected by 88 percent, and the difference between "infer" and "imply" maintained by all.

Frequently the Morrises append to the verdicts the comments of individual panelists, adding spice to what might otherwise be dull reading. Asked about the confusion between "flaunt" and "flout" in a recent Supreme Court decision, Ben Lucian Burman remarked, "No wonder Roosevelt wanted to fire the Supreme Court." Said sportswriter Red Smith, "Clout the lout with a knout." (My own comment: "Let justices flaunt their opinions but not flout the Constitution.")

The panelists are not resistant to useful change. "Hassle," originally slang, is accepted by 72 percent; "hectic," originally meaning flushed or feverish, is now accepted by 78 percent in the sense of wild activity. In nearly every instance, moreover, there was a difference of opinion, with a minority voting to accept whatever new twist of syntax, whatever new solecism.

Perhaps one may ask, then, what is the point of it all? With an ever-growing, ever-changing language how can anyone say what is proper usage and what is not, and why should anyone try?

No one, least of all the Morrises, supposes that language can be frozen; that would be silly, and not in its Old English meaning of "happy." Old words vanish, new ones arrive, others change their meaning. But if there are no standards of usage, if a word doesn't mean the same thing to both writer and reader, the result is confusion if not chaos.

We are already in danger of that happening at a time when Johnny can neither read nor write intelligible English. And with political consequences, as the poet Auden remarks, because when language is corrupted people lose faith in what they hear.

So it's good to have somebody try to raise a standard to which both speaker and listener can repair. We cannot talk to one another, much less understand each other, if our words are but weathercocks shifting in every wind.

January 7, 1976

X

Persons in their Places

CHAIRMAN MAO

There are two Chinese proverbs that stick in the mind. One is: May you never live in interesting times. The other: In the steps of a great man the reeds are crushed.

They seem particularly apt these last few days as the death of Chairman Mao recalls the history of China in this century and the role he played in making it.

For if the accomplishment of prodigious feats makes a great man then he is deserving of all those eulogies. He was, as *The New York Times* called him, the architect of the revolution that made Red China. He was, as *The Washington Post* described him, "shaper of a nation and molder of a people" who strode upon a vast stage.

Perhaps he was also as he was described by an old friend, Dr. Chen Pien Li, a "gentle, sensitive man who wrote poetry." Perhaps he was for the Chinese, as one dispatch from Peking put it, the equivalent of Washington, Jefferson, Lincoln, Mark Twain and Franklin Roosevelt. Perhaps in his old age he was that benign philosopher who caught the fancy of the world and had even American college students cherishing his little red book of wise sayings.

Of the prodigious feats there can be no doubt. As the obituaries remind us, in 1920 Mao founded the Communist Party of China with a bare handful of men. Thereafter, twisting and turning with events, he nourished the party, allying himself with the Kuomintang of Chiang Kai-shek when that seemed useful, breaking with it when the time seemed right, conquering it once he had the strength.

Courage he never lacked. The long march in which he led the remnants of his defeated army from Kiangsi in the south across rivers and mountains to refuge in northwest China is now legend. Of some hundred thousand who began, only about ten thousand finished the journey, and Mao held them together by the force of his will and his personality.

He knew the uses of generosity, when it was shrewd. Once he had a chance to hold captive his arch-enemy, but Chiang was set free because Mao knew Chiang would be useful in the fight against the Japanese.

He was a superb organizer, in time building a disciplined army out of rabble. After that army and the Communist Party had mastered China, he in turn mastered party and army. In time all who would rival him vanished. In time he not only pushed Chiang across the sea but ended the influence of Soviet communism in China and made China powerful enough to send tremors through the Kremlin.

Mao Tse-tung, then, was a man who took a country, remade it by his own vision and in so doing changed the face of the world. In prodigious feats he could only be said to be matched by Adolf Hitler in Germany and Joseph Stalin in Russia, two others who shook the world.

And in one way he exceeded them both, though in a way not much dwelt upon in the eulogies.

Historians differ about the number of people who died in the great Russian purge set loose by Stalin in the late 1930s. No one kept count of the wholesale murders by the NKVD, the Soviet security service, as Stalin launched his reign of terror to bend the country to his will. Later Nikita Khrushchev denounced Stalin, and called the NKVD chief, Nikolay Yezhov, a "degenerate." But Mr. Khrushchev gave no figures on the slaughtered.

Some have put the figure at five million dead, others at a few million more. One expert on Soviet affairs, S. V. Utechin, has said that estimates of eight to ten million are probably not exaggerations.

There is equal uncertainty about the exact numbers who died in the Hitler gas ovens and before the firing squads of the Gestapo. At Auschwitz the minimum has been put at 900,000. One French investigator, himself a Buchenwald survivor, has put the total figure at 1,200,000. Some other estimates have run as high as six million.

Enough, these are figures to stun the mind and leave the world aghast. Yet they pale by what happened in China under Chairman Mao.

Here too, of course, there are no precise numbers. If the slaughtered are difficult to count in a conquered Germany, or in a Russia where there are some cracks in the curtain, they are impossible to count in a China sealed off from the rest of the world. The best anyone has been able to do is gauge the order of magnitude.

One gauge is in the figures used by the Chinese themselves at a time when Chairman Mao was trying to impress upon the people the hazards of deviationism. In one month alone Peking radio once reported that some two million Chinese had been liquidated as a warning to those who reluctantly accepted the new era. Po I-po, one-time minister of finance, is reported to have spoken of the liquidation of two million "bandits."

Other estimates range upward. The Soviet Union, admittedly not an unbiased source, has put the figure at twenty-six million. A French estimate, just for 1951–52, is three million. This counts neither the earlier period when Chairman Mao was taking power nor the period of the Great Proletarian Cultural Revolution which began in 1966.

None of these are as high as the estimate of the U.S. Senate Committee on the Judiciary after its investigation. In 1971 this committee—in the so-called Walker report—put the total Chinese death toll in all the various purges since 1949, the year Mao Tse-tung became Chairman Mao, at somewhere between thirty-two million and sixty-one million.

Take your pick. Twenty-six million, thirty-two million, sixty-one million.

As Chairman Mao has said, "A revolution is not a dinner party. . . . It cannot be so refined, so leisurely and gentle, so temperate, kind, courteous, restrained and magnanimous. A revolution is an insurrection, an act of violence. . . ." Or on another occasion, "Political power grows out of the barrel of a gun."

So along with the eulogies for a prodigious man it's worth remembering also that the Chinese have lived through interesting times with Chairman Mao. And seen how in the steps of a great man the reeds are crushed.

September 15, 1976

TWO CIVILIZED MEN

The last time a sitting president was turned out by the people in November his successor did not take office until the following March. The deepening Depression would have made that long interregnum difficult enough for the country, but the agony was aggravated because the two men, president and president-elect, could not be civil to one another.

It had been such a bitter and dirty campaign that the animosity between President Hoover and Governor Roosevelt was personal as well as political. This personal rancor aborted all efforts at cooperation, and the consequence was that for four months the country had no real government at all. Mr. Roosevelt wouldn't consult, much less share responsibility; Mr. Hoover felt too discredited to act alone.

When at last, on March 4, the new president took office, the former president was left to make his own way privately to Union Station in Washington, board an ordinary train for New York and depart without ceremony and without even Secret Service protection. Mr. Hoover, for his part, left his desk in the Oval Office bare of pad or pencil for the use of its new occupant.

This was an extreme case, but the transitions of presidential power—especially when it has been from a man of one party to another—have rarely been overflowing with civility. This makes the conduct of President Ford and President-elect Carter all the more remarkable, and all the more to the credit of both men.

Viewers of the TV series "The Adams Chronicles" will recall that neither of the two Adamses would deign to attend the inauguration of their successors, Thomas Jefferson and Andrew Jackson, respectively. Later, while civil war threatened, President-elect Lincoln and President Buchanan did not communicate with each other at all.

In more recent times relations have also been strained between incoming and outgoing presidents. Harry Truman and Dwight Eisenhower had worked closely together for years. Mr. Truman appointed Eisenhower to head NATO and once spoke to him about running for president on the Democratic ticket. Yet after the election, while Truman did ask his cabinet officers to cooperate with the Eisenhower team, between the two men personally there was neither cooperation nor cordiality.

Eisenhower, when his turn came, was ceremoniously proper with John Kennedy, but he kept referring to him as "that boy," which pretty well reflected his attitude toward his successor.

After the 1932 election we changed the Constitution so that now a new president is inaugurated in January instead of March. We will not again, therefore, face such a long period of uncertainty during the transition. Nonetheless, the gap between the choosing of a new president and his assumption of office is a peculiarity of the American political system, one that continues to haunt us.

In most countries it's a matter of "the king is dead, long live the king," with the change of power taking place in a matter of days, if not hours. In some parliamentary systems, the British for example, there is a "shadow cabinet" already in existence ready to take charge.

This peculiarity of our system carries considerable risk. Even a two-month gap is long enough for a serious crisis to arise somewhere in the world calling for clear, forceful action. Yet the incumbent is a lame duck without the political influence to match his legal responsibilities. His position is weaker still if he was himself a candidate for reelection and was rejected by the voters.

The incoming president, on the other hand, has influence as a result of his election but no matching legal power. Moreover, he rarely has even his key cabinet appointments ready until shortly before his inauguration, which further hinders consultation and cooperation between the two administrations.

It's an awkward situation at best; at worst, it could be dangerous.

Yet not until 1964 was any legislative notice taken of the problems of a transition period. That year, for the first time, federal funds were authorized to pay for the shifts of power. Until then the incoming president had to rely on left-over campaign funds or contributions from supporters to pay for these expenses.

That still leaves much dependent upon the character and personality of the two men involved, on whether they can rise above both their political differences and personal animosities, at least temporarily.

Jerry Ford and Jimmy Carter have done that in an unusual, almost unique way.

President Ford not only sent Mr. Carter a prompt offer of cooperation but followed it with firm instructions to administration officials. In a significant gesture he also put a presidential plane at Mr. Carter's disposal, set up a personal meeting and arranged for the president-elect to use Blair House, an official residence, while in Washington.

Mr. Carter, for his part, has been equally cooperative, holding a series of personal meetings with key administration officials. He also proved himself unusually foresighted for a presidential candidate, having long before the election set up a transition team to help him if he were elected. And all this has been done with remarkably good grace. Both men have put behind them the campaign rhetoric and spoken of each other with respect.

It might not have been that way. Mr. Carter might well have been a little arrogant, having accomplished an extraordinary feat in winning the nomination and election. Mr. Ford might well have sulked over his narrow defeat, believing himself with good reason a creditable president under difficult circumstances. That both have acted otherwise is a tribute to both.

All this does not remove the potential risk in that two-month gap in the transition of presidential power. We are still faced with the possibility of a crisis someday where neither the man in office nor the man about to be holds both the moral and legal authority needed for action.

But Gerald Ford and Jimmy Carter have at least bettered their predecessors and set a good example for the future. It's our good fortune this time to have on each side of the transition two civilized men.

December 1, 1976

GERALD FORD

I f there are tides in the affairs of men which taken at the flood lead on to victory, there are also ebbs which even the most valiant cannot overcome.

This week our attention is all on Jimmy Carter, who rode a flood tide on to victory and is being inaugurated as president of the United States. That is as it should be, for President Carter represents the future with all its hopes, fears and uncertainties.

But on the eve of this inauguration it seems to me we might also pause to give a moment's thought to the man who has been our president these past two troubled years. He might still be president, I suspect, if that depended only on his courage, his decency, his love for his country and the goodwill its people feel toward him. But Gerald Ford was caught in a tide which would have challenged the strongest man.

As it is, Gerald Ford will occupy a unique place in our history. For one thing, he is our only unelected president, or more accurately the only man to come to that office without having been elected either to it or to the vice-presidency. He was an appointed vice-president who succeeded to the White House because, for the first time, a sitting president resigned before his term was out.

That makes him unique in another way. He is our only president since George Washington who did not actively seek the office. The other vice-presidents who succeeded to the presidency had actively campaigned for the second office and, in so doing, had before them the possibility that it would lead to the presidency. Many of them had in fact been previously seekers of that highest office.

Mr. Ford was quietly tending his own business as minority leader of the House, having no further ambitions, when fate in the guise of Richard Nixon reached out and tapped him. Thus does fortune play its role in the affairs of men.

I don't suppose Gerald Ford will go down in those history books as one of our great presidents. One reason is that he lacks the strong ego, the personal drive and sense of overwhelming self-confidence, that marks great leaders, like Roosevelt or Churchill, and makes them want to seize the times and shake them. He proved too much the man of the legislature, conditioned by training and experience to await events rather than shape them with his own vision.

When he did try to be the mover of events, as when he proposed higher taxes to fight inflation, events outran him. The recession deepened, causing him to have to reverse himself, abandon the thought of higher taxes and propose instead lower taxes. So too another of his bold actions, the swine flu vaccine program, had to be aborted.

All that said, however, it remains true that President Ford served us well. He was the right man for the times into which fate thrust him.

It is difficult now to recapture the mood of the country that summer of 1974. But it was a time of turmoil, which saw the people divided, the government in disarray, the office of the presidency in disrepute. It is hard to think of an equally troubled time since the Civil War, save perhaps the first months of 1933.

Moreover, it was a time of a different kind of trouble. Those earlier crises called for activist leaders, men who would boldly command even at the price of causing further turmoil, as did both Lincoln and Roosevelt. What the country needed this time was a healer, and that is what it got in Gerald Ford.

It is a mistake, though, to think such times did not call equally for courage in the president. Mr. Ford has been much criticized for his pardon of Richard Nixon. For a time it even seemed to add to the divisiveness and it may have played some part in his defeat last November.

History may judge that pardon otherwise. Anyway it is not pleasant to contemplate what the country would have been put through if its former president had been dragged for many months through the criminal courts, assailed on one side by those in a vengeful mood, defended on the other by those—and they were numerous—who felt that driving him from office was punishment enough. The affair might even yet not be settled.

Be that as it may, right or wrong, President Ford's decision was certainly one that took courage, and in the end kept the wounds from festering.

It took courage also for him to send Congress that long string of vetoes, for which he was much criticized. Whatever you may think of them, it speaks well of the man that he would not sign what he could not in good conscience endorse. So also with his refusal to hypo the economy as incumbent presidents are wont to do in election years. That would certainly have been better politics. It might even have made the margin of difference last November.

That election has already been much hashed over and will be for years to come. His loss was by such a narrow margin that it can be attributed to any one of a number of causes, the Nixon pardon, the Reagan fight, the conflicts with Congress, the economy, the charisma of Jimmy Carter. Most likely it was a combination of all these together, which coming together created a neap tide on which his fortunes foundered.

The surprising thing is how close this man came to overcoming it all. And perhaps what is more remarkable is that he leaves his office with a reservoir of good feeling among the people unmatched by any other defeated president.

Of course he also leaves that office, as every president does, with unsolved problems for his successor. But people recognize, I think, that he led the country through an extraordinary time. In his two years the inflation that threatened has been dampened, the recession much abated. Most of all, his calmness, his civility, his obvious integrity, have restored to the people their trust in the presidency.

So Gerald Ford bequeaths a good legacy to the country and to Jimmy Carter. And for that President Carter and the rest of us owe him a debt of gratitude.

January 19, 1977

VALIANT IS THE WORD

It was the Sunday before the Democratic Convention in 1968. Vice-President Hubert Humphrey was on "Meet the Press" in Washington that midday and after the television program he invited some of us who had been his questioners to fly with him to Chicago.

We all knew that the convention was going to nominate Hubert Humphrey for president of the United States despite the rival candidacies of Senators Eugene McCarthy and George McGovern. We also knew, though, what Mr. Humphrey would face when he got to Chicago.

In Chicago there would be 12,000 Chicago police, 7,500 regular Army troops, an equal number of Illinois National Guardsmen and a thousand FBI and Secret Service agents to try to keep order in the city. The convention site itself would be surrounded by a barbed-wire fence with armed guards patrolling it. Around the convention hall there was a security ring several blocks wide.

Downtown, Vice-President Humphrey's hotel would be equally cordoned off by police and the Secret Service. All this to protect the city and the convention from angry Vietnam war critics who might erupt at any time into violence. For the first time in American political history a major party would meet in a state of siege to nominate its candidate for president.

It was a prospect that cast a pall over the vice-president's plane. For once the accompanying newsmen did not importune him for interviews, instead talking quietly among themselves wondering what thoughts were in Hubert Humphrey's mind.

Mr. Humphrey sat to one side, quietly speaking to his wife and now and then to one of his aides. There was a sadness in his face. He had at last within his grasp one prize he had so much sought, the Democratic nomination for president. But what it would be worth neither he nor anyone else knew.

Yet as the plane readied for landing, he got up, put on a little makeup for the TV cameras and squared his shoulders. As the ramp came down, he stepped out smiling and waving to the small crowd that had been permitted there to welcome him. His only comment to the newsmen, made with a grin, was, "Well, here we go!"

Now Hubert Humphrey is dead. His body has lain in state at the Capitol so the nation could honor him. All the eulogies have been spoken. From around the world the tributes to him have poured in. But somehow there is an unreal air about all those honors. What sticks in the mind are the little vignettes, glimpses caught of a man who could dream so much and still smile when he saw dreams shattered.

Chicago in 1968 was not the first time he had heard the sound of battle. Twenty years before, in 1948, he had been at the center of another battle at a Democratic Convention. Then the young mayor of Minneapolis, he had sponsored a platform amendment calling for congressional action to guarantee equal rights for blacks in voting and in job opportunities.

It was a cry ahead of its time. As a result of it some Southern delegates walked out of the convention and later in Birmingham nominated their own candidate for president on the States Rights ticket. Many in the sweltering press gallery that day thought Mr. Humphrey might have cost Harry Truman the election, but all of us marked him down as a man of whom more would be heard.

More, of course, was heard of him. The obituaries have told at length how many times he came near to that Democratic nomination only to see it slip away, as in the end the presidency did when at last the nomination was his. But there never was any doubt in all that time that Hubert Humphrey was an unbowed warrior. Defeated in 1968, though by the narrowest of margins, he turned again to the Senate.

The obituaries have also reminded us of his long battle with cancer, beginning in 1967 before that anguished plane trip to Chicago. In 1976 his bladder was removed, and when later a new growth was found it was described as "inoperable." The euphemism did not fool him. He knew he was dying. So too did those who saw him in this time; it was written in the gauntness of his once cherubic face. He accepted this as he accepted political defeat, but he bowed to the one no more than to the other.

I have no idea whether Hubert Humphrey would have made a good president of the United States. There was always a small-boyish quality about him. He burbled over with enthusiasm when things were going right and was still irrepressible when things went wrong. He was too much a nonstop talker to be a good listener, and there was some truth in the comment of his critics that he had solutions for problems that hadn't yet been found.

All this was part of his charm. It did leave people wondering sometimes how he would handle the presidency if he ever got it, and it may have had something to do with why he was defeated by men of more serious mien.

More likely, though, he was defeated because for him the times were out of joint. He was too early in the vanguard of the civil rights battle. He was already an old face when he tried the race against Jack Kennedy, and that at a time when the country was ready to show it would elect a Catholic president. As Lyndon Johnson's vice-president he was perforce too late in disentangling himself from the policies on Vietnam which for four years he had loyally defended.

But all that is of no matter now. History is as history was, and I will leave it to others to decide in due time what his place should be in it. There have been these past few days enough eulogies for any man.

What I am sure of, though, is that sometime near the end he squared his shoulders and said to himself, "Well, here we go!"

Valiant is the word for Hubert.

January 18, 1978

THOSE MEMOIRS

Few people, I daresay, would put the memoirs of generals or politicians on their lists for summer reading along with that Agatha Christie mystery or the adventures of Travis McGee.

So it was with some surprise, especially after the dreadful early reviews, that I picked up those memoirs of President Nixon on an August evening and found myself engrossed. Perhaps I should have paid more attention to the readers who put them on the best-seller list than to the critics.

Of course the critics were right on some points. There are no great new revelations to change anyone's mind about Watergate. Mr. Nixon does have a selective memory, and there is self-serving in much of what he recalls and recounts. Finally, he's not a sparkling writer.

But autobiographies of public figures are seldom otherwise. From U. S. Grant to Harry Truman, they offer an *apologia pro sua vita*. As for prose stylists, Winston Churchills are rare among that company.

What makes the Nixon memoirs nonetheless engrossing is simply the tale he has to tell. It is certainly full of adventures; some would call it picaresque. It ends in mystery. And it sets the mind to brooding.

Consider the bare outlines of the plot:

A young man from a poor family, spurred on by his mother, gets an education at an obscure liberal arts college and a then small Southern law school. He has a respectable but undistinguished career in the wartime Navy. He answers a want-ad for a sacrificial candidate for Congress, puts on a shrewd and tough campaign and, astonishingly, wins. A few years later he takes on a popular senator and, once again, wins to everyone's astonishment.

In the Senate he is just another young newcomer until fortune pits him against a shining Lochinvar whom he helps destroy. That makes him a national figure. It also brands him among many influential people as a rough, even unscrupulous, man of ambition, a brand that burns into his consciousness and is to stay with him the rest of his life.

Another twist of fortune propels him, at the age of forty, into the vice-presidency under a national father-figure. He tries for the presidency himself but fails by the narrowest of margins in an election still disputed. He is, so everyone thinks, a discredited, political discard.

Eight years later he miraculously returns to win the presidency in another narrow election, the first man in modern history to succeed after a first failure.

As president he is faced with the nation's most unpopular war, begun by his predecessors. Every effort to end it is controversial and increases the bitter division among the people. There are riots in the streets, and he is excoriated in much of the nation's press.

Nonetheless he is reelected in a landslide. Then at the very peak he meets disaster. He becomes the first president in history driven to resign that office.

There must have been temptation on the part of the writers helping Mr. Nixon pull his memoirs together to liven up his prose. To their credit, they seem to have resisted. One has the feeling throughout the book that these are Nixon's own words, and you are carried along by the intrinsic melodrama of the tale.

The melodrama is lightened by little vignettes of the dominant figures of his time he came to know—Churchill, de Gaulle, Khrushchev, Mao Tse-tung. These are interesting in themselves and often perceptive in their insights.

You also get an inside view, at least from one man's perspective, of some of the great events that, for good or ill, changed the world. No doubt about it, this man played a role on a huge stage.

The mystery, of course, lies in the wild improbability of the denouement. The basic facts of Watergate, I suspect, are now well known. Anyway, few episodes of like historical importance have been as subjected to so much contemporary probing. What we are left with is not a puzzle of what happened but the riddle of why.

Richard Nixon's enemies have a facile answer. To them he is simply a bad man, or a shallow one, caught in a web of his own machinations.

Yet his refusal to contest that election of 1960, with so much evidence that it was stolen from him, is not the posture of a man whose ambition is totally ruthless. He showed a deep regard for his country in his unwillingness—despite the urgings of advisers—to put it through long weeks, perhaps months, of political agony.

Nor can you follow the process that led Richard Nixon, of all men, to the gates of Peking and not see there a man of considerable vision. His account of it is fascinating as narrative and impressive in its grasp of the realities of a changing world.

Truly an extraordinary man, able, bold, idealistic, petty, at once clear-eyed and self-delusioned, confident and beset by doubt, capable of greatness and tragically flawed. There are glimpses of all in the story told by himself.

The fatal flaw was blindness to Watergate until it was too late. By then he was ensnared, and every twist and turn only sank him, help-less, deeper into the morass. If there is self-pity in his account of it, that doesn't lessen the human drama.

Indeed, the more you brood upon it the more it begins to echo an-cient myths; in another time it would have been the stuff of legend. The legend of a man driven by the furies to assail great heights and who, once upon them, begins to find all mysteriously coming apart, as Icarus's wings melted in the sun.

Not even the dreariest writing drudge could make such a story dull.

August 30, 1978

PRESIDENT REAGAN:
A REMARKABLE MAN

R onald Reagan continues to confound all who watch him, friends
   or critics.

The events of Monday were but the latest example, impressive though
that was. Here was a seventy-year-old man with a bullet in his lung,
walking under his own steam from car to hospital emergency room.
There he underwent more than two hours of emergency surgery and
emerged from it in a condition that would have been remarkable for
one half his age. Even the doctors who attended him were astonished
at the stability of his vital functions, presaging a rapid recovery. One of
them noted that his "physiological age" belied the calendar.

So much for those who feared he might be too old for the presidency. His foes tried to make his age a major issue in the campaign, his
friends and supporters were nervous that he might not be physically up
to the demands of the presidency. We are not likely to hear of that
again any time soon.

Mr. Reagan is the fifth U.S. president to be the target of an assassination attempt in this century, beginning with McKinley in 1901
and running through the two attempts on Gerald Ford. Just why this
should be so in this country, of all countries, must remain a puzzle. The
targeted presidents have been both Democratic and Republican; except for the Puerto Rican gang attempt on President Truman, all the
attempts seem to have been the work of isolated gunmen. Not organized terrorists, just individual madmen.

What is unusual in the Reagan case is that he is the first president-in-
office to be actually shot and to recover. Teddy Roosevelt, who was
wounded in 1914 and also recovered, was then five years out of office.
McKinley died within a few days of being shot, John Kennedy within a
matter of minutes. All the others escaped.

That Mr. Reagan survived is due both to his own efforts to keep his body in good shape and to sheer luck that the bullet didn't hit three inches closer to his heart. In many ways that's the story of his life, a combination of foresight and fortune.

Ronald Reagan was elected president in 1980 because, in large measure, the times were right for him. He had been standing in the presidential wings since 1967 when to everyone's surprise he was elected governor of California. But not until last year had disillusionment with a generation of liberal Democratic policies shifted the public mood enough to make Reagan a strong presidential possibility. Before that he couldn't even win the Republican nomination.

But when the tide of fortune turned Mr. Reagan was ready to greet it. What the voters had come to feel about the state of the country, and what ought to be done about it, he had felt for a long time and he was able to articulate the people's feelings.

Indeed, for a politician, President Reagan has been remarkably consistent in his political advocacy. Ten years ago while still governor of California, he would express to any visiting journalist essentially the same thoughts, frequently using the same words and homely parables, that he used so skillfully in his successful campaign. He did not have to change his rhetoric to fit a new political mood. He waited patiently until the public mood matched his own.

Since his election his consistency of thought and action has been equally remarkable. Every new president in the past quarter century, seeking the office, has talked of reducing government spending, with a balanced budget promised in the near future, and of cutting the people's taxes. To everyone's astonishment President Reagan from his first day in office actually set out to do what he said he would do.

What's more, he seems to have thus far carried the people with him, in defiance of the conventional wisdom that cutting the government's budget is politically impossible. At least, his friends have been surprised, his foes confounded.

President Reagan is no deep philosopher or intellectual giant. What president of our times has been? But he has proved more than a match for the intellectual snobs who have sneered because he was once a movie actor and scoffed at his use of the copybook maxims. What has been overlooked is that this man has lived a long and varied life, and somewhere along the way found out who he is, what he thinks and why he thinks it. That's a rare thing for any man.

Two small incidents from Monday: When Mrs. Reagan rushed to

the hospital and asked him what had happened, he replied, "I forgot
to duck." And as he was wheeled into the operating room he looked
up at the surgical team and remarked, "I hope you are all Republicans."

One-liners, to be sure, and not even too original. But not lines fed by
any gag-writers, to whom his scorners attribute his wry humor. These
are the words of a man a little frightened by what he faces but determined to face it with grace, a man who has come to terms with death
as well as life, which is the measure of true courage. Such a man is not
easily bent with every wind.

So the suspicion grows that there is more to Ronald Reagan than
has met anyone's eye. I will no longer be surprised if he proves to be
both a strong and successful president, one who in the end captures
the country's imagination and turns its direction around as no president has done since Franklin Roosevelt.

April 1, 1981

CENTENNIAL: REMEMBERING
FRANKLIN ROOSEVELT

It's incredible. For thirteen years the man bestrode his nation like a Colossus, something no man before had done so long and no man will do again. For many of those years he was a dominant world figure. He revolutionized the way his country conducts its affairs. He remade the map of Europe and Asia.

Yet as the centennial of his birthday approached he was almost forgotten. Harvard, of which he was a preeminent graduate, forgot. The Smithsonian Institution, curator of much of our history, forgot. So did the National Archives. So did the Library of Congress. So did Congress itself. So indeed did the keepers of his own papers in their library along the Hudson.

Now that forgetfulness has been rectified, thanks to the interest of a young man named Peter Kovler, born too late to remember Franklin Roosevelt or his times. Come January 30, we will be inundated with ceremonies. There will be a torrent of panegyrics matched only by those for the centennial of Abraham Lincoln. There will also be, here and there, an outpouring of obloquy. FDR, even in the grave, can arouse strong emotions.

What may well happen, all the same, is that the man will be lost in the oratory. No one under forty can remember either him or those times. It's hard for those who do to be dispassionate. One can only try.

My first close-up look at Franklin Roosevelt was in the spring of 1936 at a presidential press conference, in those days small and informal affairs held in the Oval Office. As a twenty-two-year-old reporter I was overwhelmed at being there. I remember mainly being impressed that he was larger in shoulders and chest than I imagined from his pictures and that he exuded physical vigor and inner confidence. It was also plain he was a consummate actor enjoying his place on center stage, comfortable in the role as if it belonged to him by right.

In time I came to see that the essence of the man was his aristocratic heritage. Not only had he a kinsman before him who had been president, but his whole clan had deep roots in America and by virtue of "old money," by education and by tradition came as close to being an aristocracy as we have. In this he was unlike any other president of my years and it affected every way he conducted the office. None of his successors, with the possible exception of Eisenhower, felt as confident of who he was, as unawed by the office.

This aspect of the man led to both triumphs and disasters. He was not a man of great intellectual capacities. He came to office with no clear idea of how to deal with the Depression, as early zig-zagging showed. Historians such as Arthur Schlesinger, Jr. have recorded two "New Deals," the first embracing the cartelism of the NRA, the second the free-spending and the experimental period that saw the birth of the WPA, the PWA and other alphabetical agencies as well as the injection of the federal government into every aspect of national life. The effects of that second New Deal remain with us.

It's not easy now to take the measure of all those experiments. Many of them have been distorted by his heirs and successors. The Social Security program has become a monstrosity; his "pump-priming" has become deficit financing gone mad. None of them solved the problem of the Depression; it remained with us until the coming of World War II.

It doesn't follow, though, that all the New Deal measures were misguided, even injurious, as some would have it. In the context of the times many had much merit. Many of the public works projects endured to the nation's benefit. The "make work" programs for the young provided jobs they would not otherwise have had, leaving fewer to mill aimlessly on the streets. He's not to be blamed for excesses done in his name.

Of late years the Securities and Exchange Commission, to use another example, has been justifiably criticized for its dead, bureaucratic hand. In 1934, in the wake of scandals, it was high time for some regulation of the securities market. They are healthier now for its coming.

This aside, it's hard to explain to new generations that FDR really did for his country what Churchill did for his at a later time; he held up the people's spirits in a time of trouble. It was, as the history books say, a time of radical ferment; many were tempted by Marxism, attracted by Soviet communism. Yet the astonishing thing is that there was so little of it, especially among the young and the dispossessed, including blacks, who had the best excuse for it. Much of this was due to FDR.

Roosevelt's oratory was no match for Churchill's but his jauntiness, his air of confidence, dampened much despair by giving people the feeling he would never surrender to the economic foe however badly the battle went. For holding up the nation's morale in those years, if for nothing else, Roosevelt deserves the appreciation of his countrymen.

That he was able to do so was largely due to the fact that he had little fear of mistakes. If one thing didn't work, try another. No other president has changed course so frequently and abruptly, and with so little apology, as did he. This want of fear of mistakes, bred no doubt from his aristocratic feeling, is a rare quality in any leader. It can be a great strength in a statesman. It can also lead him to tragic blunders.

That was the case with FDR and World War II. Like the country, he refused for long to see the war clouds gathering; then he swung abruptly from neutrality to belligerence. He must share the blame that war thus came to us as a surprise and found us unprepared, not only at Pearl Harbor but everywhere. For that, many men died unnecessarily.

Yet once war came Roosevelt was a superb war leader. He rallied the country, pushed it to boldness faster than most admirals and generals were ready for. He had the imagination and the will to launch the uncertain atomic project which ultimately would bring us victory sooner with less cost in lives. But most of all he gave the country the confidence that we would win it, even in the darkest days of 1942. And win it we did.

With no inner insecurity Roosevelt had an easy tolerance for conflicting opinion but nothing could shake his confidence in his own judgment once he had made one. Thus in earlier times he plunged ahead with his plan to "pack" the Supreme Court, to "purge" the Democratic Party, despite all advice. Both were mistakes. Neither was irremediable.

It was this same quality that led him to those tragic blunders in making the peace. His self-confidence assured him he could "handle" Stalin. No one, not even Churchill, could deter him from his plan to divide Germany and carve up Europe, to partition Korea, to treat Chiang Kai-shek as if he ruled China, to leave Southeast Asia prey to chaos.

Roosevelt thus left his successors, from Harry Truman to Ronald Reagan, a terrible inheritance. They have been left, needlessly, to face a

Soviet Union which holds half of Europe in its grip and threatens the other half so that an American army must remain permanently on the eastern ramparts. In Asia, Communists were allowed to do what, with much bloodshed, we wouldn't let the Japanese do, conquer all of China. First Korea and then Vietnam followed.

World War II was begot in the peace of World War I. If there's ever a World War III it will have been begotten in the peace of World War II wrought by Franklin Roosevelt.

When he insisted on those post-war plans FDR was old and sick; part of his personal tragedy was that he outlived his time. Part of it, too, was the *hubris*, the overweening pride, bred by too much success, something which can entrap all but the wisest men and that kind of wisdom was not among Roosevelt's qualities.

Such, then, in his many dimensions was President Roosevelt. If a great man is one who puts a great impress upon his times then surely he was a great president. If greatness is that quality of being larger than other men, seeming larger than life, he was that too. So also if greatness lies in the ability to make one's mark indelible.

This country and the world will never again be what it was before Franklin Roosevelt walked upon the stage. Men will debate for years to come what of his work was good and what bad for the country and the world. But how is it possible for anyone to forget him?

January 20, 1982

REMEMBERING HARRY

It's hard to realize that few people under fifty have memories of Harry Truman as president. And for us elders, the years of his seven successors—Presidents Eisenhower to Reagan—have dimmed our memories.

Yet Harry Truman was one of the more interesting presidents of modern times, presiding over the turbulent years after World War II. Abroad these embraced the Korean War, the Berlin blockade, the founding of NATO, the launching of the Marshall Plan for Europe. At home they saw political controversy everywhere: inflation, labor troubles, the beginnings of the civil rights disturbances, the incredible election of 1948, the return of the Republican Party to national power in 1952.

Through all that Mr. Truman himself was a figure of controversy, but withal he remained—and remains—one of the most personally "likable" of any of those post-war presidents. To forget him is to lose a crucial period in our history.

One who hasn't forgotten, and who would remind us, is Robert J. Donovan. As a Washington reporter for the *New York Herald Tribune*, and White House correspondent for most of the Truman years, Bob Donovan has given us a two-volume history of those years, scholarly in research but lively in narrative style. The first of these taking the story through 1948 was published in 1977. Now comes *The Tumultuous Years*.

It says something about the publishing business today, and the attitude of the media, that pre-publication publicity has centered on the account Mr. Donovan gives of Chief Justice Fred Vinson's advising President Truman on the constitutionality of seizing the steel industry in 1952. Scandalous "revelations," I suppose, are thought to sell books. Without them who would read history?

That's a pity. For one thing, conversations between Supreme Court justices and presidents aren't unprecedented, whatever the propriety. For another, it misrepresents the virtue of Mr. Donovan's work, which is not a book of revelations (the Vinson episode is only a few paragraphs) but an evocative recalling of an exciting period and a three-dimensional portrait of a fascinating man.

Harry Truman is not an easy man to pin down. Beginning his political career as a product of the Pendergast machine in Kansas City, he was a surprising (and compromise) choice for vice-president under President Roosevelt, then left by FDR in almost complete ignorance of policy decisions. He was thrown suddenly and unprepared into the presidency.

He floundered at times, was inconsistent and feisty, sparking one controversy after another; all that is not surprising. What is surprising is that he did as well as he did and, in the end, left a record of accomplishment that would be a credit to any president.

My own recollections of President Truman, whose time was my time also, are as vivid though not as well ordered as Bob Donovan's. I remember sitting in the House press gallery when he proposed drafting railroad workers into the Army. I remember the fateful Sunday when he impulsively launched the Korean War, the morass it became and his firing of General MacArthur. I remember also his perception of Stalin, which was clearer than Mr. Roosevelt's, and his gutsiness in refusing to lie down before the Berlin blockade by the Soviet Union.

I remember that tumultuous 1948 convention when in the wee hours of the morning he galvanized the Democrats with a fighting speech that would lead him and his party to an upset electoral victory unforeseen by the Republicans, the pollsters and the political journalists, myself included.

Then there are memories of brief encounters reaching back to his early days in the Senate. One, while he was in the White House, is of speaking to him at some reception when his political fortunes were at low ebb. Out of politeness I said I hoped he felt well. He took it as a political question and replied with a grin, "I never trouble trouble until trouble troubles me." When he walked away I noticed that he walked ramrod straight as if in his mind's eye he was still Captain Truman of Battery "D" of the 129th Field Artillery at the Meuse-Argonne offensive. I thought later it was a revealing glimpse of the man.

Harry Truman also stirred up non-political flaps that seemed important at the time. There were, for example, those wild shirts he wore in public, the letter from an outraged father to a music critic who panned his daughter's singing.

But time has a way of filtering the immediate from the durable; those things now seem trivial. If President Truman must carry the burden of beginning with Korea the policy of "containment everywhere," which would end in Vietnam, his is also the honor of treating vanquished Japan with magnanimity and rebuilding a devastated Western Europe, friend and former foe alike. That Europe remains divided is none of his doing. That he was not beguiled by the Soviet Union spared us worse woes.

It was the good Dr. Sam Johnson who remarked that when a writer is alive he is judged by his worst work, and when he is dead we rate him by his best. So it often is with our presidents, although sometimes it's the other way around.

Much of what Mr. Truman's critics said of him was true. He was unsophisticated in economic policy. He was impetuous. He could be erratic and irascible. But there was also in him a reverence for his office, an earthy common sense, a willingness to be decisive, a toughness when a crunch came. We have been worse served by others, before and since.

Bob Donovan tells the story in engrossing fashion. For those who have memories the tale stirs them anew. For those who have none there's the reward of learning how it was.

September 22, 1982

REAPPRAISING IKE

Some years ago a television interviewer asked me whom I would name as the "greatest" presidents of my journalistic days. Caught unawares, I answered without much thinking: Roosevelt and Eisenhower.

This caught the interviewer by surprise. He had expected Roosevelt. He was puzzled by the other choice. At the time Dwight Eisenhower was perceived in the intellectual community as a nice man, a sort of hero father-figure the country might have needed at the time but neither a forceful president nor a man of any deep perceptions. So with obvious curiosity, I was asked why.

There followed a rather long pause for television, which abhors nothing so much as silence on a talk show. Finally I said, "Because he did the least damage as president, left behind the fewest problems for his successors."

Since then Eisenhower's public image has altered. First came the publication of his diaries and letters which showed him to be a man who saw very clearly the politicians and issues of his time, had given them much thought and rendered reasonable, if private, judgments.

The result has been a reevaluation of Eisenhower in the press and in academia. The latest of these is *The Hidden-Hand Presidency: Eisenhower as Leader* by Fred L. Greenstein, professor of politics at Princeton. Professor Greenstein documents his conclusion that there was more depth to Eisenhower than anyone gave him credit for.

But my earlier impulsive answer wasn't without reason. I've been struck by how often presidents must wrestle with problems left by their predecessors and then, even if they are successful with those, leave new problems for those who come after.

Franklin Roosevelt inherited the Depression, which he was never able to solve until war did it for him. Then after that war he left Harry

Truman a terrible inheritance, a world divided—and still divided—by the peace plans Roosevelt insisted on.

Truman met this challenge with courage, clear eyes as to Stalin, and with bold action. He didn't hesitate to use the atom bomb to end the war in Asia, saving millions of lives for the thousands who died at Hiroshima and Nagasaki. He defied the Soviet aggression at Berlin. He had the vision to resuscitate even our former enemies.

Unhappily he didn't recognize the limits of boldness. Once he proclaimed the doctrine of resisting aggression everywhere, a Korea somewhere became inevitable. To his successor he left that war unresolved and in addition a raging inflation unchecked by all his efforts with wage and price controls.

More recent presidents have left equally troubling inheritances. Kennedy, cut off in midstream, left the country mired in the bog of Vietnam from which Lyndon Johnson couldn't extricate it.

Richard Nixon struggled valiantly with this inheritance and had some other things to his credit, such as the reopening of China. But he left behind him the scars of Watergate on the body politic. In his brief time Gerald Ford could not heal them, nor could he halt the second virulent inflation sprung from Vietnam.

Jimmy Carter, man of good will, passed along both the inflation and a recession to his successor and to a discouraged country. Of Ronald Reagan we cannot yet know, but the recession is still there for anyone who may follow him.

This brings me back to Eisenhower. Imagine, for a moment, any new president being inaugurated. What would the country hope from his days in office?

First, surely, no war. Or if there were one in the beginning, that it would end. Beyond that, some years of economic stability with a minimum of inflation and, if there must be recessions, that they would be mild at worst. That this new president would give the country confidence in its government and in itself. Finally, the hope would be that when his time passed his successor would not find the country faced with huge new problems.

This, it seems to me, is what Eisenhower did for his country as president. He ended the Korean War, brought on no other. While he couldn't eliminate the effects of wartime inflation, by boldly ending wage-price controls he let the country adjust to past inflation. He met racial troubles at Little Rock with firmness, setting a precedent to keep later turmoil from being worse. President Kennedy inherited no new problems of Eisenhower's making. In retrospect the eight years of Eisenhower seem a halcyon time.

Until lately all this was put down to "Ike's luck." The credit always went to luck, from the Normandy landings to the Battle of the Bulge, with little credit for what he may have done to create it.

Now that view is changing. Professor Greenstein is not the only one who, burrowing into the hidden record, perceives behind the "luck" the skills of an exceptional leader who saw clearly what he wanted to do and knew how to do it. Even the tangled ambiguities of his press conferences, for which he was much belabored, are being recognized as "deliberate vagueness" carefully calculated to avoid unwise confrontations. Once he told his press secretary not to worry about expected tough questions: "Jim, I'll just go out there and confuse them." There was, in fact, little thoughtless stumbling about anything he did. The "luck" was well planned for.

I welcome all this reappraisal by men more scholarly than I. Yet even after time for reflection I'll stick by my own appraisal those years ago. Lucky will be the country if it finds another president who leaves behind him so few problems for others to resolve.

November 17, 1982

JESSE THE FORERUNNER

Jesse the Bethlehemite, so we are told in the Book of Kings, was favored by the Lord. He was destined, all the same, to be only a forerunner for those who came after. To others fell the honor of wearing the crown.

The feeling grows that a like fate awaits his modern namesake, the Reverend Jesse Jackson. He doesn't seem destined to win what he seeks, his party's nomination for president. Even his fellow blacks lend their political support elsewhere; some wish he had never entered the lists. Yet Jesse Jackson, no doubt about it, has made an impress not only upon his own people but upon the whole country.

He has boldly reached for what none before him have dared, not even Martin Luther King, Jr. He has put himself forward as more than a spokesman for his own people, as a national leader to whom attention must be paid. And on that score, at least, he has succeeded. When the Democratic Party assembled on a single stage eight men who vie to lead it, there among them sat Jesse Jackson.

That in itself is remarkable, for unlike the others, he has held no public office. He put himself on that stage solely by the force of his personality. Some of that personality—its flamboyance—is as much hindrance as help to one who aspires to the heights. But the simple fact that he was there, a black man to whom other presidential aspirants must pay attention, surely will have consequences for those who come after him. A different man, a different time—who can say what those consequences may be?

Whatever they may be, Jesse Jackson is indeed a remarkable man. He has certainly been favored with the gift of tongues. Few there are in our time who can speak so eloquently to the multitude. Before a crowd, the words come out in the cadences of the evangelical preacher, which in fact he is. He understands the force of rolling periods as phrases build, one upon another, until they form a hypnotic refrain.

He is also shrewd enough—and bold enough—to speak so persuasively at the seats of the mighty as to open the gates of a foreign prison. His physical presence is such that he draws all eyes in any room he enters.

If charisma were all it took to be an American political leader there would be no stopping him. It is when people begin to wonder what his words mean that the force fades. If oratory were enough, William Jennings Bryan would have been president of the United States.

There is no mistaking his emotion when he tells his people "we can't ride to freedom on Pharaoh's chariot." Or when he sounds the tocsin for excellence in education, particularly for black students. Or when he laments the millions who are unemployed, the millions on welfare. Or when he says salvation for the poor does not lie in more government handouts. What remains hidden is what he means by those words.

If Jesse Jackson were president, what would be the nation's economic policy? What would be its posture in the world? What would the country be asked to do about taxes or defense? What, that is, would a President Jesse Jackson propose for the ills he laments?

In fairness, it must be noted that the same questions posed of many other candidates also would have uncertain answers. But there are at least clues in their pasts as congressmen, senators or governors. With Mr. Jackson there is no political past to judge by.

There's another reason why his candidacy troubles his own party and even other black leaders. To many, he appears to be a maverick, more ambitious for personal attention than for any political cause. Certainly, he has been changeable, launching projects or programs and then abandoning them. His critics claim that, in that sense at least, he is untrustworthy.

Finally, there's the conviction that the times are not ripe for a black presidential candidate and that Mr. Jackson's campaign can only be divisive among the voters, Democrats as well as others, especially if he is carried away by those ambitions for attention.

For all these reasons, Jesse Jackson is apt to prove a shooting star, flashing across the political sky and then burning out.

But it does not follow that his passage will be without consequences. The time will come, however far off it may be, when a black candidate will prove acceptable to the country. When that time comes, it will be a person of a different breed.

It will likely be someone who has already made his mark as congressman or senator, as mayor of a major city, perhaps even as governor of a state. Along the way he will have proved himself capable of dealing with the complexities of public problems well enough to commend himself to a wider constituency.

As always, an attractive personality will be a necessary ingredient, as well as an ability to hold and articulate an appealing political philosophy. It will not, however, be a flamboyant personality in manner or in speech. Such people may fare well in gaining lesser office. In American politics they do not climb the heights. The list is long of would-be presidents who rose and like meteors burned themselves out.

In short, I do not think that person, when he comes, will be a Jesse Jackson. Yet when he comes, he will owe a debt to the Jesse who went before and made the nation pay attention.

February 1, 1984

A 'RETIRING' BARRY GOLDWATER?

Looking back on it, Sen. Barry Goldwater never had a chance of winning the presidency in 1964.

To begin with, the times were out of joint for a conservative president. The U.S. was still under the spell of the martyred John Kennedy and taken with Lyndon Johnson's promises of the "Great Society." It would be twenty years before disillusionment set in and the political pendulum swung.

Then Senator Goldwater didn't help himself. He chose for his running mate Rep. William Miller of New York, lifted from total obscurity and destined to return to it. Senator Goldwater also rejected advice to conciliate his opponents within his party, the so-called moderate wing. Instead he flung down the defiant words, "Extremism in defense of liberty is no vice . . . moderation in pursuit of justice is no virtue."

There was nothing retiring about Barry Goldwater, a trait that left him vulnerable to his enemies. There are many possible selections for the "dirtiest" presidential campaign, but 1964 certainly rivals the 1928 personal attacks on Al Smith.

Remember that "daisy" commercial on TV? It showed a child peacefully pulling petals off a daisy when suddenly the picture dissolved into a mushroom cloud. Senator Goldwater, you see, had taken a tough stance on Vietnam and the intended implication was that he would casually toss around atom bombs.

Meanwhile, President Johnson scattered promises of peace about that far-off war. We wouldn't get tied down in a land war in Asia. "There can be, and will be as long as I am president, peace for all Americans." A year later, of course, we were mired more deeply in that Asian war. So much for his political promises.

These recollections are sparked by Senator Goldwater's announcement that he will retire when his term expires in 1987. That's a while off but the news inspires some musings on the part this most unretiring man has played in our national life.

We forget sometimes the major roles played in our political history by men who never reached the White House. Webster, Clay, Calhoun come to mind.

Daniel Webster, who served in Congress from both Massachusetts and New Hampshire, was known as the great expounder of the Constitution and did as much as any man to inspire people to regard that document with reverence. He was twice secretary of state, respected by all, but the presidency eluded him.

So it also eluded Henry Clay, best remembered perhaps for his remark, "I would rather be right than be president." So renowned was he as an orator that one day the Senate adjourned so the members could go to the House to hear him speak on the Seminole War. He too made it to secretary of state but no further.

John Calhoun, a South Carolinian, was in public service for more than forty years, as congressman, senator, secretary of war and—yes—secretary of state. He was vice-president under two presidents, John Quincy Adams and Andrew Jackson. He resigned that office solely because he disagreed philosophically with President Jackson, who favored a more powerful federal government over the states.

No one would put Barry Goldwater down as a great orator, and all his career (save for that abortive run for the presidency) has been as a senator. But that career already spans more than thirty years.

When he first came to the Senate in 1952, he was regarded as one of those oddities—a businessman in politics; he was president of Goldwater's Department Store in Phoenix, Arizona. Before long he was regarded as even more of an oddity, an unashamed conservative in a country still dominated by the New Deal–Fair Deal politics of Presidents Roosevelt and Truman. By contrast, he made even President Eisenhower seem like a liberal.

In the beginning, of course, he was pretty much dismissed by the press and his fellow Republicans as a passing curiosity. But, curiously, more and more people began to pay attention to his views. While not a great speaker, he is a literate writer. He was already the author of two volumes of Arizona portraits and an account of a journey down the river of canyons. Anyway, in 1958 when the Republicans suffered a sweeping disaster, Barry Goldwater bucked the Democratic tide and won re-election decisively.

That propelled him into national attention. In 1960, he published *The Conscience of a Conservative*, an articulate and rational presentation of that philosophy that gave it political respectability. That propelled him to the 1964 nomination.

Ever since then Barry Goldwater has been a respected spokesman for the political views that ultimately elected Ronald Reagan. But, as that 1964 campaign illustrated, Mr. Goldwater has also been something of a maverick, a man who has his own thoughts and goes his own way undeterred by what others may say. It's not too much to say that, like Henry Clay, he'd rather believe himself right than be president. He won't trim his opinions to the winds of public opinion. So he's never been "a good party man."

He isn't today. Though he's generally in sympathy with President Reagan, he doesn't hesitate to differ publicly when he differs. On Lebanon, for example, he says we should never have sent in the Marines and he urged their removal long before the president did so. That this may have aided Democratic critics of President Reagan didn't trouble him. Because that's what he thought, that's what he said.

Such men—the Websters, Clays, Calhouns—aren't destined for the White House. Possibly they wouldn't make good presidents if elected. I'm not sure Barry Goldwater would have. All the same, it will be a sad day when this most unretiring man retires to join the others in the history books. For such men are rare enough to be treasured.

February 15, 1984

XI

The Sexes

OF WOMEN AND MEN

All happy marriages resemble one another, every unhappy marriage is unhappy in its own way. Which probably explains why poets, playwrights and television producers find the one too dull for their arts and in the other the stuff of drama.

Anyway, this slight variation in Tolstoy's aphorism about families leapt to mind the other evening while watching three hours of an NBC special on the ways of women and men.

It was an interesting program and it told us much about the human condition, circa 1975. We got glimpses of women in politics and in such "men's sports" as boxing, football and hockey. We watched a couple talk of phasing out their marriage with that air of reason that is the mark of today's sophisticated people. We saw an example of modern role-reversal, the wife as a police-person in the prowl car while the husband helped tend home and children.

And, of course, much candid talk about sex. The young discovering it and presumably freed of all those hang-ups of ages past. The middle-aged exploring its infinite variety. Even a couple in their seventies whose continued sharing of it gave encouragement to viewing sexagenarians.

Yet for all of that, it was three hours with an aftertaste of sadness that has been haunting me ever since. Save perhaps for those septuagenarians, whose years had taken them past the storms, there was hardly anybody on the program who seemed to be happy.

Certainly not those men sitting around talking about how they had freed themselves from the male machismo. Certainly not Viveca Lindfors with her mournful monologues about being a woman. Not the divorcing couple whose reasoned discourse could not hide their regrets and tensions. Not that understanding couple who had reversed roles—NBC had to add a footnote that they had separated between interview time and program time.

And the young least of all. In their new-style openness about sex they seemed no less uncertain and confused about life than were the young in those days when inhibitions and restraints were supposed to have been the cause of all adolescent tortures. Freedom too, it seems, brings its hang-ups.

There was hardly a hint that there could be anything else between a woman and a man except an unrequited searching, coupling and un-coupling. If marriage, then divorce was almost the inevitable end of it. Even the septuagenarians, happy in their sex, were the survivors of previous marriages.

So from this three hours on the modern condition you would find it hard to believe it possible for a woman and a man to join their lives and live them out together. Little there was to say, that is, of happy marriages.

Perhaps that is understandable. For one thing, you would have to answer the question, what is a happy marriage? Is it one only of per-petual bliss where life runs untroubled? If so, there is the difficulty of giving dramatic interest to what seems dull. If not, there is the harder task of saying what is happiness.

That is why novelists, like fairy-tale tellers, do not know what to say after the line "and they lived happily ever after." And why documen-tary makers think love stories are for sentimentalists and not for pro-bers of the human condition.

Documenters must deal with the statistic that one in three modern marriages ends in divorce, an aspect of the human condition that has not escaped notice by those of us of a certain age. There is also the observable fact that today the passing alliance is often the design for living.

Yet there is also the statistic that well over two-thirds of all *first* mar-riages endure; it's the repeated failures that swell the statistics. Surely among those two-thirds there are some who found their lives enriched. And maybe with a little probing among them you might find, here and there, a tale to tell.

Start with a boy of seventeen and a girl of sixteen. Have them meet, romantically, on the fourth of July. Follow them through the torments of adolescence, groping with the wonders of emerging sexuality, rebel-ling against the constraints of parents, exploring the world to find out who they are—separating, returning, quarreling, reconciling.

Set them down, married, in a third-floor walkup with a bathtub for a kitchen sink; she earning more than he, and neither much, in the times of depression. Bring on a baby and then a war, a war giving him an excuse to run away to sea, all in the name of patriotism but answering to who knows what subconscious yearning for adventure and escape from domestic responsibility.

Follow them through the war. He repeatedly absent for a year and a half at a time, she left to raise a daughter, with only fleeting reunions in drab and distant places; a turbulent time that left in its wake a string of wrecked marriages.

Afterwards, now with no money and two children, watch them try to put their lives back together; he restless at the drab return from high excitement, she fighting down recriminations. Uproot them several times, moving from one place to another, new neighborhoods, new schools, not all of them of the best.

Since this is the after-part of a fairy story, let them grow slowly more prosperous. These, so we are told, are dangerous years as a husband finds new excitement in success and a wife needs to find a new way of life with her role as mother ended.

Do not pretend that all passed without hurts, without quarrels, without days of strain. Note only that somehow the commitment to each other withstood the strain, and that with the years what grew were the shared moments, a lifetime of memories. Finally let it come to pass that the strain is in the days apart, that that boy of seventeen and that girl of sixteen are only whole in the same bed, at the same table, beside the same hearth.

A tale too banal for television, no doubt. But it did happen once, I know. And are we sure it does not speak for others and that it has nothing to say about the human condition?

January 22, 1975

THE ERA FOR ERA?

It's been four years now since Congress proposed to the states the Equal Rights Amendment, or more accurately the women's rights amendment, and four years later it still hangs in limbo.

That was not the expectation in 1972. Within a few days of congressional approval Hawaii ratified it. In the next two years nineteen other states added their approval. By 1974 the total was thirty-four. Only four more states need to ratify it to make it the Twenty-seventh Amendment since the Constitution was adopted in 1789, and it was thought they would soon be forthcoming.

It hasn't worked out that way. Eleven states have officially rejected it, and two of those previously approving, Nebraska and Tennessee, are seeking to withdraw their ratifications, although whether they can legally do so is doubtful. At the moment the other five states seem little disposed to act one way or another.

What happened was that a good many people, including a goodly number of women, began to have second thoughts. What the proposed amendment says is simply that "equality of rights under the law shall not be denied or abridged by the United States or by any state on account of sex." But to the critics a number of booby-traps seem to be lurking behind those simple words.

It has been said, for example, that ERA would make it illegal to have separate toilet facilities in public places for men and women, even if they were equal as well as separate. That it would void state statutes making it a crime to rape women or seduce girls under sixteen. That husbands could not be held primarily responsible for supporting wives or their children. That women could no longer be exempted from military conscription in time of war or even from combat. That in factories women could no longer be protected from hazardous working conditions.

These objectors, including many vocal women's groups, are not quarreling with the announced objectives of the amendment—to provide in law equal opportunities for women in jobs in industry and the professions, to eliminate many discriminatory practices, such as in pay differentials or in obtaining credit. What they fear is that it will strip away many protections that the law, wisely in their opinion, has long provided for women.

Some of these fears, as the one about mixed toilets, seem a bit farfetched. But one does not have to be a male chauvinist, or a fearful female traditionalist, to have some uneasiness with the sweeping nature of the ERA language. If it's adopted we will have at the very least a long period of uncertainty about many things until the courts have disentangled all the statutes from the new constitutional provisions.

Yet if the second thoughts about ERA are understandable it is also time to give it some quiet third thoughts. One who has done that, and whose thoughts are worth pondering, is Professor William B. Aycock of the University of North Carolina law school.

Professor Aycock begins with an analysis of that phrase "equal rights under law" and concludes that neither in law nor in common sense does equal rights always mean identical rights. "Statutes regulating abortions will not be struck down," he concludes, "on the grounds that such laws do not apply to men." Nor will statutes designed to determine fatherhood be abrogated "because they do not apply to women."

That is to say, no court in his opinion will apply the language of ERA to achieve an absurdity. "Some laws beneficial to women will survive as long as there is factual justification for their continuance," he observes, because "there are differences between men and women that the law cannot eliminate or ignore."

But if Professor Aycock allays the worst fears of the ERA opponents, he also warns that the highest hopes of its supporters will not automatically be realized. After examining recent Supreme Court decisions affecting sex discrimination in employment, in minimum wages, in the extension of credit, he concludes there is no law "Congress could pass after ERA that it cannot enact now under existing provisions of the Constitution"—if it wants to.

All the ERA amendment does, he suggests, is affirm in constitutional language a philosophical principle—that women are not to be denied the rights and privileges of full citizenship in the community simply because they are women. As in the case of every other principle stated in the Constitution—the right of free speech or of a fair trial—there is a long road from its stating to its fulfillment.

If that is the case, one may ask, what then is the use of ERA? What purpose would it serve if it is not necessary to give Congress new power to legislate women's rights? What is the point of a constitutional amendment merely to state a philosophical principle?

The answer to that, or so it seems to me as I have my third thoughts about ERA, is that ours is a country whose greatness lies in stating philosophical principles, as aspirations if not always as achievements. When we declared "all men are created equal" under the law it was at most an aspiration; in fact slaves were not included, nor Indians. It took us a hundred years to make a reality of the proclaimed principle that the right to vote should not be abridged on account of race, color or previous condition of servitude.

As for women, two hundred years ago they could not vote, hold office, serve on juries, own property apart from their husbands or act as guardians for their own children. As late as one hundred years ago they could not practice law or medicine if a state chose to exclude them. It was only fifty years ago, and then after battles more bitter than those over ERA, that women won the right to vote.

Yet as that record shows, ours has been a long journey toward a philosophical principle, toward making "all men" mean all men. The law's mazes are too intricate for me, but somehow I cannot think that in our Bicentennial year we would do wrong to that principle to declare in candor to the world that all persons are equal in their rights under our laws.

January 14, 1976

SEX, SOLDIERS AND ERA

I must confess that in spite of the evidence to the contrary I've always thought of members of the female gender as the gentler sex. I'll also admit to such anachronistic gestures as opening doors for them, holding their coats and rising when greeting one of them.

That confession seems advisable before offering my confused thoughts on ERA, the drafting of women, females in combat, sexual harassment and in general on that gender's role in society, their rights, privileges and obligations.

Not that I expect candor to disarm those who anyway will see male chauvinism beneath every thought. But the admission may help explain the seeming contradictions not only in my own views but those of the country generally in the latest skirmishes in the battle of the sexes.

Take ERA. My view is that passage of the Equal Rights Amendment will change the legal situation very little. That is, it won't bring the benefits foreseen by its supporters or the ills (unisex toilets and the like) feared by its opponents. The legal gains promised by ERA have already been made, or will be made anyway, by court decisions, legislative actions and the shifting views of our society generally.

Nonetheless, had I a vote I would vote for ERA. So, I suspect, would most male members of state legislatures were they not confronted with a large and vocal opposition to it from many women. It's not male chauvinism that's blocked ratification of the amendment.

If I seem here to be inconsistent I can only explain it by saying that while ERA won't change much in a legal sense it would be a formal expression of a public policy that has in fact already been accepted by society, male and female. It would be worthwhile for its symbolism if nothing else.

There are equal inconsistencies, I fear, in my views on the controversy over drafting women and then assigning them to active combat roles.

To say that women should be exempted from a general draft hardly jibes with the idea of ERA. Equal rights surely also means equal obligations. I would have expected the women's rights movement to be outraged at this discrimination, but I have seen no women's march on Washington demanding they be drafted, much less demanding the right to battlefield bayonets.

Before I complain, however, I have to admit my own confusions. Although I see no reason to exempt anyone from some form of military service on the grounds of sex, I am made queasy by the idea of using women as combat soldiers.

My objection to that has nothing to do with the ability of women to fire a gun or drive a tank. History is dotted with examples of women fighting alongside their men. But rare is the society that hasn't at least tried to shield its females from armed combat, abandoning the effort only in desperation. The reason is rooted in biology. The preservation of any species requires many females but only a few males. So deep is this biological instinct that even in hunting we decree different rules for killing does and bucks.

In modern war all of us, civilian and soldier, male or female, are endangered. But I cannot believe that American society is in such dire straits that it must suppress this deepest of human instincts and deliberately throw its women into battle.

If there are inconsistencies here they arise, I think, from the confusion which today surrounds our view of men and women. We assume that if they are equal as human beings they must also be alike. No differences. Particularly no differences in their roles in society. To concede such differences, so runs the catechism, is somehow to concede inequality.

Nowadays to hold a lady's coat or open a door for her is thought by many to be an insult. Male chauvinism branding her as helpless. That's ridiculous. It's no more than a gesture of respect to her sex, and no more demeaning to her sex than we demean a president of the United States when we rise upon his entrance.

It's equally absurd, and infinitely more harmful, when we denigrate the role of mother and homemaker, or think the man who is home provider is a male chauvinist treading on women's rights. Equal rights, after all, just means the right of everyone to choose their own way.

Women who choose to be mothers and homemakers deserve not scorn. Can you think them less useful to society than those who would be auto mechanics, lawyers or business executives?

Then there's the hub-bub over "sexual harassment." Insofar as that refers to sexual demands for favors, jobwise or otherwise, it should be rigorously stamped out. But I read where some women complain of harassment if they are winked at, whistled at or ogled. At that I rise to object, in self-defense if for no other reason.

All this might be funny if it didn't suggest we've somehow lost our bearings. We've forgotten that while all of us, male and female, belong to the same species and so are one, we also remain either male or female and so are different. The differences are physical, psychological—yes, also cultural. But we cannot be sure that even those cultural differences, rooted in the antiquity of society, can be ignored without peril.

Being alike as humans we all equally have rights and obligations. Being different as males and females we don't all have the same role to play in society. Once we recognize this paradox all those inconsistencies disappear.

Anyway, I won't feel insulted if young ladies rise in deference to my venerable years. But I'd much prefer being winked at, whistled at or ogled.

April 19, 1980

WEEP NOT, DEAR LADIES

D irges have already begun to be heard as state legislature after legislature has sounded the knell over the Equal Rights Amendment. Barely a week is left for a miracle to resuscitate it.

So it is hardly surprising that there are tears and lamentations from those who worked so hard for it over a decade. They did win it one respite when the time limit for ratification was extended from 1979 to the end of this June. Now to them there seems to be nothing left except to mourn.

But as one male who gave ERA such support as he could, I hope the ladies will quickly wipe away their tears and after the funeral think of what was won, not just of what was lost.

For in all truth, what was sought through the ERA has almost all been won without it. Indeed, it's hard to think of what more could have been done for the cause of women's equality in society if it had been adopted.

The catalog of what has already changed is long.

Begin at the top. Scarcely a hundred years ago the U.S. Supreme Court held that women had no constitutional right to be lawyers, noting in what now seems such quaint language that "the natural and proper timidity and delicacy which belongs to the female sex evidently unfits them for many of the occupations of civil life."

Now Madam Justice Sandra O'Connor sits upon that selfsame court, and if she perchance retains some of that delicacy of the female sex she certainly has none of the timidity of which her antecedent colleagues spoke.

So it is also in other parts of public and political life. I have no exact statistics but it's been estimated that from 12 percent to 15 percent of our elected officials, from local aldermen to state governors to federal congressmen (pardon me, congresswomen) belong to that no longer gentler sex.

Whether that influx of women into politics has brought the improvement in government once so promised, must remain moot. As for the promise of those long-ago suffragettes, who claimed that giving women the vote would end those wars men kept getting into, a glance overseas at the present prime minister of Great Britain will make you pause. There can be, it seems, iron women as well as iron men in the chancelleries of state. And also, as we can see in this country, women as gung-ho to be warriors as any male of the species.

In fact, in aspects other than biological, women show themselves not much different from men given the power to be so, something we might have noticed from studying Queen Elizabeth I or Catherine the Great of Russia.

But proving that, after all, was the whole point of the women's movement, was it not? Anything a man can do a woman can do—and perhaps a little better?

Anyway, ERA or no ERA, women everywhere are showing they can do a man's job if they wish. Today they are driving eighteen-wheel rigs, going down in coal mine digs, climbing skyscraper girders, riding firetrucks, handling air-hammers and proudly showing their callused hands and weather-beaten complexions.

Nor is that all. Others are taking out gall bladders, trying lawsuits, training as astronauts, directing movies, programming computers, teaching genetics and managing enterprises of some pith and moment.

They complain, to be sure, that there is not enough of this and that women's ways are still blocked in the line of advancement by resisting male bodies. There may be female vice-presidents at IBM, the Chase Bank or Dow Jones but few CEOs anywhere.

My own craft, journalism, is flooded with women reporters, some of whom are off covering wars amid falling shells, questioning heads of state or grappling with the syntax of the secretary of state. Rare are those who have yet risen to the majesty of managing editors.

Be patient, ladies. It's a long road from bottom to top even for frailer males. And look at what's burbling up from below. Many college campuses now have more women than men in the student body and every year the number grows of women masters of business administration, doctors of philosophy, holders of Phi Beta Kappa keys and winners of awards in mathematics or microbiology.

In fact, in another generation or so, I suspect we men will be overwhelmed and we'll have to start a men's liberation movement.

I confess a certain sadness at that doleful prospect, although I'm at an age where I will escape the full consequences of this overturning. Even so I note there's no more men's bar at the Plaza and even the few private sanctuaries of male companionship, such as the poker tables and sauna baths of our clubs, are being relentlessly invaded. Soon there will be no place to hide.

Before long, I doubt not, we will even be deprived of our reproductive function, that being fulfilled by sperm banks, fertilization in vitro and transplanted motherhood. That done, what will be left of the men's privileged world once so complained of?

If there's compensation in all this, I suppose we men will be freed from the centuries' burden of supporting the family, feeding and clothing it, with endless daily labor. In the end we may find that burden good riddance. But how then will we escape the kitchen, the nursery and the readying of children for school, which we are told is so repressive?

All this, dear ladies, lies in the omens, with or without the ERA. It would be at most a symbolic gesture. For when the tide turns in the affairs of men—or women—it cannot be stayed until it reaches the flood.

June 23, 1982

XII

Of Earth and Energy

THE FIRE-BEARERS

In the ancient myths the story of Prometheus is told in many ways. But in every telling, from Aeschylus to Shelley, it was he who stole from the gods the secret of fire and gave to man his greatest scourge and blessing.

In every telling he is punished by the gods, tied to a rock and condemned forever to have his liver gnawed by vultures, for thus revealing the power that brought man his first great mastery over nature. But never could the gods, the secret once disclosed, hide it again from mortals.

Myths, so they tell us, often teach lessons sprung from our deep subconscious. So the legend of Prometheus haunts us to this very day.

Since the secret of the atom was first wrested from the unknown at Alamogordo it has promised both horror and hope. Hiroshima taught us the horror. We have the secret, if men are mad, to destroy our earth and all upon it.

We know also though, if men are wise, that we have the secret of boundless energy to serve us long after all the other fire-supporting resources of the earth—our coal, our gas, our oil—have been exhausted. What haunts us is the fear we cannot use the secret wisely.

The other day, at a place called Three Mile Island, the fear struck anew. This time it was no holocaust in which thousands died. Instead it was the fear of mystery. The new Prometheans were reminded of the limits of their knowledge. They could not assure us that they could control the fire within their atom furnace, nor tell us even what would happen if they failed.

It was inevitable, then, that we should begin to question again whether the blessings of this atomic secret were worth its terrors. The whole future of atomic energy was thrown in doubt.

Meanwhile, another haunting fear. The government is afraid that an article for *The Progressive* magazine will give away the secrets of the hydrogen bomb and it seeks to halt the article's publication.

It's all very depressing. The government may have a legal case (or will we soon have how-to-do-it articles in home handicraft magazines?) but it's hard to escape the feeling that it's a futile case. For years after Hiroshima we tried to keep the secret of the uranium bomb but it wasn't long before others knew it too.

Once men know that something can be done the secret cannot be hidden, for what some men's minds can learn so can others. As the gods found with fire, once the book of knowledge is opened it can never again be closed. The depressing fact that others will learn what we have learned must be lived with.

What makes Three Mile Island depressing, on the other hand, is its lesson that we do not know as much as we thought we did. The nuclear power plant there incorporated, or so we thought, every reasonable safety precaution. Yet one faulty valve, one small human error, and we skirted the edge of disaster.

The experience should be humbling. It should give us pause. It should remind us of an eternal truth; the more we know, the more the mystery, the more we have to learn.

No man, then, should decry those who say we should not be complacent about what happened at Three Mile Island because this time disaster was averted. We need to go back to the beginning, reexamine the designs, restudy the engineering, reshape the operating precautions in order to be safe playing with that ultimate fire. It may even be wise, as many say, to postpone new plants until we have absorbed the lessons learned.

But those who cry that we should stop altogether, build no more plants and dismantle those we have, are men of little vision. In any event, theirs is a futile cry. They will not have their way.

For one thing, they overlook the blessing within the curse. Every mastery over nature, though often tempting us to misuse and sometimes proving a scourge, has lifted us a little further. Even the deadly instruments of war—the steel to make swords, the dynamite to kill, the airplanes and rockets to spew death farther afield—have also made it possible for more of us to live on this little earth a little freer of hunger, of want, of dread disease. Without them we could not now be reaching for the stars.

There's another reason. Whether or not it is wise to know the power of the atoms and to seek to put the knowledge to use, we will do it anyway because there is something in our species that makes us do it. Fear, even fear of wholesale death, will not stop us.

One needs to think only of ancient Pompeii, destroyed by earthquake, rebuilt, buried deep under volcanic ash only to see men building again atop the rubble. Or to see on television those homes, whole towns even, swept away by flood, knowing that when the waters have receded the survivors will return. Or know that men digging coal in the earth die by the hundreds, bury their dead and go back to digging.

Or, for that matter, to look today at the city of Hiroshima.

The fear at Three Mile Island, to be sure, was different because it was fear of the mysterious, not of known and experienced dangers. But in all our long history danger has never deterred men either in their search for knowledge or accepting the risks of it.

So, I am confident, it will be here. The promise of nuclear energy, once harnessed to men's will, is too bounteous to be rejected when other resources dwindle. The pressure of foreseen need will drive us forward. But even if that were not so, we would go forward anyway simply because that is in our nature.

There may be times when we wish the fire-bearers had never given us this secret. But now not even the gods can lock it away again.

April 11, 1979

FOREWARNINGS

Do you remember that oil embargo back in 1973–74? What state it brought us to and how we all reacted to it?

We suffered less than most of the industrial countries, including Japan, when those small oil-producing countries of the Middle East, abetted by a few others, shut off their wells and pipelines. But it was bad enough here, with those long lines before the gasoline filling stations, the squeeze on factory and home fuel and the tightened supply of electric power.

So we cussed the Arabs and the oil companies and the filling station operators and the government. The Arabs and the oil companies, so we said, were getting rich off our misery and why hadn't President Nixon done something about it?

But while we cussed we did actually do something about it. At the president's urging Congress passed the Alaska pipeline bill, heretofore stalled by protests from environmentalists who said it would spoil the Arctic tundra. A 55-mile-an-hour speed limit was established on our highways and we all obeyed it. We started buying smaller cars instead of those traditionally American big gas-guzzlers. We organized car pools and turned down our thermostats.

All that lasted just as long as the oil embargo. Once that was lifted and the oil again was available, even at a higher price, we all went back to our accustomed ways. Once more we tootled along the highways at 60 or 70, the car pools disbanded, up went the thermostats, and the big comfortable touring cars regained their popularity.

And before two years had passed we were using more oil, and were more dependent on foreign oil producers, than before that brief crisis.

Now comes this frigid winter of '77. Half the nation is buried in snow and ice, three-quarters of it freezing for lack of natural gas. Across the land, schools, factories and office-buildings are closed down. This time we are cursing the greedy gas-well producers and the pipeline owners, and wondering why the government let it all happen.

But once more, as is our wont in times of crisis, we are trying to do something about it. The president and cabinet have met in emergency session. Whole states have been declared disaster areas. At the request of the president, Congress has rushed through new laws; the president was even granted authority to lift temporarily the price controls on interstate gas.

So this time you might think that we really are going to do something about it. That we are not just going to have a program to equalize misery during our wintry discontent but do something about the long-range danger that faces us, which is in essence the fact that we no longer have cheap energy to waste.

Maybe I've grown cynical, but I fear that despite President Carter's plea this mood too will last only as long as the winter's discontent. Give us a pleasant summer and a milder winter next year, and once more back to our wasteful ways.

When the president, as he has promised to do, offers a long-range energy program the Congress will debate it endlessly. There will be voices raised to say the shortage is all contrived anyway. We mustn't decontrol natural gas prices because that would just let the gas companies earn ill-gotten riches. For the same reason we musn't change oil industry regulations or taxes to encourage new oil well digging.

We can't dig more open pit coal, it will be said, because that will mess up the countryside. We can't build dams for hydro-electric power because they too will spoil natural beauty. We can't turn to more nuclear power because that can be dangerous.

Yet what we have had here, in the space of four years, are two dramatic forewarnings of troubles yet to come. We are faced with the fact that the era of cheap and plentiful energy from the fossil fuels of the earth is coming to an end. We are faced with the fact but we will not face up to it.

I do not have the slightest idea how large are the untapped reserves of oil and gas in the earth; every expert has a different opinion. But it is clear already that the easy pools have been tapped; we are now digging in the Arctic wilderness and in the deeps of the ocean at costs so high that we can hardly grasp the figures. It is madness to think we can draw on these supplies and by some magic of price controls have energy cost no more than before.

There is something else equally clear. No matter how large these re-serves, they are finite. We do not know when, but at some point in time they will be exhausted. Coal will last the longest, so the experts say, but it too will someday have a stop. This is also true, incidentally, of nuclear power as presently produced, since the supply of uranium is also finite.

Thus we face a series of interlocking problems. One is that for the first time in our history we are not independent of the rest of the world; we cannot maintain our industry, much less fight a war, from our own energy resources alone. This means we must develop an immediate program of conservation combined with one to increase the imme-diately available supplies of oil and gas. Both of these will involve higher prices for consumers, personal and industrial, and a govern-ment policy that encourages, not discourages, new exploration.

That part of the problem lies within our reach, if we will accept it politically. The long-range problem is immensely more difficult.

It's been barely two centuries since the modern energy age was intro-duced with the development of the first practical steam-engine. Less than a century that most of man's work has been done by the power of fuels from the earth. It will be a short-lived era if we make it so by our profligacy in exhausting those resources with none to replace them.

What must be now is what the president asks, a determined effort to conserve and to develop other energy sources: solar energy, geo-thermal power, atomic fusion, breeder reactors or perhaps something yet undreamed of. This will require human ingenuity, political leader-ship and the public will to support it.

We have two forewarnings of what otherwise lies ahead. How many more will we need?

February 9, 1977

PARADISE LOST

In the beginning, whether you follow the stories of the Bible or the myths of the Greeks, it was an age of innocence and happiness for mankind.

Then, according to Genesis, Adam and Eve ate of the forbidden fruit. God had told them they might eat of every tree in the garden save one, but the serpent said that this was only God's jealousy because, if they did, their eyes would be opened and they too would be like gods. So they ate of the tree of knowledge and indeed their eyes were opened.

Whereupon the Lord God said, Behold, Man has become as one of us. And He said unto them that henceforth the tree would bring forth thorns and thistles and sorrow would they eat all the days of their lives.

In the Greek myth it was Prometheus, himself one of the Titans, who revolted against the gods and gave fire to men, the gift that made them more than a match for the animals, that enabled them to make tools with which to cultivate the earth, that warmed their dwellings so that they might escape the cold—the same fire, though, that burned their dwellings, scorched the earth and made the swords with which they killed one another.

It was Prometheus, too, who gave to his brother as a wedding gift a small box full of mysteries, with the caution to beware of opening it because it contained the secrets of Jupiter. But curiosity proved too much and Pandora opened the box to let loose all the ills to plague mankind. And once the box was opened she could not put them back again.

The point of both stories is the same. They remind us that we differ from other animals in that we are determined to seek knowledge, to know the mysteries that are hidden but from the gods, and that knowledge is a blessing mixed with woe.

Of late these stories have been haunting me.

For much in the news has been the controversy over whether scientists in their laboratories should be allowed to probe further into the mystery of life itself, into the genes which govern every living thing and say whether the living thing will be a microbe, a bird, a fish or a human being. To experiment with DNA, to see what new genetic combinations man may make, seems to many to open a Pandora's box of terrifying dangers.

And it was much from the same fear that President Carter the other day ordered a stop to all further work on plutonium. The United States, he said, will halt its work on plutonium in the hope that by our example other nations will also stop.

Mr. Carter's fears are well founded, for plutonium is very much a dangerous blessing. On the one hand it promises an almost unlimited supply of energy for an energy-starved world. On the other it carries the greatest risk of nuclear proliferation, of nuclear blackmail or nuclear accident, because of the explosive power from even the smallest amounts.

Unlike uranium-235, the fuel for present nuclear power plants, plutonium is not used up; in a breeder reactor the more plutonium you use the more you make, a wonder of physics that makes it unlikely that man would ever exhaust the energy resources of the earth. But it is also a terrifying radiological poison (absorbing a few thousand microcuries can be fatal) and because even small amounts can easily be made into bombs it poses incredible problems of security. With it, the smallest country could become an atomic power. It could also easily fall into the hands of terrorist groups, with all the horrors that implies.

So you can see why President Carter wants to stop further work on plutonium. But, as he has said, we cannot stop others from going ahead, and if the past is any guide we cannot expect that they will stop.

For one compelling reason, there is the promise of the blessings plutonium can offer. That alone will impel others, if not ourselves, to learn to use it. But there is also that other reason. The deep, driving instinct for knowledge so deeply bred into the human species. We are driven to unlock mysteries simply because the mysteries are there.

This same drive, unless the nature of men has changed, will impel them onward in genetic research. There is no doubt that techniques to overcome the natural barriers to genetic exchange can be dangerous; we cannot know what hazards may lie in genes transplanted from one microbe to another. A normally harmless bacterium might be transmuted into a deadly pathogen.

No wonder, then, that even prominent scientists have issued warnings against such experiments and that our National Academy of Sciences has called for a moratorium on recombinant DNA research.

But here too knowledge holds its promises as well as its dangers. This same research can let us glimpse mysteries heretofore hidden about how the genetic structure of an organism affects both its form and its function. Somewhere in that mystery could be the key to the genetic cause of diseases such as cancer.

That promise alone will drive others onward, no matter what we forego in our own laboratories. Moreover, that instinct to know is so bred into our species, confined to no race or country, that it will be stilled by no presidential order nor by the alarums of the fearful.

If that be so, and everything in the history of our species says that it is so, what is there to calm our fears? Is there no way we can save ourselves from knowing too much? From someday in a moment of careless rapture over our knowledge destroying ourselves and the earth as well?

To such questions, we cannot know the answers. The future is the last mystery reserved to the gods. All we can say is that it is a peril that has been with us since Man's first disobedience and the fruit of that forbidden tree, the price we pay for seeking dominion over earth and sky.

And as those stories long ago foresaw, once out of Eden there was no escape. Once eyes have been opened, there is no way to blot out the sight. Or, if you prefer the clairvoyance of a myth, no way to put knowledge back into the box whence it came. Our fate, for good or evil, is that the paradise of innocence has been long since lost and it will not be regained.

April 27, 1977

THE MALTHUSIAN THEOREM

The late Thomas F. Woodlock, whose thoughts on things were once a regular feature of *The Wall Street Journal*, used to warn the youngsters around the shop never to argue with the followers of Henry George or the believers in Thomas Malthus.

He was convinced both men were wrong, he would say, but you can't win an argument with their supporters because the logic of George and Malthus was impeccable.

Henry George has long since been forgotten. No economist today, and certainly no government, would have any truck with his argument that the only tax should be levied on land. Yet it is not easy to dispute the premise of his "single tax" theory that all material progress derives ultimately from the land, what lies on it or under it. So he thought idle land wasteful and should be taxed the heaviest, while labor, which tills the fields or shapes its raw materials, shouldn't be taxed at all.

On the other hand Malthus has had repeated reincarnations, and the echoes of his doctrines are heard today when President Carter warns us that the people of the earth are outstripping its natural resources of energy.

The Malthusian theorem, stated briefly, was that populations tend to grow faster than the growth of production necessary to sustain them. So population, he contended, will always expand to use up the means of subsistence unless it is checked by some force such as the catastrophes of war, famine or pestilence. Without such a check it inevitably reaches a point where the consequences are poverty and hardship as too many people struggle to live from too little production.

History has often seemed to refute that Malthusian prophecy. In his time the earth supported about 900 million people, which he thought near the limit of its food production. Today the world population is somewhere around four billion, a huge increase thanks to a forgotten

300

ingredient, the ingenuity of man in exploration and technology. The earth now produces food in quantities once unimaginable.

Still, the Malthusian argument is not so easily disposed of. For the essence of his argument was that no matter how much production increased, population would expand faster until once again it overloaded the means of subsistence. The human species, he said, was caught in a logical vise.

Naturalists are familiar with the phenomenon. Put a herd of animals in an area of plentiful food supply and where they are protected from predators, and they will soon overload their paradise. Then their numbers will have to be thinned, their numbers reduced by an artificial "catastrophe" to protect the group.

The same population phenomenon can be observed among people, even today, in some parts of the world, notably in India and areas in Asia.

Malthus, of course, was concerned primarily with food in 1798, since the industrial revolution lay nearly a century ahead. But in modern advanced societies "subsistence" embraces more than food. We need energy in huge quantities to sustain both industry and agriculture. More, we need quantities of other things dug from the earth—copper, lead, zinc, aluminum, phosphates, the raw materials of civilization circa 1977.

So the interesting question is whether the Malthusian theorem applies here too. Is it possible that we, the human species, by our number and our insatiable demands are outstripping the physical resources of our little planet?

The premise of the president's energy policy is affirmative with regard to fossil fuels. The premise is that however large the supplies, all of them are finite and exhaustible some day. Some day even coal, give or take a few hundred years, will be gone.

What, then, of other resources upon which our present civilization depends? A few are renewable; manganese, cobalt and nickel are continuously being formed on the ocean floor, though available only at great cost. Even these, though, will be available only so long as we do not violate the Malthusian equation: that is, only so long as the rate of use does not exceed the rate of formation.

Others, so far as we know, are nonrenewable, although for some of them—iron and aluminum—the exhaustion date lies far in the future.

Uranium and thorium are relatively abundant, at least for our times. But the phosphates, a major ingredient in fertilizers, are being consumed at a rate that may exhaust them in the not too distant future.

Over all of them, of course, hangs that Malthusian threat. That is, even if we were suddenly to discover some huge new pool of oil, would that merely multiply the rate of consumption? Something like that seems to have already happened with the discovery of oil in Alaska and the North Sea. Even with water, which is both nonexhaustible and nonrenewable in our biosphere, the demand of an expanding industrial world is pressing upon the readily available supply.

A grim picture? Certainly. Only an intellectual ostrich would deny the possibility that we can exhaust the physical resources of this earth upon which we live. Or, even before that happens, that we could put such a strain upon those resources that the modern industrial society could not sustain itself as we know it. It behooves us all to pay attention to our profligacy.

A despairing picture? Not necessarily. For what has always been left out of the Malthusian theorem is the ingenuity of the human species. Alone among animals we can, by conscious thought, control our numbers. We alone can alter our environment, for good or ill. We alone can probe the mysteries of our earth, and even of its universe.

This, indeed, is what has been left out of President Carter's energy program so far presented. It is so fearful that we cannot master the problem of energy that it proposes only to hoard what we have, not to search for what is yet to be discovered.

As that thoughtful man told me long ago, if your premise rests only upon what is known at a given moment, then the Malthusian logic is impeccable. But you cannot predict human destiny merely by extrapolating the present into the future.

May 11, 1977

XIII

Nights at the Opera

RETURN TO ENCHANTMENT

Every man has a few remembered things that retain their powers of enchantment. This Wednesday evening I returned to one and found it had lost none of its magic in a score of years and three.

Lily Pons made her debut at the Metropolitan in January 1931 as the ill-omened Lucia di Lammermoor. Between that January and this she sang the same arias from the same stage for ninety-nine times, so the statisticians say. It is not sentiment alone that brings the wish this hundredth performance shall be a happy omen of many more.

Miss Pons is no longer the dark lass of the moors but a blonde lady of the castle. She no longer, in her madness, floats down the grand stairway with such ethereal ease. She seems, at times, to have to call upon her fullest efforts to bring out the soaring echoes of the flute which make Lucia the ultimate test of a coloratura. But though twenty-three years may have added to the effort they have not subtracted from the song. There is no Lucia standing in the wings, not even Miss Munsel, to replace her.

Fausta Cleva, who conducted the orchestra, gave to this the testimony of a peer. Donizetti's instrumental music is itself a delight, but Mr. Cleva never let the orchestra intrude upon Miss Pons; the mood and the tempo were hers to declare. Only when others sang, and particularly in the choral numbers, did Mr. Cleva feel any need for offering the support of the orchestra.

The only pity of it is that Manager Bing has no one to sing beside her since Tagliavini went home to Italy. In the shadow of Miss Pons, Jan Peerce's Edgardo seemed a dull and shabby thing.

January 15, 1954

NIGHT TO REMEMBER

One afternoon in the late spring of 1930 Giulio Gatti-Casazza and Otto Kahn, manager and president of the Met, sat in a closed rehearsal hall listening to the Mad Scene from *Lucia*, the Bell Song from *Lakmé*, "Je suis Titania" from *Mignon* and "Caro Nome" from *Rigoletto*. On January 31, 1931, they presented the unheralded, and almost unknown, singer to the Metropolitan audience as Lucia di Lammermoor.

On January 3, 1956, Lily Pons sang again at the Met. And once more the program included the Mad Scene from *Lucia*, the Bell Song from *Lakmé*, "Je suis Titania" from *Mignon* and "Caro Nome" from *Rigoletto*. The second occasion was no less a triumph than the first.

Let me say quickly what a critic must. Not even the most poignant memories can wash away a quarter of a century. The years have taken away some of the freshness of the voice, if very little from that elfin face and figure. Where once the music poured forth with ease, it now comes with effort, if no less with grace and pride.

Yet saying that is to say too little. For last Tuesday evening was not a debut but a jubilee. Everywhere the silver sparkled, and not the least upon the majestic little lady who, so far as the oldest memory runs, is the first to span so many years on the stage of this house.

Manager Bing, a newcomer, gave her the Met's brightest honors. He provided a full-scale production of the second act of *Rigoletto* and of the great hall at Lammermoor. To dress the stage was the full chorus and the corps de ballet. To sing with Miss Pons were Jan Peerce, Robert Merrill, Nicola Moscona and Thelma Votipka. To assure musical perfection, the orchestra conductors worked in shifts. Pietro Cimara for *Lucia*, Fausta Cleva for *Rigoletto* and Max Rudolf for the arias from *Mignon* and *Lakmé*.

Finally, to evoke memories there was John Brownlee, who sang with

Miss Pons that quarter century ago, and a host of others to present her with silver keepsakes.

But withal it was Miss Pons—and the audience—who made the evening shimmer. Whatever trophies she may have given to time, she has yielded nothing in showmanship or in the mastery of musical timing. She dominated, as is her wont, every scene.

And that is the way her audience wanted it. At the end of *Lucia* there were old men who stood in the aisles to cheer and at least one young man who was moved to tears. For it was plain to all that we shall have to wait our own good time for her successor, unless there be some other Tetrazzini unheralded in the wings.

It was truly a pity that through television or some other magic all the myriad lovers of Miss Pons could not share the evening. It was a night to remember.

January 5, 1956

NEW GIFT OF MUSIC

The Metropolitan this week added another refurbished opera to its repertoire and a new Italian soprano to its roster. The combination of the two added up to one of the most brilliant musical events of many seasons.

Miss Renata Tebaldi, who sang Desdemona in Verdi's sweeping version of *Otello*, was already the darling of Milan's La Scala where her roles included such varied parts as Mimi in *La Bohème*, Tosca, Madame Butterfly and Aïda. Monday evening she made plain the reason why. A beautiful voice, expertly controlled, and a statuesque stage presence marked her as the most exciting dramatic soprano to hit the American opera and concert stage in recent memory.

Manager Bing gave her a setting to show off her qualities to best advantage. He has had *Otello* completely restaged by Dino Yannopoulos and Ellen Meyer, and he provided Miss Tebaldi with Mario Del Monaco to sing the title role and Leonard Warren as Iago. Then he put the whole under the sure musical direction of Fritz Stiedry.

That makes it difficult to be conservative with the superlatives or to know just where to begin using them. *Otello* starts out with the advantage of a truly dramatic story, unlike the soap-opera plots of most grand opera, and if anything the dramatic impact of the Shakespearean story is enhanced in the Boito libretto by having parts of it cut away. Attention can focus sharply where it belongs, on Otello's tormented jealousy under Iago's malevolent scheming.

Verdi then provided the somber and passionate music to fit this theme. It is essentially mood music, which may not give it the easy popularity of the more singable melodic operas. But from the first crashing chords with which he opens the first act, without benefit of overture, the sense of ominous tragedy is never lost. It is perhaps music to be sung only by masters, but in their hands it is masterly indeed.

Mario Del Monaco sometimes seemed prone to ham up the acting of the desolate Moor, but it is a role that calls for the grand manner. Anyway, in voice he was superb, and no one less than Miss Tebaldi could have outdone him. Leonard Warren made a cherubic sort of Iago, which must have been a little disconcerting at first to Shakespearean devotees. Yet before he was finished he had provided this somewhat corpulent villain with enough malevolence to satisfy anyone.

This three-cornered tale was told before some very striking sets. In the background of the first and third acts was a distant sea, first angry and then calm, in as an effective a bit of illusion as you might find at the Radio City Music Hall. These spectacular effects helped to emphasize the somberness of the final set which displayed only the murder bed in a bare chamber.

But above all this, the big event of the evening was still the debut of Miss Tebaldi.

To listeners accustomed to finding the voices of dramatic sopranos somewhat heavy in the higher registers, Miss Tebaldi's ability to reach up softly as well as surely will come as a delight. Her control of timbre and volume is almost miraculous; she can go from a peal to a whisper, and back again, with no perceptible effort and without the least loss of beauty in tone.

She may have been a little bit nervous in the first act. If so, it was understandable and as far as anyone could tell it had all disappeared by the final scene, which is the one that puts her to her greatest test. Here she was magnificent. And for all that she is a large woman, she handled her body with such expert stage presence that none of the emotional impact of the scene was lost.

This reviewer doesn't know as yet what other roles Mr. Bing plans for her this season or what her concert plans may be after it is over. But if Miss Tebaldi's Desdemona is a true sample of what she can do, the Met and American music lovers have a grand new gift from abroad.

February 2, 1955

BRILLIANT PAGEANT

An opera that is more oratorio than opera, more pageant than drama, was returned to the Metropolitan's repertoire last week after an absence of many years. And the brilliant performance which Mr. Bing's company gave to Gluck's *Orfeo and Euridice* offers a fine example of why it is so rarely staged.

For here is a moving musical work that cannot be carried as a piece of theater by its music alone, either vocally or orchestrally, and certainly not by its story. It requires what is known in modern theatrical parlance as a "production"—a combination of music, dancing, singing, costumes, sets and staging, all blended together in perfect balance. But this difficult task well done can provide, as the Metropolitan has proved, an enchanted evening.

To begin with, Manager Bing provided an excellent cast. Rise Stevens sang Orpheus, the lover out of Greek mythology who undertook the task of bringing his dead wife back from the depths of Hades. Hilda Gueden, one of the loveliest sopranos on any opera stage, made an entrancing Euridice and Roberta Peters was almost a perfect personification of the Goddess of Love.

If there was a single star of the evening it was not a singer but a dancer, Alicia Markova, who led the corps de ballet. Most of the music is non-vocal and it was Miss Markova and the ballet corps who made the long stretches of orchestral music theatrically effective. There was a spectacularly macabre Dance of the Furies in the first act, a light and airy Dance of the Blessed Spirits in the second act, and for the climax of the last act a breath-taking pageant that featured a complete classical ballet.

Yet when all is said, what made a rewarding evening was the way all the parts were put together. The credit for this not only goes to Mr. Bing, but to Mr. Herbert Graf, recently of the Music Hall, who did the staging, to Pierre Monteux who directed the orchestra and to Zachary

Solov who created the choreography. Harry Horner designed some sets that were simple but striking.

In lesser hands, or in ones that worked with less care, *Orfeo and Euridice* would be disappointing; the story has no action and the music, while pure and haunting, lacks dramatic passion. But handled as it was last week it was a delight and adds another gem to Mr. Bing's crown.

February 28, 1955

PRIMA DONNA AT THE MET

Maria Meneghini Callas of Brooklyn has made her debut at the Met. The occasion was also the opening of the Met's 1956–57 season, but for once the glittering first night audience was out-dazzled on the stage.

Let it be said at once that Miss Callas is not the greatest soprano of all time, or even of these times. Her voice has neither the lilt of Lily Pons, the sweetness of Renata Tebaldi nor the old quiet ease of Rosa Ponselle. In her singing the other evening there were noticeable imperfections. Her breath was audible in the pauses. There was a little jerk when she shifted registers. And in off moments her tone was a bit piercing.

But no matter. However you balance the critical niceties, Miss Callas is a splendid soprano. She is also a personality.

Norma is not the finest opera to display a personality. Its theatrics are poor; for the most part the leading characters just stand around in poses and pour out their troubles with nothing much happening. It is not even the most powerful opera musically; Bellini has written some gorgeous music for it but it is all of a piece, with hardly a variation in mood (musically or emotionally) from beginning to end. It isn't fiery theater.

But no matter about that, either. Miss Callas took charge from the moment of her entrance and never let go.

Since Norma is on stage and singing almost continuously, the role is an endurance test with few peers. It isn't even attempted by the mediocre. It can only be pulled off by that rara avis, the true prima donna. That is Miss Callas.

It is difficult to explain how she does it. She knows how to make a grand entrance and to use the grand gesture. But she rescues what might be hamminess, and turns it into a thing of emotional impact, by a personality that makes these things seem natural. She has disciplined her body as well as her voice so that she has the grace of a ballet dancer. Her face is extremely mobile so that the emotion comes not alone from the voice but from the whole person.

And she thoroughly understands that opera calls for a combination of sound musicianship and the theatrical arts. Without her splendid voice she would still be an actress ready to step into the role of Lady Macbeth with the Old Vic.

About the voice, much is left to be learned. In the soft duet with her rival, sung by Fedora Barbieri, it was truly magnificent, soft and in perfect balance. In the usual last act finale, it showed tremendous power. But her reputation is for a wide-ranging talent; Lucia is one of her roles. Her countrymen will have to wait to see how she handles coloratura roles before that reputation is assessed.

Manager Rudolf Bing certainly gave her a prima donna's reception. He put Mario Del Monaco, the best Italian tenor around, in the lover's role. And besides Miss Barbieri, he supported her with Cesare Siepi and, in the orchestra, Fausta Cleva. The only thing drab was the set. Miss Callas took care of lighting that up.

October 31, 1956

FAMILY AFFAIR

It is not often that a Lucia—especially such a Lucia as Joan Sutherland—has to share attention with the stage sets and the orchestral conductor. But that was the effect the other evening when the Met staged its first *Lucia* in the new opera house with Richard Bonynge making his debut in the pit.

It troubled her not. Miss Sutherland could be dismissed with a sentence. In natural voice, in training and in her ability to fulfill them both, Miss Sutherland stands supreme among the sopranos of the day. But even that is not enough to say of her performance the other evening..

Whether due to the fact that Mr. Bonynge is her husband or to the fact that time has matured both voice and talent, Miss Sutherland surpassed all her past performances here. There was an electric quality about her, proceeding as much from personality as from voice, that lit sparks everywhere. After the Mad Scene it took a full quarter hour for the audience to calm down enough for the performance to go on.

The best word for Mr. Bonynge is inconspicuous. He kept both himself and the orchestra out of the way and seemed to follow his wife more than to lead. While that might be a fault on some occasions, here it was a virtue for which he deserves credit. He showed off her performance by not trying to show off himself.

The sets, however, are quite conspicuous indeed and well adapted to the expanse of the new house, showing off here much better than in the old one. Indeed, except for the unfortunate lighting of Rudolph Kuntner this was a production as exciting to the eye as to the ear.

The other principals were also quite good indeed, especially John Alexander as Edgardo. It wasn't their fault that they were overshadowed.

August 14, 1966

AIRY DELIGHT

Every once in a while an opera company, like a football team, will come upon a day when fortune decrees not only that every member will surpass himself but that all will blend together in mysterious perfection. On such rare days the great operas touch nobility and lesser ones become a marvel of delight.

Such was the occasion last Thursday evening when the Metropolitan gave the season's first performance of *La Sonnambula*. This fairy-like tale of a young lady who sleepwalks her way into scandal and then sleepwalks her way out of it is as fluffy as *Up In Mabel's Room*, and Bellini's music is as airy as a soufflé. But delight is the only word for the way it was served by Joan Sutherland, John Alexander, Giorgio Tozzi, Jeanette Scovotti and their colleagues backstage and in the orchestra.

Miss Sutherland, it's hardly necessary to say, was the brilliant star of the evening. Hers is without doubt the most superb all-around soprano voice extant, at once powerful and soft, rich in timbre. But her contribution was more than that of a prima donna's voice, for while she let go with dazzling pyrotechnics in her own arias, in the duets and ensembles she blended her singing to the enhancement of the whole.

In this, we suspect, she was the inspiration for what can only be called the perfect togetherness of the total performance. At any rate, that was the effect, so that Mr. Alexander, Mr. Tozzi and Miss Scovotti seemed to shine even more than is their accustomed way. One mark of this, perhaps, was that Silvio Varviso, the conductor, kept the music lilting and appeared to enjoy the performance as much as did the audience.

There was the proper airy lilt, too, to the choreography of Zachary Solov and just the right fairy-like quality to the new sets of Rolf Gerard, although we must note in passing that some of Mr. Gerard's stone steps looked insubstantial enough to risk tumbling Miss Sutherland down the stairs.

All in all, it was such a performance as is not likely to be duplicated with quite the same perfection, even with the same cast. That kind of magic cannot be conjured up on order. But Miss Sutherland and her colleagues prove how right Rudolf Bing was to return *La Sonnambula* to the Met's regular repertoire. In these hands it is sure to prove always a delight.

December 9, 1963

AÏDA AND THE BELLY DANCERS

In its ninety-two years Verdi's *Aïda* has been staged with everything from chariots to elephants. But so far as we can recall or discover, the new production which the Metropolitan this week offered as its opening performance of the season is the first one to decorate the grand triumphal scene with belly dancers.

The innovation was not wholly a triumph. For if *Aïda* was intentionally designed to be super-colossal (a sort of pre-cinematic *Cleopatra*), it was also intended to be grand in theme as it proved grand in music. And the trouble with the belly dancers, like some of the other self-conscious touches in Nathaniel Merrill's staging and Katherine Dunham's choreography, was that they brought yaks instead of ahs from the audience.

That was a pity, too, for the rest of the new production was dramatically interesting and musically superb.

With the exception of the last act set, which was not as striking an arrangement as in the older production, the sets and costumes of Robert O'Hearn were imaginative and colorful. The principals—who included Birgit Nilsson, Carlo Bergonzi and Irene Dalis—offer as fine voices as one is ever apt to collect at one time. And few conductors can put as much fire into Verdi's music as Georg Solti.

Miss Nilsson may lack some of the physical accoutrements ideally associated with a beautiful Ethiopian slave girl, and Miss Dalis is not so slinky an Amneris as, say, Blanche Thebom. But there are no soprano voices around to match the magnificent control of Miss Nilsson's. When it's required she can cut through the full orchestra with the greatest of ease; she can also drift up to the highest registers with a soft and moving pianissimo. If she was suffering from illness at the opening performance, as reported, she gave not the slightest sign of it.

As for Miss Dalis in the role of Amneris, whatever her difficulties with her body movements there were none with her vocal movements. Her voice is dramatic, and in her last act scene in which she sings of her tortured remorse at having condemned her lover Radames to a living tomb, she is emotionally moving.

Mr. Bergonzi, not a personality of great fire, let himself be overshadowed by the ladies for a good part of the evening. Yet given the chance, he was an excellent Radames, notably in his opening aria to the heavenly Aïda and in the final entombed love scene.

The secondary roles, as is so often true at the Met under Rudolf Bing, were rewardingly sung. John Macurdy made a royal Pharaoh; Giorgio Tozzi, with his deeply resonant voice, was an impressive high priest; Mario Sereni, as Amonasro, was in both voice and bearing a properly proud captive king.

All of which added to the little disappointments of the production, for they were small ones on the total scale of things. The first act set, for example, was a striking one and established at once both the atmosphere of ancient Egypt and the mood of brooding tragedy. Amneris's apartment in the palace at Thebes, where the second act opens, was luxurious enough for Elizabeth Taylor yet without being so overdone as to seem either vulgar or impossible for the times.

But there was small reason, so far as we could see, to set the meeting between Aïda and her father, and later with Radames, amid temple ruins. It does not accord with Verdi's stage directions, and hardly accords with the fact that at the time of the story Egyptian power and wealth were at their highest.

There was more excuse for the introduction of a fertility-rites dance, we suppose, since ancient Egypt was not noted for its Puritanism. Still, we found it a bit odd to have these rites take place in the scene in which Radames is being armed and girded for a great martial endeavor.

The rest of the choreography, too, struck us as more imaginative than intelligently tasteful. Some of the show-piece dances before Amneris, while properly African, seemed more appropriate for a modern jazz festival than the era of Isis. And the introduction into this scene of a tiny little girl, cutely mimicking her elders just for laughs, brought lifted eyebrows from the highbrows in the audience and plain boos from the real Verdi lovers standing behind the back rails.

The trouble, we think, was just not knowing when to stop. But if that was a mistake, it is one easily rectified by just a little more restraint, a little "pulling back" on the excesses. When that is done, and we suspect it will be in subsequent performances, then the Met will have a fine new production of *Aïda* for its repertoire.

October 16, 1963

OPERA SPOOFFA

For the enjoyment of satire two things are necessary. One is that you know the thing being satirized well enough to recognize parody. The other is that you have a sense of humor.

Fortunately for Gian Carlo Menotti the premiere last week of his *The Last Savage* was not a special gala but a subscription performance for the Metropolitan's regulars, who found it delightful. Unfortunately a number of the local critics apparently have no sense of humor about opera, missed the point entirely and greeted it with dismally pompous reviews.

For it was eminently clear from the first curtain that Mr. Menotti was writing a spoof of classic opera, particularly the nineteenth-century Italian variety. Librettist Menotti used every tangled plot cliché available. Composer Menotti picked up the musical mannerisms of Verdi, Puccini and Donizetti and crossbred them with Sir Arthur Sullivan and Richard Rodgers, adding a dash of Sigmund Romberg. Then producer Menotti staged the result with such an outlandish exaggeration that his tongue-in-cheek ought to have been visible from the back row.

Yet all we got from most of the critics were somber complaints about an unimaginative plot and "derivative" music. For our own part, we joined the audience in finding it all pleasant fun.

The fun begins when an American millionaire by the name of Scattergood is trying to make a business-deal marriage between his modern-minded daughter and the modern-minded son of an Indian Maharaja, each of the fathers trying to hedge against the inroads of socialism in their respective countries.

The obstacle is that the young lady, having studied anthropology at Smith (or Vassar or Wellesley), is searching for an aboriginal savage as a contribution to science, and the Prince believes in democratic love for a caste-less Indian maid. So the fathers cook up a scheme to make a fake savage out of a stableboy, let him be captured and taken to Chicago for display in order to get all that foolishness out of the young lady's system.

Thereafter things get as complicated as you could wish. Naturally the young lady falls in love with the savage. Naturally it turns out that the Prince is actually the son of the American millionaire and the Maharaja's wife (the result of a forgotten tryst on the Nile in the days of their youth). Naturally the Prince, being half-American, marries the serving maid and sets out to scatter good among the oppressed Indians.

To accompany this operatic tale Mr. Menotti has put together a light-hearted musical mélange. There's a quartet, a sextet and two septets, a grand triumphal march replete with thundering trumpets, and a couple of coloratura arias drowning in cadenzas, a lush tenor love song, and a baritone lament fit for Emile de Becque on some South Pacific isle.

Nor is opera the only thing that's spoofed. The second act ends with a Chicago cocktail party that's the wildest thing since Auntie Mame, with satirical darts at modern art, Bohemian poetry and atonal chamber music.

And it's all obviously fun for the performers. Roberta Peters enjoys herself immensely, giving just the right exaggeration to the coloratura pyrotechnics. George London, as the savage stableboy, seems a mite sheepish at first in his Tarzan leopard skin but he carries it off with good grace and humor. Ezio Flagello and Lili Chookasian, as the Maharaja and Maharani, are simply superb comic figures, both in voice and acting.

The orchestra too has caught the mood. Thomas Schippers, ordinarily the very picture of the proper young conductor, waves his arms and jumps about on the podium for all the world like Danny Kaye conducting his Television Symphony with Art Carney at the piano. And at one point one of the flautists was puckered in such a grin that he missed a cadenza entirely.

The serious critics are right, of course, that Mr. Menotti has not written here anything worth serious consideration as an opera. Even as opera buffa it doesn't belong in the first rank because it depends too much on easy parody and lacks anything that might be called creative humor. The Metropolitan will have to wait, as it has been waiting since

1909, for a new American opera to gain a permanent place among the old beloved treasures.

But it's possible to love the old operas, as one loves old friends, and still be able to laugh at a spoof of their foibles. What's wrong, once in a while, with a bit of simple fun on your night at the opera?

January 27, 1964

XIV

Purely Personal

EUROPE REVISITED:
A NOSTALGIC TOUR WITH
GRANDCHILDREN

There is something to be said for Robert Benchley's grumpy remark that there are two kinds of travel—first class and with children.

As my wife and I discovered, taking two young granddaughters on their first trip to Europe can be wearying to the flesh and discombobulating to travel habits. Not for us, this time, leisurely dinners at starred Michelin restaurants, the afternoon nap or the lazy morning of a dreary day. Because of the young's pressure for movement, we were up betimes to repeat what we had thought we were long since done with—standing with the throng at Buckingham Palace for the Changing of the Guard or making the pilgrimage to the Eiffel Tower.

So be forewarned: Traveling with grandchildren is not a placid holiday. You will find surprises, and you can expect some misadventures. But Benchley notwithstanding, such a journey is also a time of many delights. There is an especial pleasure, to be understood only by those of a certain age, in introducing your grandchildren to a whole new world, of returning to familiar places and seeing them anew through fresh eyes. You are reminded of that wonderful excitement of first seeing Piccadilly Circus from atop a bus or strolling the vast expanse of the Champs Elysées.

For my wife and myself the pleasure was enhanced because it was also a sentimental journey. Just twenty years ago we took our own two daughters to Europe and this time we repeated it as nearly as we could.

This meant, first of all, that we decided against a grand tour, flitting from country to country in a jumble of days. We would rather our granddaughters, Heather, thirteen years old, and Shelley, eleven, come to know two of our favorite cities, London and Paris, with time enough to absorb them.

Being a sentimental journey, we also had to start our twenty-five-day trip on the *Queen Elizabeth 2*. The new Queen may not have the grandeur of the old dowager but she remains a civilized anachronism in the age of the airbus. We wanted Heather and Shelley to have at least a taste of gracious travel before this species vanishes, something to tell their grandchildren of how it was in the olden days.

It meant, too, splurging on first class, although the *QE2* does not make a sharp division between first and tourist except in the dining room. Somewhat to our surprise, the two girls took delight in seeing Grandfather in dinner jacket and Granny in a long dress and in nightly doffing their own jeans for ladylike dresses.

So the *QE2* made a good beginning. On our crossing there were children of all ages aboard and by the second day out we had two shipboard "romances" under way. These gave the girls companions for swimming, Ping-Pong, movies and, in Heather's case, an escort for late-night disco dancing, which saved Grandfather from having to endure the ear-shattering din.

It was convenient for the old folks in other ways, too. With the young people's time well occupied, we could relax in our sedate way, storing up energy for the shore-side excursions ahead.

It was on the *Queen*, though, that we met our first crisis. A day out of Southampton a mysterious bug struck down Shelley with a high fever, and it was a heart-stopping time for grandparents overwhelmed by responsibility. Fortunately, a shipboard doctor banished our fears of appendicitis, meningitis or other imagined disasters, and the trouble subsided with the marvelous recuperative powers of youth. Put the incident down as one of the hazards of traveling with grandchildren.

We arrived in London in an inauspicious downpour but otherwise in eager good spirits. Good spirits are needed when travelers are confronted with the logistics of moving four people with six large bags and innumerable handbags, packets and miscellaneous gear. Porters become not a luxury but a necessity, and we were to discover that not all European taxis are large enough. Sometimes it took two, confirming the wisdom of confining our itinerary to just London and Paris. Moving proved a bit like shifting the Ringling Brothers Circus.

We also confirmed our decision to select, in both cities, a central hostelry near a subway stop instead of less expensive lodgings on the outskirts. We found that this strategy saved wear on the nerves, especially Grandfather's.

London, of course, is a cornucopia of sightseeing treasures. The problem is to choose among them those most likely to appeal to the young. Some are obvious, but in our case there were some surprises. Obviously, Buckingham Palace and the Tower head my list. I had forgotten, however, how much stamina each requires.

From the entrance of the Tower at Traitors' Gate to the top of the White Tower is a stiff climb, especially if you detour to join the long queue snaking around the Crown Jewels, and then have to stand and stare at endless armor, crossbows, swords and muskets. The older visitor is then ready to find a quiet sitting place and allow the granddaughters to explore the spot where Anne Boleyn lost her head.

They tell you that the Changing of the Guard at Buckingham Palace takes only half an hour, but the crowd gathers an hour ahead and if you are laggard all that your grandchildren will see will be the top of a guardsman's plume.

I had forgotten how hard all such sightseeing is on the legs; a little more spring training would have been helpful. If your grandchildren are as eager as ours, you will also have before you Madame Tussaud's wax museum (the Chamber of Horrors is a bit disappointing), the London City Museum (the Royal Coach and an animated panorama of the Great Fire of London are worth the trip) and Kensington Gardens (the children's playground is a happy discovery).

By the time you are ready for Hampton Court I recommend the Take-a-Guide Service, which provides guides who use their own cars and make an easier day of it. Windsor Castle can be thrown into the bargain. Of course, visitors still have to climb the castle hill or wander in the maze at Hampton Court, but the reward is a glimpse of royal living from Henry VIII to Elizabeth II.

That experience is even better if your grandchildren have been persuaded to read a little history before the journey. It was a pleasant surprise to have a thirteen-year-old straighten out Grandfather on the order of English kings and the wives of Henry VIII, and at the British Museum (wear your walking shoes here also) to discover her unexpected familiarity with the Rosetta Stone.

Happily, London is not all hiking and history. Some evenings we would catch a quick supper (Fortnum & Mason's dining room is useful) before going to the theater. There our reward was watching sparkling young eyes at *Annie* or *Oliver*. Another night we went to the cavernous Albert Hall for a military band concert, bright with regimental uniforms, crackling with trumpets and a rousing rendition of the Battle of Waterloo, complete with exploding cannons.

Afterward we would enjoy a nightcap of ice cream and sugar wafers. Being indulgent is a privilege of grandparents; if we indulged the girls in sweets and late hours we also knew that they would return soon enough to a proper routine.

Somehow we also found time to show them the lights of Piccadilly Circus and the quaintness of Shepherd's Market, and to introduce them to the ritual of afternoon tea at the Dorchester. We also stumbled upon an exotic place called the Great Chicago Pizza Factory, tucked in a lane off Pall Mall, and spent an afternoon feeding the pigeons in Trafalgar Square.

It was not until the end of our London visit that we met another crisis. Our careful planning included the night train to Paris, the one where the sleeper cars are put aboard the cross-channel ferry. Alas, British Rail chose that night to cancel the train.

The result was a series of misadventures. Substituting the day train involved transferring our baggage from the train to the ferry, off the ferry onto the French train, and then from that train into two Parisian taxis. To top it off, the rough passage on the English Channel was shared with hordes of seasick children, including one of ours.

But Paris redeemed itself in Gallic fashion, despite a spell of rainy days. The children learned, somewhat to their astonishment, I think, that French was not just an annoying schoolroom chore but something people actually spoke. Out came the traveler's phrase book and before long the girls were asking for the room key in an intelligible accent and correcting Grandfather's barely intelligible one.

We had arranged to stay near the Rue de Rivoli, which is in walking distance of the Place de la Concorde, Place Vendôme and the lower reaches of the Champs Elysées. Walking distance meant walking, and we had hardly settled in before, once again, Grandfather's legs were wobbling. The young have energy we only remember!

Have you been to the Eiffel Tower on a summer's day? It may have been only an illusion but it seemed to me that not since the sixteenth century has Europe been in the grip of such a Children's Crusade. The elevator cages were packed with them and, once on top, there seemed hardly room to peer over the parapet at the panorama below.

For some reason the distance between the Eiffel Tower and Les Invalides, where Napoleon lodged, has been stretched since my last visit.

Still, the Champs de Mars, lying between, offers a good vista and, once arrived at Napoleon's crypt, it was another pleasure to discover that our thirteen-year-old had at least a nodding acquaintance with the emperor's battles and his love affairs.

As a result of the breakdown of the night ferry, we had lost a day from our Paris schedule, but thanks to the vigor of the young and an indefatigable grandmother we still managed to crowd in Notre Dame and Sainte-Chapelle, the Jeu de Paume (a museum the mind can encompass) and the Louvre (a museum it cannot), to stroll the Left Bank and to take the funicular to Sacré-Coeur.

Versailles, of course, was also on our schedule. Unhappily, the day before our planned visit an extremist group chose to blow up part of it, and with all the excitement it seemed wiser to go elsewhere. This was a disappointment to the girls, whose romantic interest in Marie Antoinette had to be satisfied by showing them where the guillotine stood. Catching a sunny day, however, we took a cruise on the Seine aboard a *bateau mouche*, where we could sit down, and, thanks to my weariness, we also did some sitting in sidewalk cafes.

Our visit would not have been complete without a visit to the Folies Bergères. Twenty years ago when we took our daughters there the performance could have been considered risqué. Today its scantily clad dancers raise no eyebrows even on children's faces but it remains a fast-paced show with spectacular scenic effects to keep youthful eyes agog.

As for Parisian dining, the Tour d'Argent would be wasted on grandchildren but we found more modest places like La Bonne Fourchette on Rue St. Honoré, which gave a satisfactory taste of French cuisine, and our young were delighted with Le Soufflé, a tiny place on Rue du Mont Thabor. When they grew too nostalgic for familiar food there was always Le Drugstore at the Place de l'Opéra or pommes frites at McDonald's.

We reached home after a final misadventure. The jam-packed, uncomfortable 747 ran short of even ice for Cokes, and we arrived to find a baggage foul-up that left Heather without her clothes, carefully kept diary, treasured mementos and all her gifts for family and friends. They were recovered about three weeks later.

I have no way of knowing what memories will be most vivid for Heather and Shelley, but I do not think they will be only of misadventures or only of such delights as breakfast in bed on the *QE2* or feeding those pigeons in Trafalgar Square. There will surely be many others for time to sort out and enrich them in ways they cannot now realize.

As for my wife and myself, we came back weary in body and exhausted in pocketbook. A budget calculated long ago was wrecked by inflation abroad and the depreciating dollar. And that tiredness made us wonder at times if we were not too old to travel with the energetic young.

Yet we came back refreshed in spirit. We experienced not only the pleasure of giving young eyes a glimpse of new worlds to be explored but also the good fortune simply to spend some weeks alone with our grandchildren at a time when they stand on the threshold between childhood and adolescence. It was a once-in-a-lifetime opportunity to get to know them.

With capital gains taxes and inheritance taxes—and the one piled atop the other—we cannot expect to leave much to our grandchildren except memories. These, at least, cannot be taxed away.

The New York Times, January 28, 1979

FIFTY YEARS AFTER

School reunions are as American as apple pie. Every year at high schools, prep schools, colleges and even the advanced institutions, such as law and medicine, old graduates drift back to renew old acquaintances or relive old memories.

But there's one particular reunion that brings an old grad up short. That's the fiftieth. By that time the numbers have dwindled, old dreams have faded and life has become whatever it is.

So when I first heard there would be a gathering to celebrate the fiftieth anniversary of my high school graduation I felt somebody must be kidding. A half-century? Impossible.

Then I looked in the faded yearbook. And there was my smooth-faced, cherubic picture as a senior in the Hugh Morson High School, Raleigh, North Carolina, class of 1929.

The gathering proved more fun than I expected. It was, of course, dripping in nostalgia. People went around staring at name tags (written in large letters for tired eyes) and recalling ancient adventures. There was the night, for example, when in the midst of play rehearsal some miscreant found the central switchboard and turned out all the building lights. I smugly noted that the statute of limitations bars chastisement for such misdemeanors and admitted to enjoying the ensuing chaos.

Graduation night replayed itself in a haze of memories, of the boys in their best suits with jackets and ties, the girls in something called "period dresses" of white organdy with corsages of pink roses on their arms. Very lovely they looked indeed.

Someone recalled that a nickel then would get you a Hershey bar, an Eskimo Pie or an ice-cream cone at Brantley's drug store. The movies (*Wild Party* with Clara Bow, *Dreams of Love* with Joan Crawford) cost a quarter, ten cents if you sat in the second balcony, which is where couples nestled in the darkened back row.

But sometime during the evening other thoughts began to intrude upon the nostalgia. Our graduation speaker, as graduation speakers will, had told us we had the making of our lives in our own hands. He was right in part and wrong in part. He in his ignorance and we in our innocence knew not what lay ahead.

We had all been born before the war to end all wars. We grew up in the roaring twenties, when everyone thought prosperity would be for-ever. Happily we didn't know that the curtain was about to come down. Just ahead of us, that autumn, lay the stock market crash— which would change our country, our town and our lives. Suddenly amid the reunion revels came a somber thought: We, we here of the class of '29, were survivors.

Our youth passed, we faced the greatest depression in history, not of our making but through which we had to make our way as best we could. Beyond lay another great war, which many of us would join and from which some of us would not return. In fact our lives have spanned four wars, two of them such world wars, one of them the most domes-tically searing for our country since the Civil War.

We were also to see our country torn apart by the labor riots of the 1930s, the race riots of the 1960s. We have already endured three peri-ods of inflation and stand now in the midst of another.

In our lifetime we have gone from the horse and buggy, familiar in our childhood days, to soaring jets spanning the oceans, to a landing on the moon. We have seen the secrets of the atom unlocked, with what consequences none can yet foretell.

We have also lived through a revolution in morals and manners. Some of it we welcome, like that in the relations between the races. Some of it makes us uneasy, like the sexual revolution; not for the rea-sons you might suppose (a new name has simply been given to some-thing old) but because of the shadow it casts on the social order (now, naturally, called the "nuclear family") in which we grew up.

Some of it truly alarms us, like the revolution that has brought vio-lence not only to the streets but to the classrooms of memory. The schoolhouse pranks of long ago have yielded to mayhem, and even murder, in the corridors where children gather.

We hear it said this is a socio-economic phenomenon, brought on by unemployment or other economic dislocations. It's an explanation that only puzzles us. For in our time unemployment was measured in double-digit figures, as inflation is today, and none escaped economic dislocations. Yet in the deepest part of the Depression you could walk the city streets and there was no need of armed guards in schoolhouse halls.

Perhaps it is only weariness, but to those of a certain age it has not seemed a tranquil half-century. There's a popular book by Alvin Toffler called *Future Shock*, warning today's young of the assault that changing times will make upon their lives. Those of us gathered upon a summer's evening could tell today's young—our children and our grandchildren—that we have survived past shock.

No doubt things are, as the newspapers and television tell us, in terrible shape, with the shape of things to come even more foreboding. But it seems to us they always were. And somehow we have survived.

That, I suspect, is what gave the evening such a festive air. We paused for a moment to remember those who didn't make it. Then the revels resumed. There was dancing to soft, long-forgotten music. For a brief time, anyway, that gray-haired man was once more the star football player and the dowager lady once more May Queen.

So I recommend your fiftieth reunion, should you be a survivor. A half-century can't pass without being crammed with memories. Even being with all those old people won't spoil the fun.

September 12, 1979

FIFTIETH ANNIVERSARIES—FIFTY

Somewhere out there in that mysterious computer land where our names are stored by mail-order salesmen, and they're bought and sold like pork bellies, there must be a special asterisk by my name.

Anyway I've been getting some peculiar mail lately along with the catalogs from L. L. Bean, Bloomingdale's and Hammacher-Schlemmer that usually stuff the mail box.

One just recently was a special offer for a lot in a cemetery—pardon me, a Memorial Park. When I figured out the price on a square-foot basis I thought they were offering me a parcel in Manhattan. What I couldn't figure out was how I manage to get recompense from the grave if they don't live up to the promise of perpetual care around the tombstone.

This was followed by a proposal for life insurance especially designed "for those between sixty and eighty." No physical exam required. Working out the annual premiums on my handy-dandy calculator I concluded I'd have to drop off pretty soon if I wanted to come out ahead on the deal.

Now my mail tells me there's a whole magazine just for those of us in what's euphemistically called the prime of life. If I subscribe it will tell me about all the booby-traps to look out for in retirement homes and thereafter in nursing care centers.

Obviously the computers have got me well tagged. I never seem to get any catalogs for hip-hugging jeans or scuba diving equipment. *Yachting* magazine did slip up with a special introductory subscription rate. No come-ons, though, from *Playboy* or *Hustler*.

A friend who teaches embryonic MBAs says this illustrates the way modern technology helps pinpoint marketing targets in a nation of changing demographics. Nobody's abandoned the huge youth market, but overall the population's aging. That means worries for the Social Security system but opportunities for business. Those of us in that "prime of life" generally have more money than kids and make good customers for the right goods.

We get pinpointed in a number of ways. My professional friend points out that a couple of years ago I wrote in *The Wall Street Journal* about my fiftieth high-school anniversary. That, he said, got me reclassified onto the gerontology list, proving the *Journal*'s slogan it carries "news you can use."

If that's the case, the worst is yet to be. A few weeks ago the lady at my house had her own fiftieth high-school reunion where I had to wear a name tag that read "Frances Claypoole's Husband." I learned that in the springtime of '31 she was voted "most attractive girl," which it seemed to me she still was. Next thing you know, though, she'll be on mailing lists for widow's weeds.

The trouble with fiftieth anniversaries is that once begun they multiply. That same lady, who remembers such things, reminded me just the other day it was the fiftieth anniversary of our first "date"—a word that itself has an antique ring. Upcoming, if I live so long, is a fiftieth college reunion followed shortly thereafter by like remembrance of a wedding day, at which point the newspaper will want one of those pictures of the ancient couple for the young to marvel at.

Fiftieth birthdays can be pleasant affairs. Just mid-life, so you can look forward to much ahead. Fiftieth anniversaries bring on a backward look and you start talking to the young about things that happened half-a-century ago, which leaves their eyes glazed.

What does that young *Journal* reporter, fresh from questioning Ronald Reagan, care about my tales about talking to Franklin Roosevelt? Come to think of it, ere long there'll be a fiftieth anniversary of my first story in that then small newspaper, circulation 35,000. That means, I fear, a "memorial dinner" where the reluctant attendants will have to wear name tags of large type so I can tell the publisher from the editor.

Already I've a problem with a granddaughter who, studying history, gets the impression from my meandering talk that I must have been a contemporary of the emperor Franz Josef of Austria. Which, in fact, I was.

I'm well aware, of course, that this is better than the alternative. How could I not be when there are so many from olden days who no longer answer the roll call, and when I find myself turning first to the obituary page of the morning paper?

But is it really necessary to mark every milepost with public commemoration to remind us with what speed the fiftieth anniversaries mount? You reach a point, you see, where everything marks fifty years since something. After a while it gets to be deadly monotonous.

It's all very well to recall from classroom days old Seneca's remark, "Iucundissima est aetas devexa iam." Life seems more delightful on the downward slope, however, before the incline gets so steep you begin to suffer acrophobia.

Mind you, I find it a pleasant custom to honor age, as with a septuagenarian president. All the same, I sometimes feel like that fellow who, being tarred and feathered, remarked that if it warn't for the honor of the thing he'd as leave do without it.

July 15, 1981

TO BE A QUEEN

"You can't be a Queen, you know, till you've passed the proper examination." So the Red Queen warned Alice just as she thought she already was and imagined the golden crown heavy on her head.

Not long before Alice had seen her White Knight tumble off his horse, though whether while playing polo or racing a steeplechaser the childhood tale doesn't say. Still, he picked himself up unhurt and afterwards Alice would remember the bright blue eyes and kindly smile, the sun gleaming through his hair. He told Alice she could be queen someday if she didn't give up, went right ahead and crossed the last brook.

"To be a Queen!" exclaimed Alice, as she stood on the edge of that last obstacle. "How grand it sounds!"

And how grand it seemed last week as another little girl took the last step that could someday make her queen. Her name was Diana, about to be Princess of Wales. No matter. To most of the millions watching she was the Alice of fairy-tale dreams. Especially to the other little girls on the dull and workaday side of the looking glass.

Queens have to be dignified, of course, as Alice told herself. For Diana that meant no more tears if clicking camera lights flashed in her eyes, or if her White Knight again fell off his horse. That would be part of her examination. And dignified Diana was, all the way to St. Paul's and back again.

I don't know what you thought about it all, whether you took the trouble to arise at 5:00 A.M. to watch. It helped to face the predawn dark if there were little girls, daughters or granddaughters, in your house to stir sleepy heads and watch in wide-eyed wonder. I have to confess that even with all our little girls off in other nests my wife and I were up betimes.

You may think that takes explaining, although in the morning dark I noticed lights winking on in neighbors' houses.

That our household stirred so early was due in part to the fact I was on a holiday and weary of summer TV reruns. But there was also the tug of nostalgia.

It was only yesterday—a mere twenty-eight years ago—that two little girls in our house stayed past their bedtimes to see a queen crowned, mother of today's White Knight. There were no satellites then to whisk the pictures instantly across the seas. They were flown by special couriers upon whose coming all had to wait.

What I remember of that time is not only the shining eyes watching the midnight pictures but the sight next morning of a thirteen-year-old with the newspaper spread on the living room floor avidly reading about what she had just watched. That was comfort for a father wondering if the new age would outmode the printed word.

But some other thoughts also ran through my head the other morning.

Queens aren't what they used to be, or kings either. No more of that "off with their heads!" at any displeasure. You can forgo a curtsy and still keep yours. Indeed, nowadays it's the kings and queens who may lose their crowns if not their heads at the displeasure of their subjects. They're as rare as crinoline and antimacassars.

We've had no truck with royalty in our country since we sent old George packing. We choose our presidents by public lot. True, we house and feed presidents well; that office costs as much as any royal court what with helicopters at beck and call and a summer palace more comfortable than Windsor. But we tolerate them for no more than eight years and often fling them out much earlier.

Moreover, we permit them no airs. We allow no privacy in their personal lives, give them no minister to shield them from the whips and scorns of political life.

Being a democracy (one person, one vote, equality for everybody and all that sort of thing), we pretend we want our presidents to be ordinary folk like those next door. No frills and furbelows. But I noticed that President Carter won no plaudits by carrying his own suitcase across the White House lawn, by banishing "Hail to the Chief" to announce his coming.

The truth is we view a president through bifocals. Through one lens he's that haberdasher, peanut farmer or actor. Through the other he's the president of the United States. When we grumble it's Harry, Jack, Jimmy or Ronnie. We hunger, though, for a personage above the political fray when the ruffles and flourishes sound.

That's where kings—and queens—come in handy. They can no longer send courtiers in disfavor to the Tower (ah, what president doesn't long for such power!). But there are recompenses. If the realm is in sad estate, or riots disturb its peace, nobody blames Elizabeth II. They lay all that on Maggie. And while prime ministers come and go, a crown remains to show all the realm still stands. A small thing, no doubt. A comfort nonetheless.

Not for us, of course, such make-believe. All the same, all over the world, here as well as elsewhere, millions by the hundreds the other day watched plumed horsemen, gilded coaches, gentlemen in antique scarlet, a girl in a tiara pronounced a princess. And all, I think, hoped she and her White Knight would live happily ever after, as it always is in fairy tales.

With the harshness of the day the realities returned. Hidden only briefly by the pageantry, Britain is indeed a troubled realm. We are left to wonder whether the little princess will ever wear a crown beside her prince. Camelot was long ago and never was except in dreams.

But what if it was all make-believe for a brief and shining hour? The heart need not disbelieve in fairies because the eyes have never seen one this side of the looking glass.

August 5, 1981

PURELY PERSONAL

The smartest thing I did as a young man was to take to wife a secretary in the State Department.

It was thanks to her that as newlyweds we could afford more than bare subsistence, this being in the depths of the Depression, which some readers may remember. Frances was paid more by the government than I was by my newspaper.

In time the newspaper gained more prosperity, or at least more generosity, and when our first daughter arrived Frances could escape that dreary office job.

All she had to do then was nurse a baby, change diapers, keep a house, do the laundry and the shopping, cook the meals and wash up afterwards, a dishwasher not being among our home amenities. With her spare time she could sew on buttons or iron her husband's shirts.

In those pre-television days she could even enjoy the soap operas on radio while tending to such intermittent chores. As best I remember, she seemed happy with this change in circumstance.

Then just as she was settling down to domesticity a war came along—World War II, that is—and the circumstances changed again. This time it was I who went to work for the government, traveling all over the world at taxpayers' expense. Unfortunately, at that time the Navy pay scale didn't match the civilian State Department's; newly hatched ensigns weren't expected to support a wife and child until they had served at least a year.

So once more Frances had to rescue us from penury by putting her stenographic skills back to work. Neither she nor I anticipated that this state of affairs would last five years, but she seemed to bear up being head of the household alone.

The war over, she retired again. Not at once, to be sure, because her returning sailor brought no money with him, not even enough to buy civilian clothes; my "civies" were Navy blues with the stripes removed.

Nonetheless, some prosperity gradually crept up on us, and we could support two daughters. A VA loan got us shelter and the newspaper's pay arrangements improved.

All this, of course, was forty years ago. I mention it because of late my Frances has had to dust off those ancient stenographic skills, brushing up on her shorthand and typing.

This time not for financial reasons and not in some 9-to-5 office. The best way to describe her job now, I suppose, is as a live-in secretary, all because last summer I had what doctors describe as a vascular "episode."

It was a lucky stroke, if there is such a thing. That is, I am still mobile and I can still talk in what has been described by others on these pages as a "pugnacious" manner. But the fingers on my left hand don't work the way they did and should. That's not a good thing for a man who makes his living at a typewriter.

So for the last several months the essays you've been reading on this page have been transcribed by that former State Department secretary. She's slower and not as efficient as she once was, but she's cheaper and a lot more convenient than a hired outsider. One disadvantage, though, is that I can't grumble at her over a misunderstood word or a typo scattered here and there. Fortunately, she always could spell better than I.

The only other problem arises, I think, from the women's lib movement. Now I'm the one who fetches her coffee in the morning and tea in the afternoon. She's also picked up notions about working hours, vacations even.

Although I take her to New York and such places as a traveling companion (handier than a Dictaphone), she has been muttering lately that she needs a whole month's vacation now that Christmas approaches. At least one of the daughters will be home for the holidays. That means a house to be festively decorated, a larder to be stocked. It also means presents to be purchased and I'm reminded that only one is my responsibility while she must buy for children, grandchildren, sundry kinfolk and assorted friendly neighbors.

Then, too, there are Christmas cards to distant friends that must be addressed, inscribed with little notes and mailed promptly. The postal service isn't as speedy as it used to be.

I don't need to tell any business executives among my readers that labor isn't as tractable as it used to be, either. Secretaries especially must be humored if you're to avoid the confrontation of a strike. Freud may have been confused by what women want but the modern woman makes her wishes known in no uncertain terms, as I have lately learned.

The point of all this discursive account is to inform my editors (and my readers) that there will be a long holiday hiatus in the appearance of these weekly essays. It's all very well to say that I should resort to the hunt-and-peck system of typing them myself, but I've tried it and the result is unintelligible to any compositor. I find myself at my age as dependent on my lady as in the days of my youth and find her less docile than in that long-ago time.

The unsettled question in this labor dispute is how long the holiday vacation will last and when I will once more have secretarial service available. I trust that as soon as the New Year's celebrations are past and the house has settled into its accustomed pleasant routine, any thoughts I may have on the state of the world can again be committed to paper and find their way onto these pages.

Until then all I can do is beg your patience. My Frances will tell me when she's ready to put an end to idleness and go to work again.

November 30, 1983

A GREAT-GREAT-GRANDMOTHER

There hangs framed on our family-room wall a faded and stained clipping of an obituary of a forebear of mine, now more than a century old. The account it gives of this lady's life will fall strangely upon modern ears, but I think some of it is worth quoting for what it says of the relationship between women and men, both that which has changed and that which endures.

"Died in this city [Raleigh, N.C.] on October 25th, 1864, Mrs. Susan Royster, consort of David Royster, aged 85 years. Sixty-two years ago she came to Raleigh as a bride and her funeral was preached in the same room she first entered as a bride. In the sixty-two years of her married life, she never left home without her husband and children. In that long period she and her husband were never separated a week at a time until death took away from the old man 'the light of his eyes' and left him alone.

"She has also left to mourn her loss eight children, forty-four grandchildren and fifteen great grandchildren, all of whom except three grandchildren reside in this city. In addition, four children and twenty grandchildren have 'gone before.' All of those except three sleep in the burying ground of this city. Mrs. Royster was of cheerful disposition even while drawing near the close of her long life suffering much pain. . . .

"She was for more than forty years a consistent member of the Baptist Church and leaves to her large and sorrowing family her example of patience, resignation and piety. . . ."

You do not see obituaries in this style anymore. Nor would your newspaper, even if it tried, likely find such a tale to tell.

I was moved to take Susan down from the wall so that my tired eyes could read the fading print because it so happens that my wife and I celebrated a wedding anniversary yesterday. A mere forty-seventh, which leaves us, I hope, a long way to go.

343

But that is not the only difference. It's hard to think of twelve children, living and dead, from one union. We have only two, with two
grandchildren. The population experts would approve, but all the
same, I wonder.

I wonder too about sixty-two years in the same house with so much
living to fill it up, including all those birthdays. I wonder what she
thought of her new nation, younger than she. Or of the war that was
tearing it apart as she died, not knowing that it would survive her.

Most of all, I wonder if she was happy with her life. She never traveled as much as a hundred miles from home. She never had but one
husband to share her hearth and bed. She never knew any great prosperity, her husband earning his living as a cabinetmaker. Certainly she
never knew much leisure time with such a family and a house to care
for. She was well acquainted with sickness and death, there being no
hospital and only primitive medicine.

So the differences between Susan's time and my own are glaring. My
wife and I have lived in six different homes in five different places.
Twice during World War II we were separated for as long as a year and
a half. Twice my wife had to work outside the home to help support it
and her family. We have both traveled over most of the world. We have
known some prosperity as well as hard times. We have enjoyed some
leisure hours free of the drudgery of life.

There are other differences between the times. In Susan's day a
woman's only place was in the home, as homemaker for husband and
children. If there was more than one marriage it was because one or
the other was left a widow or widower. Partners were not changed
casually.

And of course there were none of those trappings we can hardly
imagine life without. No automobiles, no airplanes to whisk us away
from home. No radio, no television, no telephones. No dishwashers or
clothes washers to lighten the burdens. No opportunity for a woman,
if she chose, to have a different lifestyle. Hardly surprising that Susan
was honored for her patience, resignation and piety.

All the same, there is much that endures from her time to mine. We
read much about the death of the "nuclear family" with the burgeon-
ing divorce rate, and about children reared by stepfathers and step-
mothers. We hear much about women so busy with their occupations
they have no time for either motherhood or homemaking.

Yet as I look about me I see among my contemporaries that there are several reaching golden anniversaries, not from necessity but from choice. The newspaper is full of forthcoming marriages, often by those who tried before, made mistakes and yet are drawn to try again. A phenomenon of our time is the number of women near the end of the childbearing years who now wish to fulfill their womanhood.

What endures, I think, is the age-old relationship between women and men. Not simply that of coupling and uncoupling, as the fashion has it, but a seeking of what is imbedded in our genes and in our history as a species, the fulfillment of male and female by pairing for the making of nests in which to rear another generation.

It's true that this is not so for every person. We should be grateful that society no longer demands it and that there is a choice for every person. Whether Susan would have preferred another choice, I do not know. But I doubt it. I think when her time came, after eighty-five years, she could feel fulfilled by all those children, grandchildren and great-grandchildren. My sorrow is for the old man left alone when "the light of his eyes" was gone.

Susan is now back on the wall, and my wife and I are looking forward to reaching together that golden marker of a life long shared.

June 6, 1984

THE AUTHOR

VERMONT ROYSTER took a "temporary" job with *The Wall Street Journal* in 1936, at $15 a week. With time out for four years of wartime Navy duty, he has written for the *Journal* ever since, as Washington correspondent, senior associate editor, editor from 1958 until 1971, and since then as weekly columnist.

A native of Raleigh, North Carolina, he is a graduate of the Webb School in Bellbuckle, Tennessee, and of the University of North Carolina at Chapel Hill. In his long journalistic career he has known and written about every American president from Roosevelt to Reagan. He was awarded a Pulitzer Prize in 1953 for his editorial writing, and another Pulitzer in 1984 for his commentary. He has been president of the American Society of Newspaper Editors and recipient of the Fourth Estate Award of the National Press Club of Washington "for a lifetime of service to journalism."

In 1972 he became William Rand Kenan, Jr. Professor of Journalism and Public Affairs at the University of North Carolina at Chapel Hill.

His autobiography, *My Own, My Country's Time: A Journalist's Journey*, published by Algonquin Books of Chapel Hill in 1983, has gone into a third printing. His other books include *Journey Through the Soviet Union* and *A Pride of Prejudices*, which went through three printings when published by Alfred A. Knopf in 1967 and has now been reissued by Algonquin Books of Chapel Hill.